BUSINESS ISSUES, COMPETITION AND ENTREPRENEURSHIP

# PROMOTING INVESTMENT AND PROTECTING COMMERCE ONLINE

## LEGITIMATE SITES V. PARASITES

## (PART I AND II)

# Business Issues, Competition and Entrepreneurship

Additional books and e-books in this series can be found on Nova's website under the Series tab.

BUSINESS ISSUES, COMPETITION AND ENTREPRENEURSHIP

# PROMOTING INVESTMENT AND PROTECTING COMMERCE ONLINE

## LEGITIMATE SITES V. PARASITES

## (PART I AND II)

WILLIAM T. PRIETO

snova
New York

**Library of Congress Cataloging-in-Publication Data**

ISBN: 978-1-53613-711-8

*Published by Nova Science Publishers, Inc. † New York*

# CONTENTS

# PREFACE*

For more than two centuries, America's economic strength has been built on a firm foundation. However, in an increasingly connected world, threats have arisen from different parts of the world which have jeopardized our ability to sustain the incentives needed to foster growth and development and advance human progress. These threats create challenges for us in both the physical world and the virtual world where the systematic and willful violation of intellectual property rights poses a clear, present and growing danger to American creators and innovators, US consumers and our collective confidence in the Internet ecosystem. This book examines copyright issues and provides recommendations on how to tackle "online parasites" and cut off these sites from US based revenue.

* This is an edited, reformatted and augmented version of Hearing on: "Promoting Investment and Protecting Commerce Online: Legitimate Sites v. Parasites, Part I" Serial number 112-153, dated March 14, 2011.

*Chapter 1*

# HEARINGS

## PROMOTING INVESTMENT AND PROTECTING COMMERCE ONLINE: LEGITIMATE SITES V. PARASITES (PART I)

MONDAY, MARCH 14, 2011
House of Representatives,
Subcommittee on Intellectual Property,
Competition, and the Internet,
Committee on the Judiciary,
Washington, DC.

The Subcommittee met, pursuant to notice, at 4:05 p.m., in room 2141, Rayburn House Office Building, the Honorable Bob Goodlatte (Chairman of the Subcommittee) presiding.

Present: Representatives Goodlatte, Smith, Coble, Chabot, Reed, Griffin, Marino, Adams, Quayle, Watt, Conyers, Berman, Chu, Deutch, and Lofgren.

Staff Present: (Majority) David Whitney, Counsel; Olivia Lee, Clerk; and (Minority) Stephanie Moore, Subcommittee Chief Counsel.

Mr. Goodlatte. Good afternoon. The Subcommittee will come to order.

I will recognize myself for an opening statement.

For more than two centuries, America's economic strength has been built on a firm foundation. The rule of law, respect for individuals and private property and the promotion of industry through policies that reward creativity and innovation are essential virtues that helped a fledgling Nation encourage the initiative of its citizens and in time emerge as the most advanced and prosperous on Earth.

But these virtues are not universal. In an increasingly connected world, threats that emanate from areas where they are not shared can jeopardize our ability to sustain the incentives needed to foster growth and development and advance human progress.

These threats create challenges for us in both the physical world and the virtual world where the systematic and willful violation of intellectual property rights now poses a clear, present and growing danger to American creators and innovators, U.S. consumers and our collective confidence in the Internet ecosystem. Within that ecosystem today, there are legitimate commercial sites that authorized goods and services. Indeed, many exciting new technologies and websites help content owners distribute music, movies, books, games, software and other copyrighted works in ways that were not even imaginable 10 years ago.

However, there are also what might he called online parasites, or rogue sites, that steal the intellectual property of others and traffic in counterfeit and pirated goods. The Merriam-Webster Dictionary defines a parasite as "something that resembles a biological parasite in dependence on something else for existence or support without making a useful or adequate return."

In a very real sense, that is an apt description of how these sites operate. They depend upon the investments, creativity and innovation of others while offering nothing of benefit in return.

Indeed, according to the Motion Picture Association of America, websites that peddle stolen digital content represent, "the most pernicious forms of digital theft," and they present a two-pronged threat. They simultaneously weaken the film and TV industry by undercutting, eliminating or reducing the market for film and television production, which millions rely on for jobs, and discourage legitimate companies from investing in new business models to provide high-quality content and more consumer choice online.

Frederick Huntsberry, the chief operating officer of Paramount Pictures, who is with us today, believes these sites, left unchecked, will decimate the motion picture industry. He describes an online shadow economy that distributes stolen property on a revenue-generating basis, diverting consumer spending from the creators into the hands of criminals often outside the United States and further robbing Americans of jobs and investments in new productions, while depriving governments of tax revenue.

In recent years, these websites have evolved. They have become increasingly sophisticated and rival legitimate sites in appearance, operation and indicia of reliability. U.S. consumers are frequently led to these sites by search engines that list them among the top search results. After clicking on a site, they may be immediately reassured by the logos of U.S. payment processors and the presence of major corporate advertising supporting the site.

But just how popular and profitable are these sites? One cyberlocker, that is used to store and stream copyrighted content, ranks as the 51st most popular website while a business analysis provided by Paramount estimated a minimal annual profit of 41 to $304 million for one infringing cyberlocker. Who says crime doesn't pay?

At the request of the Subcommittee, the Acting Register of Copyrights, Ms. Maria Pallante, who is also with us today, has been meeting with stakeholders to consider the issues associated with online parasites. One of her conclusions is that these sites exploit highly creative and economically valuable copyrighted works because there is no real expectation of enforcement. She notes that the most pressing issue is how to tackle sites based in foreign jurisdiction and observes that the continued evidence of widespread global Internet copyright infringement suggests that international cooperation alone cannot be the only solution to this global problem.

Ms. Pallante recommends that copyright enforcement follow the money within the Internet ecosystem and cut off these sites from U.S.-based revenue. She warns these sites undermine the incentives for legitimate commerce and threaten to weaken the robust innovation-based markets that exist in the United States today.

This matter has been a top priority and will become a principal focus for the Subcommittee in the coming months. Today's hearing marks the first of two oversight hearings we will conduct to make certain we are fully acquainted with the range of issues involved.

I intend to take the time necessary to build a complete record and balance appropriately all the interest before introducing a bill that will contain meaningful and effective new authority. As this process progresses, I look forward to working with Members on both sides of the aisle and with our colleagues on the other side of the Capitol, as well as stakeholders in the private sector. With 19 million Americans employed in IP intensive industries, we owe it to them and to ourselves to ensure any legislation we send to the President will be effective.

It is important to note that whatever legislative product we enact will be only one solution to this problem. It is my strong hope that the stakeholders in content, technology, financial and Internet communities will see any legislation we enact not as the end of this debate, but as the starting point for more discussions among the private parties to find additional innovative solutions to the threat of online piracy.

It is now my pleasure to recognize the Ranking Member of the Committee, the gentleman from North Carolina, Mr. Watt.

Mr. Watt. Thank you, Mr. Chairman, and thank you for convening this hearing. There is little disagreement that online theft of intellectual property is increasing and negatively impacting the rights holders and our economy.

As the GAO found last year, the problem is sizeable. The Internet has provided an explosion of e-commerce and a new marketplace for American innovators. Industries with heavy intellectual property interests have powered the American economy as the Internet has become a dominant venue for commerce.

Today's hearing explores how to promote this commerce online by protecting the legitimate sites, but addressing the problems that have arisen as what the title to this hearing refers to as "parasites." I actually think a more appropriate term for them would be pirasites, pirasites, rogue websites, mostly foreign, engage in illicit conduct and are generally designed to pirate others' property for economic gain.

A study from Frontier Economics estimates that in 2008 alone, over $650 billion was lost internationally from online counterfeiting and piracy. Counterfeit goods sold online on these pirasites posed serious health and safety concerns. Just last night, 60 Minutes featured a segment on the sale of fake and tainted medicines and medical products that often come from illegitimate, online pharmacies.

Congress must take heed or run the risk that criminals and organized crime cartels who profit from piracy and counterfeit products hijacked the Internet to the disadvantage of law-abiding citizens.

At a time that intellectual property intensive industries provide more than 19 million U.S. jobs and account for more than 60 percent of U.S. exports, pirasites and the theft of intellectual property represents probably, far and away, the largest criminal enterprise in the world, and we are probably spending less to prevent it than we spend to counter old-fashioned bank robberies. In fact, electronic bank robbery is a much more significant threat now than armed bank robbery ever was.

How we preserve due process and free speech rights, as well as confront this problem, will be critically important as we move forward. We cannot just go around and take sites down without due process or probable cause any more than we could arrest old-fashioned bank robbers only on suspicion.

I look forward to hearing each of the witnesses' perspectives on the scope of the problem, and I hope that we will also hear concrete proposals for legislative solutions to help remedy this significant drain on our economy.

I yield back, Mr. Chairman.

Mr. Goodlatte. I thank the gentleman. It is now my pleasure to recognize the Chairman of the Judiciary Committee and one who has been deeply concerned and a leader on this issue, the gentleman from Texas, Mr. Smith.

Mr. Smith. Thank you, Mr. Chairman.

This important hearing will point out the destructive effects of online parasites, those rogue entities that generate huge profits from the theft of intellectual property.

The Internet is a wonderful tool that has forever changed the way we communicate, conduct business and relate to one another. Most users want a safe computing experience and only use the Internet for lawful and legitimate purposes.

But others employ it as a tool to perpetrate fraud, steal identities, traffic and counterfeit or pirated goods or engage in even more disturbing crimes such as child pornography. Today our focus is on the illicit trade in counterfeit and pirated goods. This Committee has long recognized the positive contributions of America's intellectual property industries. They contribute 19 million jobs, more than 60 percent of U.S. exports, support tens of thousands of small businesses and generate tens of millions of tax revenue for communities across our Nation.

IP enterprises drive our productivity, produce our entertainment and promote our economy, but these industries face a threat in the form of exponentially increasing counterfeiting and piracy. A recent study revealed that one-quarter of global Internet traffic infringes on the rights of IP owners.

Internet piracy is so profitable and pernicious that it discourages investments, innovation and licensed content from legitimate companies. It is clear that existing laws are inadequate and we must do more to confront the problem.

Just over 2 years ago, then-Chairman Conyers and I worked with other Members of this Committee, including the Chairman and Ranking Member of the Subcommittee, to enact the prioritizing resources and organization for the Intellectual Property Act of 2008 or PRO-IP. The purpose of that law was to strengthen American industry and protect American jobs by improving the government's response to the threats posed by counterfeiting and piracy.

When considered on the House floor PRO-IP, passed by a vote of 410-11, a result that demonstrated our bipartisan commitment to IP protection. PRO-IP was a good start, but much more needs to be done. We will work to strengthen the law to ensure criminals who operate online are not able to harm U.S. consumers and steal from American innovators.

Mr. Chairman, it is appropriate that Frederick Huntsberry, the COO of Paramount Pictures, is a witness today, since the present situation reminds me of a 1987 Paramount motion picture that starred one of my favorite actors, Sean Connery.

In The Untouchables, Connery played Chicago Detective Jim Malone. In a memorable scene, Malone tells Eliot Ness that if he is serious about getting Al Capone, then he must be prepared to pull a gun if one of Capone's gang pulls a knife. You all have heard that.

For IP onlies and other legitimate companies who have had to rely upon ineffective online enforcement regimes for far too long, it must seem that they have been forced to take a knife to a gun fight. It is time we help them fight back. We can no longer tolerate a state of affairs that requires U.S. citizens to be subjected to the illicit importation of infringing goods in violation of Federal law, and the constitutional protections that are designed to promote innovation and creativity.

Mr. Chairman, I look forward to moving strong and appropriate legislation through this Committee, and I appreciate the witnesses here today and their helping us accomplish that goal.

I yield back.

Mr. Goodlatte. I thank the Chairman. The Chair now recognizes the Ranking Member of the full Committee, the gentleman from Michigan, Mr. Conyers.

Mr. Conyers. Thank you. I wanted to congratulate you. Chairman Goodlatte, on the way all of us have come together on this important subject. I will put my statement in the record, but I would like to get this started by offering a definition of rogue site and it will be distributed.

An Internet site is a "rogue site" if it is primarily structured in order to, and has no demonstrable, or significant commercial purpose or use other than to offer goods or services in violation of title 17, including by offering or providing access to, in a manner not authorized by the intellectual property owner or otherwise by operation of law, copies of, or public performance or display of, works protected by title 17, in complete or substantially complete form, by any means, including by means of download, streaming or other transmission.

Because that is what I think is going to be the important consideration for this Committee.

I join in welcoming, particularly the chief operating officer of Paramount Pictures, our register of copyrights and our two distinguished experts, David Sohn and Daniel Castro.

Thank you. Chairman Goodlatte.

[The prepared statement of Mr. Conyers follows:]

# PART I: OPENING STATEMENTS

## STATEMENT OF THE HONORABLE JOHN CONYERS, JR. FOR THE HEARING ON PROMOTING INVESTMENT AND PROTECTING COMMERCE ONLINE: LEGITIMATE SITES V. PARASITES, PART I

Monday, March 14, 2011, at 4:00 a.m.

2141 Rayburn House Office Building

Thank you, Chairman Goodlatte, for convening this hearing. I expect that today's discussions will prove highly useful as I and other Members of the Judiciary Committee craft legislation to get at the crux of protecting America's intellectual property on the Internet.

First, I would like to note that with regard to intellectual property and the economy: the stakes are only growing higher.

Trillions of dollars and millions of American jobs stem from the intellectual property industries, and this sector is fast becoming our economy's most powerful engine for growth. Just as these industries have powered the American economy, so has the Internet risen as a dominant venue for commerce.

But a study from Frontier Economics estimates that in 2008 alone more than $650 billion was lost across the globe due to online counterfeit and piracy. For the United States, economists estimate that annual copyright theft costs our economy $58 billion in lost output and denies us nearly 400,000 jobs. For the U.S. auto-industry, for example, counterfeit auto-parts drain $3 billion and approximately 250,000 jobs each year.

Beyond economic indicators like these, however, counterfeit goods sold online have jeopardized the health and safety of thousands of Americans who have received fake and tainted medicines and medical products from illegitimate online pharmacies.

The Internet has regrettably become a cash-cow for the criminals and organized crime cartels who profit from piracy and counterfeit products. A study released in

January by the research company Envisional revealed that nearly one-third of global online traffic involves copyright infringement. With an estimated 2 billion people accessing the Internet annually: this translates to a devastating amount of property theft and job-destruction.

Secondly, I would note that the problems we are talking about have a social and cultural dimension. The sad truth is that many people don't make the connection that when they download a camcorded movie through a "cyberlocker" while that same movie is playing in a theater a couple of blocks away, they are watching stolen property and may be enriching foreign criminal syndicates. Moreover, the peer-to-peer and cyberlocker technology used to access copyrighted entertainment and software are also notoriously exploited by identity-theft criminals to access people's financial and personal data.

Coalitions of businesses, educators, and political leaders have much more to do when it comes to educating Americans - particularly our school-age children - about online safety and respect for property rights.

Finally, I believe that the situation has grown so grave for American workers that legislative action has become warranted. While I have several concerns about the details of some of the legislative proposals that have been put forth - namely I want to make sure that due process and free speech rights are adequately protected, I am encouraged that this hearing is entitled "Part I" on this issue.

I look forward to hearing each of the witnesses' perspectives on the scope of the problem, and I also hope that they will help us to craft legislative solutions. I would like to see Congress act to protect property rights and American jobs by carefully targeting the truly bad actors, and do so in a way that continues our nation's commitment to due process and freedom of speech.

Millions of American jobs will rely on our ability to do this because the current situation is untenable.

Mr. Goodlatte. I thank the Chairman emeritus for his remarks. We, by special request and agreement, are going to recognize one additional Member on each side of the aisle for an opening statement, and then we will ask all of our Members to put their statements into the record.

So the Chair at this time recognizes the gentleman from New York, Mr. Reed.

Mr. Reed. Thank you very much, Chairman, for this special consideration. I would like to thank Chairman Goodlatte and Ranking Member Watt for calling this important hearing today, as well as thank our witnesses who have agreed to participate.

I firmly believe that criminal domestic and offshore websites dedicated to the online theft of music, movies, books, pharmaceuticals and other intellectual property harm the U.S. economy, our balance of trade, U.S. employment and put companies, consumers and other individual artists in New York and throughout the country at a severe disadvantage.

What was once more about college students downloading music in their dorm rooms, online piracy has now grown to the point to where many U.S. companies and small creators are at risk of surviving. I am pleased to see bipartisan legislation introduced into the 111th Congress and the U.S. Senate by Senators Lee and Hatch. I look forward to working in a bipartisan fashion in the House to address many of these same issues.

Many have said that legislative activity aimed at reducing piracy could prevent free speech and shut down the technological infrastructure which the Internet was built upon.

I, however, remain convinced that the popularity of the Internet, in the first place, is driven largely from the availability of high-quality copyrighted content, including films and TV programs that are delivered to users in innovative ways. I remain concerned these claims have yet to be fully vetted and hope this hearing and those that follow touch on these claims.

Finally, I am hopeful for an open dialogue with all stakeholders in the Internet ecosystem as it relates to any potential legislation out of the Judiciary Committee.

I am particularly concerned that inclusion of private right of action language and the prospective negative impacts on any legislation that we put forward. In addition, I am hopeful that the Committee will be open to having discussions on search engines and how they relate to the popularity of various pirated websites.

I look forward to any comments on these topics at today's hearings and I thank the witnesses again, and I thank you, Mr. Chairman.

I yield back.

Mr. Goodlatte. I thank the gentleman, I think the award for earliest riser and greatest distance traveled to be with us today goes to the gentleman from California, Mr. Berman. And in appreciation for that, we want to recognize him for his opening statement as well.

Mr. Berman. Well, if that is the price of having an opening statement, I will exercise it rarely.

Mr. Goodlatte. I think the strategy, actually.

Mr. Berman. Thank you very much, Mr. Chairman for holding the hearing. I want to associate myself with yours and the other opening comments.

In investigations you follow the money, which is why many of us have invested time in trying to understand how those involved in the unlawful distribution of trademarked, copyrighted works are able to profit from their crimes. Five or 6 years ago, we worked with Visa and MasterCard to stop the misuse of their financial networks by the notorious Russian music site, allofmp3.com.

We also need to turn a spotlight to online advertisers that are hoping that effective mechanisms are put in place to ensure that some of America's best-known companies and brands are not unwittingly helping to make piracy profitable.

The fight against these parasites or rogue sites is difficult, especially when many operate from servers and registrars located outside of the U.S. with the goal of selling pirated material into the U.S.

In the Foreign Affairs Committee, the IP coordinator, Victoria Espinel, and the ICE Director John Morton describe the Administration's innovative efforts to combat counterfeiting. They are trying new tactics because the anti-piracy tools we adopted in the past are inadequate to confront the crimes of today. As we evaluate new legislative tools, I have been wrestling with how to define the targets narrowly enough so that we can, on the one hand, rein in truly knowing infringers without leaving loopholes that provide a roadmap to criminals or, on the other hand, to put law-abiding sites at risk.

I am also wondering how we set up a streamline process to address the whack-a-mole problem for seized sites that pop back up under a different name. By and large, I trust prosecutors to exercise their authority and discretion. Given the growth of online theft, the Justice Department may have even been too cautious for too long, but we must balance aggressive enforcement with real due process.

And, lastly, as a special and an especially tough question for me is whether, due to the lack of resources and competing priorities at DOJ, we should take some of the responsibility off law enforcement by setting up a mechanism that allows private parties to bring the kinds of actions that ICE is now bringing to protect their own property. There aren't any easy answers, no silver bullets, but it is long past time for saying "no" to every new idea.

Thank you, Mr. Chairman.

Mr. Goodlatte. I thank the gentleman. We have a very distinguished panel of witnesses today. Their written statements will be entered into the record in their entirety, and I ask the witnesses to summarize their testimony in 5 minutes or less to help you stay within that time, there is a timing light on your table. When the light switches from green to yellow you have 1 minute to conclude your testimony.

When the light turns red, it signals your 5 minutes have expired.

And before I introduce our witnesses and as is customary for this Committee, I ask that they stand and be sworn.

[Witnesses sworn.]

Mr. Goodlatte. Our first witness is Maria Pallante, a senior adviser to the Librarian of Congress and the Acting Register of Copyrights, a position she temporarily assumed at the beginning of 2011.

The Register of Copyrights is a unique and important position. Among other duties, the register serves as the principal adviser to Congress on matters of copyright policy. Ms. Pallante has spent much of her career in the office where she previously served as the associate register for policy and international affairs, deputy general counsel and a policy adviser.

In addition, Ms. Pallante spent nearly a decade as intellectual property counsel and director of licensing for the Guggenheim Museums in New York. She earned her JD from George Washington University and her bachelor's degree from Misericordia University, where she was also awarded an honorary degree of humane letters.

Our second witness is David Sohn, senior policy counsel and director for the Center for Democracy and Technology, CDT's project on intellectual property and technology. Prior to joining CDT, Mr. Sohn worked for nearly 5 years as commerce counsel to Senator Ron Wyden. Before that, he practiced law at a Washington D.C. Law firm. He earned his JD from Stanford Law School and his BA degree from Amherst College. Mr. Sohn has also a degree from the London School of Economics.

Our third witness is Daniel Castro, a senior analyst with the Information Technology and Innovation Foundation, ITIF. Before joining ITIF, Mr. Castro worked as an IT analyst at the U.S. Government Accountability Office where he audited IT security and management controls at various government agencies.

Mr. Castro was also a visiting scientist at the Software Engineering Institute in Pittsburgh. He earned an MS in information security and management from Carnegie Mellon University and a BS in foreign service from Georgetown.

Our final witnesses is Frederick Huntsberry, the chief operating officer of Paramount Pictures, where he is responsible for strategic planning and operations for the studio. Prior to joining Paramount, Mr. Huntsberry spent nearly a decade serving in a wide variety of executive and senior management positions at NBCUniversal and affiliated companies as well as at Vivendi Universal.

He also spent over a dozen years with General Electric's Europe division. Mr. Huntsberry has a bachelor's degree with a concentration in finance from Boston University.

We welcome all of our witnesses to the Subcommittee on Intellectual Property, Competition and the Internet today, and we will begin with you, Ms. Pallante, welcome.

*Chapter 2*

# WITNESSES

## TESTIMONY OF MARIA A. PALLANTE, ACTING REGISTER OF COPYRIGHTS, UNITED STATES COPYRIGHT OFFICE

Ms. Pallante. Thank you, Mr. Chairman. I would like to express my gratitude to you and Ranking Member Watt for having this hearing today, and for elevating the importance of copyright protection in the context of online commerce.

I also would like to say that my office greatly appreciates the support of Chairman Smith and Ranking Member Conyers on these issues.

As you know, the U.S. Copyright Office is undergoing a leadership transition following the retirement of Marybeth Peters, and I want to take a moment to assure you that our staff is very busy carrying out the work of the office, including registering copyrights, eliminating the backlog, securing works for the Library of Congress and, perhaps most relevant for this hearing, studying and advising on domestic and international copyright issues.

Copyright promotes innovation, by extending the number of exclusive rights to creators, including the rights of reproduction, distribution, the right to make derivative works, and in some instances, the rights of public performance and public display. Our law grants these rights, but they are of little value to anyone if they cannot be effectively enforced.

There is nothing redeeming about parasites or rogue sites that are entirely or substantially committed to infringement. They exploit copyrighted works with impunity, because they have little or no expectation of enforcement. And to be clear, we are talking about activity that does not constitute fair use and cannot qualify for any other defense available to good faith actors under the law.

In support of the Subcommittee's work on this issue, my staff and I have met with a broad spectrum of stakeholders, and we will continue to do this in the weeks ahead. The issues are complex but they present an opportunity for Congress to manage the relationship between technology and intellectual property as it has done many times before.

Rogue sites can be located anywhere in the world and have a devastating effect on U.S. books, software, music, movies and television programming. Unlike traditional brick-and-mortar infringers, they can be quite difficult to identify and locate and, when pursued, may simply and quickly reappear under another domain name.

Those based outside the United States lack sufficient ties to be compelled to appear before U.S. courts, or to allow the enforcement of a judgment against them. It can be difficult for rights holders, especially small rights holders, to litigate in foreign countries or to enforce a judgment abroad.

So what can be done? Solutions that follow the money, for example, sales, subscriptions and advertising revenue, may be most successful. Payment processors like credit cards and PayPal are essential to the Web-based commerce we all enjoy, but rogue sites have no business using trusted companies to process profits. Likewise, many rogue sites display advertising, allowing them to run lucrative businesses using copyrighted works as the hook.

Search engines are perhaps the most important, perhaps the most impressive player in the ecosystem. Without them, the Internet would be almost impossible to navigate. Unfortunately, both paid and unpaid search results routinely point people to rogue sites.

One solution might be to give enforcement entities like Immigration and Customs Enforcement increased authority. For example, ICE could request a court order requiring the payment processors and ad networks to sever their financial ties to rogue actors. Congress might also review the role of domain registrars, registries and Internet service providers.

A harder question for Congress is whether it is reasonable and viable to ask search engines to participate in a solution by suppressing search results that send users to rogue sites.

Safeguards are important. Some have warned that some of the proposed remedies would risk fragmenting the Internet's global domain name system. These assertions would require careful examination. It might also be helpful, however, if the dialogue that Congress seeks includes the counsel of experts who can objectively evaluate these relevant technical facts.

Principles of due process and freedom of expression are also critical. Even the worst of the worst should receive notice as well as an opportunity to be heard, and relief should be narrowly tailored. However, injunctions have long been used in copyright cases, and we do not believe that an order that shuts down a web site dedicated to infringement would violate the First Amendment.

Mr. Chairman, thank you again for inviting me to testify, and I await any questions that you or the Subcommittee may have.

Mr. Goodlatte. Thank you, Ms. Pallante.

[The prepared statement of Ms. Pallante follows:]

# STATEMENT OF MARIA A. PALLANTE, ACTING REGISTER OF COPYRIGHTS, BEFORE THE SUBCOMMITTEE ON INTELLECTUAL PROPERTY, COMPETITION, AND THE INTERNET COMMITTEE ON THE JUDICIARY UNITED STATES HOUSE OF REPRESENTATIVES 112TH CONGRESS, 1ST SESSION, MARCH 14, 2011 "PROMOTING INVESTMENT AND PROTECTING COMMERCE ONLINE: LEGITIMATE SITES V. PARASITES, PART I"

Chairman Goodlatte, Ranking Member Watt, and Members of the Subcommittee, I appreciate the opportunity to appear before you this afternoon to testify about the importance of providing incentives for legitimate commerce in the online environment by protecting against the parasites who compete with it. We also deeply appreciate the support of Chairman Smith and Ranking Member Conyers on these issues.

As you know, the Copyright Office is the agency charged with administering the copyright law. Our duties include advising Congress and other government entities on matters of domestic and international copyright policy, including legislative proposals, participating in intergovernmental meetings and negotiations, and conducting studies, public inquiries, roundtables and rulemakings, as appropriate. We do not carry out enforcement activities, but are regularly consulted on copyright enforcement issues by Congress and the executive branch.

Copyright law, which originates in the U.S. Constitution[1] and is codified today in Title 17 of the United States Code, promotes innovation by extending to owners of creative works a panoply of exclusive rights, including reproduction, distribution, the right to prepare derivative works, and, in certain instances, the right of public performance and display. Though these rights are granted by law, they are of little value to the copyright owner if they cannot be meaningfully enforced.

The issues presented by parasites and so-called "rogue websites" raise complex legal questions but also present an opportunity for Congress to manage the relationship between technology and intellectual property, as it has done many times before. In the course of our research on this issue, we have met with a variety of stakeholders in the Internet ecosystem and will continue to do so in the weeks ahead. We welcome the opportunity to assist Congress in its continued examination of the need for legislation in

[1] Art I, § 8 ("The Congress shall have Power To promote the Progress of Science and useful Arts, by securing for limited Times to Authors and Inventors the exclusive Right to their respective Writings and Discoveries.").

this area. While we recognize the significant concerns related to trademark infringement and counterfeiting, my comments today focus on copyright law and practice.

## Rogue Websites

The Copyright Office believes the United States has a problem with a category of bad actors that build online businesses by infringing copyright and engaging in related illegal activity. Indeed, based on our discussions with a wide array of stakeholders, there appears to be widespread, although not universal, consensus on this point.

The operators of rogue websites exploit copyrighted works with impunity because, in part, there is no expectation of enforcement; they have no real fear of being brought to justice. With the global reach of the Internet, rogue websites can be located anywhere in the world and still have a devastating effect on the market for legitimate copyrighted works created by U.S. book authors, composers, recording artists, filmmakers, software companies and other creators.

While many agree on the broad outlines of the problem, the precise contours remain elusive. There are a variety of views about how to frame the issue and how to develop effective solutions that respect our core American values of due process and free expression of ideas. Moreover, there is a wide spectrum of piratical, counterfeiting, and otherwise infringing activity on the Internet, making a solution difficult. Many sites contain some infringing content alongside lawfully distributed materials, while others contain nothing but infringing content.

Still other sites - most commonly referred to as “cyberlockers” - allow users to store and share digital files. Although many users employ cyberlockers for entirely lawful purposes, some have used them as a mechanism to distribute infringing content.

We appreciate that the Subcommittee’s stated focus is the proliferation of websites built almost entirely on the business of making and/or distributing unauthorized materials. Such websites violate trademark law, engage in unfair competition and, in the case of copyright law, undermine the exclusive rights of reproduction, distribution, and/or the public performance or display of legitimate copyrighted materials.

These “worst of the worst” flagrantly engage in illegal activities. They offer consumers the sale, download, streaming of or linking to highly creative movies, music, books, and software. They may also offer devices, software and services used to circumvent access or copy controls in violation of Title 17.

Many rogue website operators make money through direct transactions with Internet consumers. In some cases, they charge a fee for the purchase of a product or service. In other cases, they charge subscription fees, in either instance, they may utilize well-known payment processors (e.g., credit cards) to facilitate the actual exchange of money, or they may falsely state that they have relationships with such payment processors and then, when a consumer actually attempts to pay, redirect consumers to other, alternative payment methods that may or may not be secure. Those rogue websites that do not engage in direct financial transactions with customers may rely on online advertising placement to fund their illegal activities.

Aside from being illegal, the existence of such websites undermines the incentives and the ability of legitimate companies to engage in the production, sale, licensing and other dissemination of copyrighted content to compete in the marketplace. For good faith companies whose livelihoods are based on the creation and exploitation of intellectual property, rogue websites present a significant threat to their core business model.

At the same time, unlike traditional brick-and-mortar infringers, rogue website operators can be extremely difficult to identify or locate, especially if they are based outside the United States. As a result, pursuing them can be hopelessly frustrating for copyright owners and law enforcement agencies alike, including because it is everybody's goal to target those whose primary purpose is to profit from intellectual property they do not own and have no reasonable basis for exploiting. (The circumstances clearly exceed a finding of "fair use" or other defenses available under the law.) Nevertheless, one of the key challenges for policy makers will be to define carefully those bad actors who are the target of additional enforcement measures, so as to avoid inadvertently capturing good faith actors.

## Current Legal and Business Environment

As a backdrop for the issues, I will provide a brief overview of current U S. law related to enforcement of copyright on the Internet.

### *Civil Enforcement and the Digital Millennium Copyright Act*

With respect to civil actions for online copyright infringement, the forms of relief provided by the Copyright Act in appropriate cases include actual damages, statutory damages, injunctive relief, costs and attorneys' fees, and impoundment. The well-established doctrines of direct and secondary liability for copyright infringement have developed through case law. Copyright owners have a significant role in enforcing their interests using civil law mechanisms. Indeed, the vast majority of copyright enforcement cases are brought by copyright owners themselves, though fewer and fewer small copyright owners can afford the costs of litigation. In the context of rogue websites, the cause of action is typically direct infringement and the availability of damages and injunctive relief would vary with the specific facts at hand.

Additionally, in 1998 Congress passed the Digital Millennium Copyright Act (DMCA),[2] which was intended to foster the expansion of electronic commerce by reducing legal uncertainties of conducting business on the Internet while, at the same time, establishing mechanisms for combating online infringement. As part of the DMCA, Section 512 of the Copyright Act provides certain "safe harbors" and limits the liability of online service providers for copyright infringement when engaging in certain types of activities. For example, Section 512(a) provides Internet service providers (ISPs) with a limitation on liability for acting as "mere conduits" and providing transitory digital network communications, Section 512(c) provides online service providers that host material on their servers or networks at the direction of third parties with a limitation on liability, and Section 512(d) provides search engines with a limitation on liability for providing information location tools.

To be eligible for these limitations under the law, online service providers (other than mere conduits) must take certain responsible steps as participants in the Internet ecosystem, including responding to the notifications of copyright owners. In general, an on-line service provider may be notified that it is providing access to infringing material. The copyright owner may request a "take-down," but must also supply to the provider a degree of factual data specified in Section 512 (such as identifying the copyright at issue, the infringing work, and the owner's contact information, among other things). If the provider removes the infringing material, the copyright owner will not be able to bring an action against the provider for allowing access to the infringing material. A similar provision applies to search engines that direct users to infringing material. Section 512 thus provides a streamlined method for copyright owners to have infringing material taken down without first having to go to court.

### *Criminal Enforcement*

Criminal copyright infringement is a federal cause of action. The Department of Justice often takes the lead on criminal copyright prosecutions, but several other U.S. government agencies have a role in investigations and law enforcement under various statutes that protect intellectual property rights, including copyright. For example, the Federal Bureau of Investigation (FBI), the Department of Homeland Security (DHS), Immigration and Customs Enforcement (ICE), Customs and Border Protection (CBP), and other agencies all work to enforce our copyright law.[3] In recent months, ICE has used

---

[2] See l7 U.S.C. §512, § 1201 et seq.

[3] A summary of recent efforts by law enforcement in the intellectual property arena has been compiled by the Office of the Intellectual Property Enforcement Coordinator, which recently issued its first Annual Report. See Office of the Intellectual Property Enforcement Coordinator, *2010 U.S. Intellectual Property Enforcement Coordinator Annual Report on Intellectual Property Enforcement.*, Feb. 2011, available at http://www.whitehouse.gov/sites/default/files/omb/IPEC/ipec_annual_report_feb2011.pdf.

existing civil forfeiture remedies available against criminal activity to seize the domain names of websites involved in extensive infringing copyright and trademark activities.[4]

We note that part of what ICE is doing is providing a level of comfort to consumers with respect to the legitimate operation of the top-level domains most commonly used in the United States. That is, ICE cannot reach all the secondary or foreign domains that lure consumers to infringing content or unsafe medicine, but they can try to make the big three (com, org and net) safe for the American public. Unfortunately, we understand (and are concerned) that once a domain name has been seized, it eventually returns to the pool of domains available to the public for registration unless it is purchased by the government. We question this result. We would also note that to the extent ICANN plans to increase the number of top-level domains available for commerce in the United States, as has recently been discussed, one consideration should be how the use of multiple domains would affect existing enforcement capabilities and objectives for customer protection.

### *Takedowns and the Domain Name System (DNS)*

One particular enforcement measure that is especially relevant in this context is the takedown or blocking of Internet domain names that are associated with rogue websites. As mentioned above, U.S. law enforcement has used existing civil forfeiture provisions to obtain warrants to seize domain names, and the service of these warrants is usually aimed at a domain name registry, and, in some cases, ISPs. These entities also respond to orders or requests from courts and law enforcement to disable or block access to domain names and websites that are used for criminal activity. DNS blocking targets the domain name itself; it does not block the Internet protocol (IP) address, which is comprised of a series of numbers that identifies a domain name on the Internet and that ultimately leads the user to the desired website.

### *Current Voluntary Practices*

Voluntary practices to combat online copyright infringement have been developing in a number of areas. For instance, we understand that there is increasing cooperation between payment processors, which include credit card companies (e.g., MasterCard) and online payment services (e.g., PayPal), and rightsholders to combat online infringement of copyrighted works including films and music. In addition to cooperation in the United States, we understand that there is progress on voluntary cooperation with law

---

[4] These actions led by ICE have been conducted under 18 U.S.C. § 2323. The Prioritizing Resources and Organization for Intellectual Property Act of 2008 strengthened existing forfeiture provisions for use in cases involving copyright infringement and trademark counterfeiting. Pub. L. No. 110-403, 122 Stat. 4256. ICE has indicated to us that approximately 140 domain names have been targeted in four operational sweeps since the summer of 2010. According to a recent conversation with ICE, to date, not a single owner of the targeted domain names has contested these seizures.

enforcement by payment processors and certain copyright owners in the United Kingdom.[5]

We have also been told that some domain name system registrars voluntarily cooperate with individual rightsholder requests to block access to domain names that are associated with rogue websites because these registrars have broad terms of service prohibiting use of domain names for various types of illegal activity, including intellectual property violations. We understand that at least one registrar is actively - and voluntarily - helping rightsholders when a domain name is being used in connection with infringing goods and services.[6]

## Deficiencies in Current Legal and Business Environment

In analyzing the legal issues relevant to rogue websites, it has become clear to us that websites based outside the United States are especially problematic. In many cases, they lack sufficient ties to the United States to be compelled to appear before U.S. courts and to allow the enforcement of judgment against them. The detrimental effect of this fact on U.S. creators and innovators is one of the major reasons we applaud the attention this Subcommittee is giving to this topic.

Indeed, the pressing issue is how to tackle rogue websites based in foreign jurisdictions. Copyright owners have few options to pursue websites that are based abroad and that do not take advantage of U.S.-based Internet registrars or registries.[7] Finding methods to address the illegal activities of foreign websites and non-U. S.-based actors who may not be subject to U.S. jurisdiction can be a challenge in many areas of U.S law enforcement, and the same challenge applies to civil efforts to combat copyright

---

[5] Earlier this month, the international recording industry announced a project with two payment processing companies and the City of London Police's Economic Crime Directorate. See IFPI press release, "Recording industry welcomes support by payment providers to tackle illegal online sale of unlicensed music." March 2. 2011, available at http://www.ifpi.coni//content/section_news/20110302.litnil. So far, the details of 24 copyright infringing music services have been given to the London police.

[6] We are also aware of voluntary efforts addressing Internet pharmacies and establishing standards for addressing trademark counterfeiting on the Internet. On December 14, 2010, the White House announced that American Express, eNom, GoDaddy, Google, MasterCard, Microsoft, Network Solutions. Neustar. PayPal, VISA and Yahoo! agreed to start a non-profit group to educate the public and begin to take voluntary enforcement action against illegal Internet pharmacies. See Office of the *Intellectual Property Enforcement Coordinator, Counterfeit Pharmaceutical Inter-Agency Working Group Report to the Vice President of the United States and to Congress,* March 2011, available at http://www.whitehouse.gov/sites/default/files/omb/IPEC/Pharma_Report_Final.pdf. Voluntary guidelines also exist in the trademark counterfeiting context. See International Trademark Association (INTA), "Addressing the Sale of Counterfeits on the Internet," Sept. 2009, available at http://www.inta.org/Advocacy/Documents/INTA%20nest%20Practices%20for%20Addressing%20the%2nSale%20oi'%20Counterfeits%20on%20lhc%20Tntcmel.pdf. Participating payment processors include American Express, Discover, MasterCard, PayPal, and VISA, working with participating Internet providers eBay, Google and Yahoo!.

[7] Internet registrars allow individuals and organizations to register specific domain names. By contrast, Internet registries do not have direct relationships with the registering person or organization, but instead manage all domain names within a specific type of top-level domain name such as "com" or "net."

infringement. In this context, the question becomes how to get at the off-shore rogue websites. We have seen the "pop up" effect of Internet piracy, as operators of rogue websites whose domain names have been seized have simply moved to top-level domains administered in other countries (e.g., ".info" and ".ru"), which may serve as more "hospitable" jurisdictions that allow them to operate, usually with impunity, or at least untouched for a significant amount of time.[8]

Copyright law is territorial and copyright owners must manage significant jurisdictional questions when attempting to pursue infringement actions against foreign actors. Copyright owners could attempt to bring suit in the United States for copyright infringement by a foreign website if there are sufficient contacts (e.g., significant advertising and sales to U.S. consumers) but it can be difficult to litigate against uncooperative foreign entities and/or to enforce a judgment abroad. The intersection of U.S. and foreign law is an appropriate topic for Congress to consider, including how these jurisdictional issues affect the remedies in successful infringement cases.

We do believe that enhanced international cooperation can play a positive role, that is, international cooperation both by law enforcement authorities and by private sector groups and Internet intermediaries. However, while voluntary efforts should be pursued whenever possible, the continued evidence of widespread global Internet copyright infringement suggests that cooperation alone cannot be the only solution to this complex problem. Cooperation on an international scale is at best a gradual process and to date has not stopped these websites from continuing to wreak havoc on the marketplace of legitimate commerce.

Finally, we note that, although copyright owners may have more options to pursue domestic rather than foreign rogue websites, domestic sites also continue to pose challenges.

The parasites who operate rogue websites in the United States often do not provide sufficient contact information to allow a copyright owner to identify or locate them and can create obstacles to moving forward with potential litigation. Additionally, even if a copyright owner targets a domestic website, there may still be the same problem as faced abroad that the website may simply - and quickly - reappear at another domain name.

## Moving Forward

The Copyright Office believes that copyright enforcement against the operators of rogue websites could be enhanced and improved with mechanisms that "follow the

[8] For example, news reports indicate that the Spanish website Rojadirecta.com, a domain name that was seized by ICE in its February 1, 2011 seizure, quickly established additional domains served by registries in other countries (e.g., Spain, Montenegro, India), and continues its operations. See, e.g., Trent Nouveau, *US DOJ and ICE seize additional domains*. TG Daily, Feb. 2, 2011, available at http://www.tgdaily.com/business-and-law-features/53884-us-doj-and-ice-seize-additional-domains.

money" within the Internet ecosystem. These parasites could be cut off from payment mechanisms and advertising revenues in the United States; this could combat their very existence, or at least substantially decrease their impact on the market for legitimate copyrighted content.

In our view rogue websites are a problem that will require mutual cooperation of many stakeholders and Congress may want to consider whether all who benefit from a healthy online ecosystem should contribute to a solution. For example, ISPs play a critical role in providing Internet access, and correspondingly the means to interrupt access, to rogue websites. Domain name registries and registrars are able to block domain names. Search engines point users to rogue websites, but technology may exist that would allow them to block such sites from appearing in search results, much as search engines have eliminated child pornography from their results.

### *Payment Processors*

Payment processors are credit card companies and payment intermediaries such as PayPal. With respect to legitimate commerce, they enable consumers and businesses to conduct transactions online. Without them, the Internet would not be the robust business enterprise it is today in the American economy.

Payment processors are structured in a variety of ways. Some have direct contractual relationships with consumers, others have relationships with merchants and banks, and yet others have mixed arrangements. They have terms of use that can be helpful in handling allegations of copyright infringement. At the same time, many rogue websites allow Internet consumers to use traditional credit cards, debit cards and other financial transaction services to purchase or access infringing materials as part of single transactions or subscriptions. Even those websites that do not rely on financial transactions can benefit from payment processors' goodwill by displaying the logos of well-known payment networks in an effort to lend credibility to the site by creating a false sense of authenticity.

Congress could grant enforcement entities such as ICE the explicit authority to request a court order requiring payment processors to stop providing these services for the website in question to consumers within the United States. If rogue websites are unable to use standard payment methods, Internet users may be less willing to use less familiar alternative payment structures, and innocent consumers might be suspicious of the absence of standard payment methods, thereby harming the financial viability of the sites.

### *Advertising Networks*

Many rogue websites display advertising, allowing them to run lucrative businesses by providing content without a copyright owner's permission. Generally, advertising networks place advertisements on websites for merchants wishing to advertise their goods and services. Such networks typically place their clients' advertising on websites that may be relevant to the clients' goods and services or that are popular with the clients' target demographic. Some networks, however, do not specifically control where all of the advertisements appear and instead subcontract at least some of their placement services to other advertising brokers that, in turn, place advertisements on various websites.

Unfortunately, the multi-layered structure of Internet advertising placement can make it difficult to determine which entity is ultimately responsible for placing an advertisement on a specific website. At this point it is unclear to us whether all the advertising networks involved in the placement of a particular advertisement would necessarily have either knowledge that an advertisement was placed on an infringing site or the ability to prevent the advertisement's placement on that site.

Legislation that could prevent advertising networks from placing advertisements on rogue websites might reduce the profitability of these sites and deter further copyright infringement. Once again, legislation could give enforcement entities such as ICE explicit authority to request a court order requiring U S.-based advertising networks to stop placing advertisements on the alleged rogue website in question.

### *Other Parties in the Internet Ecosystem*

ISPs play a critical role in providing access to and delivery of Internet-based services to consumers. Some stakeholders propose to provide enforcement authorities such as ICE with the ability to request court orders directing ISPs to block the domain names or Internet protocol addresses of specified foreign-based rogue websites for all U S.-based customers. We have also heard concerns about the technical feasibility of implementing blocking orders, especially at the subdomain or IP address levels, as well as the potential costs that ISPs might incur if a large volume of orders were presented to them for action. We believe that these issues require further investigation and analysis.

We are aware of several other countries that have issued judicial orders requiring ISPs in their jurisdictions to block national access to specific foreign websites that seem to fall within the rogue website concept here. For example, actions have been taken in Italy, Ireland and Denmark in an effort to block the website The Pirate Bay from those nations' citizens.[9]

---

[9] The Italian Supreme Court in December 2009 ruled that ISPs could be obliged to cut access to the then-Swedish-based The Pirate Bay (TBP) domain. See International Federation of the Phonographic Industry (IFPI), *Italy's Supreme Court explains ruling that ISPs should block The Pirate Bay*, Jan. 8, 2010, available at http://www.ifpi.org/content/section_news/20100108.html. In early February 2010, Italian prosecutors ordered all national access providers to block IBP. *See Block The Pirate Bay, Italian ISPs ordered*, Feb. 10, 2010, available at http://www.p2pnet.net/story/35342. Action has also been taken action against TBP in Ireland and Denmark. One major Irish ISP, Eircom, blocked access to TPB in July 2009 (using both DNS and IP address blocking). See Austin Modine, *Eircom to block Pirate Bay*. The Register. Feb. 23, 2010, available at http://www.theregister.co.uk/2009/02/23/irma_demands_irish_isps_block_access_to_piracy_sites/. In Denmark, the recording industry obtained an injunction against an ISP (Tele2, now Telenor) requiring it to block access to TPB; this was confirmed on appeal, and, in May 2010 the Supreme Court upheld the injunction. See European Digital Rights (EDRi), *Danish supreme court upholds injunction to block the Pirate*

When attempting to seize or take down domain names to block rogue websites, law enforcement agencies and copyright owners often work with registrars and registries because they can often control where a request for a domain name from an Internet user is directed.[10] We are aware, however, of the concerns expressed by some that domain name server blocking, including that used in the recent ICE civil forfeiture proceedings and other non-copyright law enforcement activities, targets only the domain name and does not block the IP address, thus allowing persistent Internet users to find the rogue website using the IP address. This Subcommittee might want to give further consideration to methods to address this concern either at the registrar and registry level or through ISPs.

Search engines are perhaps the most important player in the on-line ecosystem. Without them, the Internet would be un-navigable. Unfortunately, search engines routinely point people to rogue websites, including in situations where the customer is looking for a legitimate site. In fact, sometimes the illegitimate sites appear much higher in search results, displacing authorized sources of copyrighted content. A legitimate question is whether search engines should be involved in solving the rogue website dilemma. For example, is it reasonable and viable for search engines to suppress search results that direct Internet users to rogue websites?

The Copyright Office is very active in the realm of international intellectual property policy. In discussions and efforts with other countries, the United States seeks to be a leader in the development of standards and solutions. Moreover, our rightsholders are beneficiaries of the work done by the U.S. government globally. It would befit the leadership role of the United States to address the bad actors who undermine legitimate commerce on the Internet.

## Due Process and Other Safeguards

The Copyright Office strongly agrees with those who have stressed due process and related concerns in the context of legislating a solution to rogue websites. First, due process is a bedrock foundation of our nation's legal system, even for those who violate the law. Any remedy that impedes or obstructs access to a website must be consistent

---

*Bay*, June 2, 2010, available at http:/www.edri.org/cdrigram/number8.11/piratebay-denmark-supreme-court. The Court did not require IP address blocking, only blocking of the site's domain and sub-domains (DNS blocking).

[10] When a consumer tries to reach a website associated with a domain name, the consumer's ISP identifies and contacts the relevant registry associated with the requested domain name, such as VeriSign for ".com" top-level domain names, because the registry controls the root name servers that will direct Internet traffic to the correct website. The registry, in turn, directs the user to an authoritative domain name server, which, in most circumstances, is the registrar of the specific domain name. The registrar' then sends the Internet user to the content identified by its customer, the domain name registrant, which is housed on a specific server, identified by an TP address connected with a particular domain name (or group of domain names).

with this core American principle. The domain owner should receive notice as well as an opportunity to be heard.

Due process concerns are all the more pertinent in light of possible First Amendment implications of shutting down websites on the Internet. Care must be taken to ensure that non-infringing expression is not unnecessarily suppressed and that the relief is effective but narrowly tailored. This said, we do not believe that an order that shuts down websites devoted to infringing activity would violate the First Amendment (nor would it constitute "censorship").

We note that injunctions have long been used in copyright cases and courts have not held them to be inconsistent with free expression. Indeed, copyright itself is part of the construct of free expression in the United States. The exclusive rights of copyright allow authors and their licensees to disseminate creative expression to the public and provide incentives for them to contribute to important public discussions and the economy. Fair use and other exceptions under the law provide good faith actors with the means to make limited use of copyrighted works without permission in certain instances, such as using brief excerpts of works necessary for the dissemination of news.

Second, remedies for the rogue website problem cannot unnecessarily jeopardize the efficient operation of the Internet. Some Internet engineers have warned that some of the proposed remedies would "risk fragmenting the Internet's global domain name system (DNS) ... and seriously harm the credibility of the United States in its role as a steward of key Internet infrastructure."[11] Such assertions require careful examination and the hearing of the Subcommittee today is a very helpful means of doing so. It might also be helpful to the dialogue among stakeholders if Congress were to seek the counsel of experts who can objectively evaluate technical facts as they relate to the rogue website problem. The Copyright Office believes that all players in the ecosystem would agree with this premise, including authors and other content owners, as the Internet is an extremely important platform for the dissemination of creative works.

## Conclusion

The Copyright Office believes that the parasites who operate rogue websites undermine the incentives for legitimate commerce and if left unchecked, they threaten to weaken the robust, innovation-based markets that exist in the United States today. Though we have some successful mechanisms for copyright enforcement, there remain deficiencies in law and practice. We believe every player in the Internet ecosystem can play some role in remedying this problem, and we look forward to Congress's continued examination of the issues.

---

[11] Open Letter from Internet Engineers to the Senate. Judiciary Committee (Sept 28, 2010), http://www.eff.org/deeplinks/2010/09/open-letter.

Mr. Chairman, thank you again for inviting me to speak here today. The mission of the U S. Copyright Office is "[t]o promote creativity by administering and sustaining an effective national copyright system." We welcome the efforts of this Subcommittee and welcome any questions that you and the Subcommittee may have. As always, we at the Copyright Office stand ready to assist you in your work.

Mr. Goodlatte. Mr. Sohn, welcome.

## TESTIMONY OF DAVID SOHN, SENIOR POLICY COUNSEL, CENTER FOR DEMOCRACY AND TECHNOLOGY (CDT)

Mr. Sohn. Thank you, Chairman Goodlatte, Ranking Member Watt, Members of the Subcommittee. On behalf of the Center for Democracy and Technology, thank you for the opportunity to participate in today's hearing.

I would like to say at the outset that CDT recognizes the problem posed by online infringement. Large-scale copyright infringement affects not just rights holders, but also the growth of new media, e-commerce and online expression, all of which are values that CDT works hard to promote.

The main point of my statement today, however, is to emphasize that the tactics chosen to fight infringement matter a great deal. Some tactics might be superficially attractive, but would not work very well in practice. Some tactics could do a lot of collateral damage, for example, by inadvertently impairing lawful online speech, lawful online communications tools, or by undermining cybersecurity.

And some tactics, particularly the domain name focused tactics that I discuss at length in my written testimony, suffer from both problems. They won't have much impact on infringement, and they risk doing significant inadvertent harm.

What I would like to do with the rest of my time is briefly list some general principles that Congress should keep in mind as it considers policy approaches in this area, and then turn to the specific question of domain name blocking and domain name seizures.

First in general. One, enforcement tactics should keep the targeted focus on the true bad actors and be careful to avoid impact on lawful businesses and speech. Doing that requires a narrow focus on purposeful wrongdoers, and it requires sufficient due process to avoid mistakes.

Two, proposals for a new law in this area really, as in any area, should be subject to careful cost-benefit analysis. If there are policies that offer small or ephemeral gains at high cost, that obviously doesn't make much sense.

And, three, when the infringers are overseas, cross-border cooperation is essential to stop the illegal activity at its source, and shut down the wrongdoers for good. Congress should not assume that the best approach to foreign infringement is necessarily a new domestic law.

Now, let me turn to the specific question of going after infringement websites by blocking or seizing their domain names. As I think the Members of this Subcommittee know well, the Senate Judiciary Committee last year considered legislation to expand this practice, by, among other things, asking Internet service providers to block domain name lookup requests.

The first thing to understand about this tactic is that it does not actually remove bad sites from the Internet. Nothing gets shut down. The servers and all the infringing content they contain are still there online.

If the domain name has been seized, the site operator can quickly hop to a new one, this time using a registrar outside U.S. jurisdiction. And as for the users, my testimony lists several completely easy ways they could reach a site whose name has been blocked or changed. The ways aren't highly technical, but for those users to whom it still seems complicated, software tools would quickly spring up to automate the process.

So the bottom line is that domain name tactics will have rapidly diminishing returns. The more common the interference with the domain name system, the more these work-arounds will go viral, and the more they will become routine. And I think at the end of the day, any actual impact on infringement will be fleeting at best.

Meanwhile, domain name tactics risk collateral damage in a number of areas. First, the tactics will have some impact on lawful speech. It is important to realize that targeting a domain name affects all the content at that domain. It is different than, for example, the DMCA notice and take-down process where only the specific infringing material is targeted.

Plus there are many domains that are shared by literally thousands of individual sites, and we have already seen concrete examples of mistakes and overbreadth because of this. In February, ICE mistakenly seized a domain with 84,000 sub-domain registrations. The result was that numerous, innocent people, personal bloggers, small businesses and so forth, had their websites replaced with a banner that read, essentially, this site has been seized due to child pornography. Needless to say, that is a very damaging allegation to have made against one.

Second, there are serious technical and cybersecurity concerns. For example domain name blocking is technically incompatible with DNSSEC, which is a standard for protecting the security of the domain name system that has been a decade in the making and is just rolling out. In addition, the technologies that users—or, excuse me, the techniques that users would employ to circumvent blocking would create new cybersecurity risks as well.

Finally, targeting domain names of purely foreign sites would encourage a dangerous jurisdictional scrum internationally with each country potentially trying to use the domain name system to enforce domestic law against foreign sites so that Congress has to consider the international implications and the precedent it would be setting.

For all of these reasons, I believe that codification and widespread use of domain name focused tactics would fail any serious cost-benefit analysis, and I would urge Congress not to go down that particular path.

Thanks for the opportunity to appear here today.

Mr. Goodlatte. Thank you, Mr. Sohn.

[The prepared statement of Mr. Sohn follows:]

# STATEMENT AT DAVID SOHN SENIOR POLICY COUNSEL CENTER FOR DEMOCRACY AND TECHNOLOGY, BEFORE THE HOUSE OF REPRESENTATIVES COMMITTEE ON THE JUDICIARY SUBCOMMITTEE ON INTELLECTUAL PROPERTY, COMPETITION, AND THE INTERNET, HEARING ON PROMOTING INVESTMENT AND PROTECTING COMMERCE ONLINE: LEGITIMATE SITES V. PARASITES. PART I*, MARCH 14, 2011

## Statement of David Sohn, Center for Democracy and Technology

On behalf of the Center for Democracy & Technology, thank you for the opportunity to participate in this hearing on websites that engage in rampant intellectual property infringement. CDT is a non-profit, public interest organization dedicated to preserving and promoting openness, innovation, and freedom on the decentralized Internet.

CDT supports the goal of reducing online infringement. Large-scale copyright infringement undermines First Amendment values in promoting expression and threatens the growth of new media and e-commerce. With respect to the particular focus of this hearing, CDT recognizes that there are websites whose main purpose and activity is to enable and promote infringement. These sites are true "bad actors" and they deserve to be the target of law enforcement.

CDT believes, however, that the specific means chosen to address infringement matter a great deal. Some tactics may be attractive from a copyright protection perspective, but would carry significant costs to important values such as innovation and free speech. CDT urges members of this Subcommittee to be aware of this risk and to carefully avoid tactics that would impair lawful Internet-based media and communications tools that are of growing value to consumers, the economy, and society in general.

After a brief note regarding the scope of the problem, this testimony will offer several principles for evaluating proposed policy approaches. It will then address the significant concerns raised by a specific enforcement tactic that has received considerable attention in recent months: the idea of combating allegedly infringing websites by ordering the seizure or blocking of their domain names. In short, CDT believes that legislation targeting domain names would be ineffective at achieving the goal of reducing infringement. At the same time, a domain-name approach would threaten unintended collateral damage in a number of areas, including suppressing lawful speech; exacerbating cybersecurity risks; and encouraging a dangerous global scrum in which each country tries to use the domain name system to assert domestic jurisdiction over foreign websites. Congress should not pursue such an approach.

## I. The Problem of Websites Dedicated to Infringement

CDT recognizes the problem of websites that seek to profit by distributing copyrighted material without authorization and without paying the lawful rightsholders. Indeed, CDT has sought to focus attention on websites that masquerade as lawful online music stores when in fact they have not secured any distribution rights. In 2005, CDT filed a complaint at the Federal Trade Commission concerning two websites that charged subscription fees for what they claimed was "100% legal" access to music and video downloads, when in truth the sites merely provided gateways to file-sharing networks on which infringement was common.[12] The FTC filed suit against the operator of one of the sites and ultimately won a court injunction and settlement.[13] In 2007 and 2008, CDT, with the intent of alerting potential users, compiled a "Music Download Warning List" of 47 websites that were falsely posing as legitimate music stores.[14]

Quantifying the problem, however, is exceedingly difficult. Congress should be especially cautious about statistics and studies that purport to measure the problem in dollars and cents. Last year, the General Accounting Office released a report analyzing efforts to quantify the economic effects of counterfeit and pirated goods.[15] GAO found that three widely cited U.S. government estimates of economic losses "cannot be substantiated" and that it "is difficult, if not impossible, to quantify the economy-wide

---

[12] Complaint and request for Investigation, Injunction, and Other Relief before the Federal Trade Commission In the Matter of Mp3DownloadCity.com and MyMusicInc.com, March 8, 2005, http://cdt.org/copyright/20050308complaint.pdf.

[13] Federal Trade Commission, "File Sharing Operator Settles FTC Charges," Press Release, May 25, 2006, http://www.ftc.gov/opa/2006/05/p2p.shtm.

[14] CDT, "Music Download Warning List," last updated July 2008, http://cdt.orq/copyright/warninglist.

[15] General Accounting Office, *Observations on Efforts to Quantify the Economic Effects of Counterfeit and Pirated Goods*, April 2010, http://www.gao.gov/new.items/d10423.pdf.

impacts." To be sure, the report observed that research suggests "the problem is sizeable." But methodologies for estimating the economic impact all have limitations, and results are highly sensitive to assumptions.

I would add two additional caveats. First, parties commissioning studies often have vested interests in the results. And second, it is important to remember that the Internet and digital technologies can be highly disruptive of traditional business models for reasons having nothing to do with infringement. For example, the rise of the Internet may have enabled increased infringement of music recordings, but it also has enabled a shift to selling songs individually, new marketplace options like podcasts and music streaming services, and changing patterns in the way people consume and enjoy music. Although these changes may have harmed some incumbent music providers, the changes were the result of innovation and competition. With so much in flux, there is no easy, controlled experiment to isolate the impact of infringement.

Therefore, while there is no question that the infringement problem is real and significant. Congress should not place too much weight on statistics purporting to quantify its overall economic impact. The GAO report suggests that such statistics are generally less than reliable.

## II. Principles for Evaluating Policy Approaches to Fighting Infringement

In developing and implementing policies designed to fight infringement-focused websites, CDT believes the Federal Government should take care to observe the following principles.

### *A. Enforcement Efforts Should Narrowly Target True "Bad Actors." Policies Should Take Care to Avoid Inadvertent Impact on Lawful Businesses, Individuals, and Speech*

Enforcement policies should emphasize pursuing and punishing those persons and entities engaged in purposeful, infringing conduct on a substantial scale. Focusing specifically on such "bad actors" avoids inadvertent impact on legitimate business, legitimate free expression, and legitimate technologies.

By contrast, policies that target providers of multipurpose technologies, services, and platforms will risk significant overbreadth. Laws that affect whether and how such platforms operate can carry major consequences for the large body of lawful speech and other activity that the platforms support. Similarly, policymakers should be sensitive to the fact that there are many disputed areas in copyright; mainstream technologies that have been challenged in major copyright litigation over the years include VCRs, mp3 players, printer cartridges, video-sharing websites, online auction sites, and many more.[16] Any new policies aimed at improving enforcement of current law should be designed to target clear-cut cases and should expressly steer clear of legal grey areas.

In addition, policies aimed at "bad actors" should provide sufficient procedural safeguards to protect against the risk of mistakes. The Internet has become a crucial medium for free expression, entitled to the highest level of First Amendment protection.[17] Accidental, overaggressive, or technologically unsophisticated application of tough new policies could impair lawful speech in a variety ways, from stifling individual websites to undermining online platforms that enable speech by users. Providing sufficient due process can help ensure that measures meant for true piracy rings are not brought to bear against the wrong parties. By contrast, policies that would give law enforcement authorities great discretion in a one-sided process create fertile ground for mistakes and inadvertent overbreadth.

### *B. New Policy Proposals Should Be Subject to Rigorous Cost-Benefit Analysis. There Needs to Be a Sober Assessment of Both How Effective a Policy Is Likely to Be and What Collateral Impact It May Cause*

Concern about online infringement is understandably high. But that does not mean that any and all proposals for reducing infringement are worthy of government endorsement. As in any area of policy, proposals for new anti-infringement measures must be subject to rigorous cost-benefit analysis, asking both (i) how effective a proposed policy is likely to be, and (ii) what negative collateral impact it may entail.

Policymakers should be particularly alert to the risk that, where a measure provides benefits to one industry or group and imposes costs on another industry or group, it can be in the interest of the beneficiaries (likely the rightsholders) to lobby strongly even for a measure that offers relatively minor private gains at high social cost. Thus, careful, independent consideration and balancing of the true costs and benefits of suggested measures is essential. If a particular proposal's reduction in online infringement is likely to be of marginal size or fleeting duration (because, for example, it can be easily evaded) and the proposal would impose significant burdens on (for example) legitimate innovators or online free expression, then the proposal should be rejected.

### *C. Addressing Foreign Infringement Activity Requires International Cooperation*

Where website operators and other participants in online infringement are based outside the United States, unilateral domestic law enforcement tactics will be limited in their effectiveness. Cross-border problems require cross-border solutions.

---

[16] For a longer list, see CDT, Comments to the Department of Commerce Internet Policy Task Force's Inquiry on Copyright, Creativity, and Innovation in the Internet Economy, November 19, 2010, http://cdt.org/files/pdfs/CDT%20Comments%20to%20NTIA%20Copyright%20Task%20Force.pdf, at 2-4.

[17] *Reno v. American Civil Liberties Union*, 521 U.S. 844 (1997).

Cooperating with foreign law enforcement may carry its own challenges. But only cooperative approaches have the potential to stop infringement at its source - to hold wrongdoers personally accountable and to shut down their operations for good. As the recent annual report of the Intellectual Property Enforcement Coordinator observes, "Intellectual property crime knows no borders and effective efforts to combat infringement must involve cooperative law enforcement efforts with foreign governments."[18] The report goes on to detail law enforcement cooperation efforts with Mexico, Latvia, South Korea, and even China. In addition, the final proposed text of the Anti-Counterfeiting Trade Agreement (ACTA) includes a chapter on international cooperation. Congress should not assume that foreign infringement activity is best addressed through additional domestic law.

### *D. Enforcement Alone Cannot Offer a Satisfactory Solution to the Problem of Online Infringement*

A full strategy for reducing online infringement requires more than just the "stick" of law enforcement. Just as essential is the "carrot" of compelling legal offerings. One of the best defenses against infringement sites is the continued proliferation of lawful online distribution options that create convenient, easy-to-use ways for consumers to get the content they want in the form that they want it. When consumers have attractive legal options for satisfying their demand, the incentive to rely on illegal sources is greatly reduced.

With this in mind, policymakers should look for ways to encourage the legal marketplace. For example, about five years ago this subcommittee held hearings and debated legislation concerning possible reform and streamlining of the music licensing provisions in Section 115 of the Copyright Act.[19] Ensuring that the structure of current licensing regimes encourages the building of attractive legal services, rather than serving as an obstacle, would help reduce infringement.

Public education is another important and underappreciated component of policy in this area. Modern information technology is here to stay and will continue to put powerful digital tools in the hands of the public. Inevitably, public norms and attitudes will play a major role in shaping how people choose to use the information-age tools at their disposal. Consumers need to understand that using these tools to engage in infringement is both illegal and wrong. But copyright law can be a highly technical area, and consumers' initial assumptions about what is and is not permitted are often not accurate. If the goal is to have a long-term impact on the scope of the infringement problem, policymakers should make public education a key part of the discussion.

---

[18] 2010 U.S. Intellectual Property Enforcement Coordinator Annual Report on Intellectual Property Enforcement, February 2011, www.whitehouse.gov/sites/default/.../IPEC/ipec_annual_report_feb2011.pdf, at 20.

[19] CDT Policy Post, "Music Rights Regime Needs Updating, Should Embrace New Technologies," November 2, 2007, http://cdt.org/policy/music-rights-regime-needs-updating-should-embrace-new-technologies.

## III. Policy Concerns with Tactics That Target Domain Names

In recent months, there has been considerable focus on using the domain name system (DNS) to go after websites associated with infringement. Since late June 2010, Immigration and Customs Enforcement (ICE) and the Department of Justice have executed seizure warrants for over 100 domains as part of "Operation In Our Sites."[20] S. 3804, the "Combating Online Infringement and Counterfeits Act" from the 111 Congress, would have expanded the practice of such seizures, giving the Attorney General the ability to bring in rem actions against both domestic and foreign domain names and to compel intermediaries, including Internet service providers (ISPs), to seize or block the domain.[21]

CDT has significant concerns about both the low effectiveness and the high collateral impacts of this approach to fighting infringement. In light of these concerns, we believe that a policy that codifies and encourages large-scale reliance on domain names as an enforcement mechanism would fail any cost-benefit test. For the reasons set out below, we would strongly urge Congress not to proceed with legislation proposing domain-name focused remedies.

### *A. Ineffectiveness*

Domain-name seizure and blocking can be easily circumvented, and thus will have little ultimate effect on online infringement. The DNS performs a relatively simple function: translating text URLs (like www.cdt.org) into machine-readable IP addresses (like 72.32.6.120). This function is wholly unrelated to the content available at any given site. Importantly, neither seizing nor blocking a website's domain name removes the site from the Internet. The servers are still connected and users can still reach the site, including any infringing content.

There are a number of ways a targeted site may still be reached. First, the site's operator could simply register a new domain name for the site. This is both easy and likely. For example, most of the sports-streaming sites connected to ten domains ICE seized in February quickly reappeared and are easily located at new domains.

Second, the site's operators could simply publicize its IP address, which users could then bookmark in lieu of saving or remembering the domain name. This is exactly what happened when the provider of WikiLeaks's DNS service provider terminated the

---

[20] ICE, "'Operation In Our Sites' targets Internet movie pirates: ICE, Manhattan U.S. Attorney seize multiple Web sites for criminal copyright violations," Press Release, June 30, 2010, http://www.ice.gov/news/releases/1006/100630losangeles.htm.

[21] Combating Online Infringement and Counterfeits Act, S. 3804, 111th Congress (2010).

controversial site's account in December 2010; the IP address was immediately and widely available.[22]

Third, a site's operators could distribute a small browser plug-in or other piece of software to allow users to retrieve the IP addresses of the operators' servers. Such simple tools would make the process of following a site around the web virtually automatic.

Fourth, in the case of blocking by ISPs, users could easily switch DNS-lookup providers to avoid blocking orders. Since most operating systems come with DNS server functionality built in, savvy users could set up local DNS resolvers on their own computers, thus avoiding any DNS servers that have been ordered to block. In addition, third-party public DNS servers are widely available, and more would inevitably spring up outside the United States to avoid being subject to blocking orders. For Internet users, pointing DNS requests to these unfiltered servers would be simply a matter of updating a single parameter in their operating systems' Internet settings. Users who want to engage in infringement will thus easily be able to route their traffic around DNS providers that enforce blocking orders. For users to whom this seems complicated, software tools could easily automate the process.

All of these circumvention techniques are likely to occur if domain-name seizure and blocking become widespread. Infringement sites have a highly motivated and relatively savvy user base, and word will spread quickly as to how best to circumvent any blocking. This means that any impact on infringement from seizing or blocking domain names is likely to be ephemeral at best.

In short, the main impact of domain-name seizure and blocking would be to drive website operators to domains administered by non-U.S. registrars and registries and website users to alternative (but equally easy) Internet navigation methods. The more common the interference with the domain name system, the more the workarounds would become routine. The workarounds themselves are trivial and would quickly go viral, rendering the domain-name approach almost entirely ineffective.

### *B. Overbreadth: Impact on Lawful Speech*

The seizure and blocking of domain names would almost certainly affect lawful speech, for several reasons.

First, these methods target entire domains, which may contain a mix of lawful and unlawful content, including non-Web content like email or instant messaging connections. This stands in sharp contrast to the notice-and-takedown provisions of the DMCA. Under the DMCA process, specific infringing material is identified. That material, and only that material, is then targeted for takedown. Enforcement actions

---

[22] Rob Pegoraro, "WikiLeaks sinks, resurfaces (repeat as necessary)," *Washington Post* Faster Forward blog, December 3, 2010, http://voices.washingtonpost.com/fasterforward/2010/12/wikileaks_sinks_resurfaces rep.html.

targeting a domain name itself would not be so narrowly targeted; they would affect anything and everything associated with that domain.

The risk of impairing access to lawful content might be mitigated if there were strong guarantees that only pure infringement hubs would be targeted. For that purpose, a tightly focused definition of the "bad actor" websites would be essential. Last year's Senate bill, S.3804, failed to ensure such a narrow focus. Although that bill used the well-intended phrase "dedicated to infringing activities," its definition of that term was broad enough to encompass sites that, far from being "dedicated" to infringement, are actually multipurpose sites featuring a wide variety of content.

The risk of sweeping in non-infringing content is exacerbated if seizure or blocking orders are issued without a full adversarial hearing. When law enforcement makes its case unopposed and a domain name owner has no opportunity to defend itself, mitigating factors and overbreadth issues may not come to light before the name is seized or blocked. In a one-sided process, the risk of mistakes or overaggressive action is high.

This risk is evident from news reports about several of the recent domain name seizures conducted by ICE pursuant to the civil forfeiture provisions of criminal copyright law. Several of the domain names seized in November were for music blogs which contained links to copyrighted songs. The operators of some of those blogs claim that the songs were supplied by the record labels themselves, for promotional purposes.[23] To be clear, CDT expresses no opinion about whether these blogs were authorized to post links to these songs or whether that activity was infringing. But there are significant questions about whether these blogs were such "bad actors" that their entire domain names should be seized, and it seems under ICE's seizure process these questions were not fully considered. In addition, seizing the domain name affected not just the links to potentially infringing songs, but all of the commentary on the blogs.

In another example, in February ICE seized domain names associated with a Spanish site that had been ruled lawful and non-infringing after extensive litigation in Spain.[24]

Again, CDT expresses no opinion about whether the site's activity violates U S. law. But the outcome in Spain suggests that the site operator, rather than being a clear-cut infringer, might at least have some serious legal arguments that it could offer in its defense. Its domain names were seized nonetheless. The end result was that a domain that Spanish courts had declared to be lawful was seized by the U.S. Government.

---

[23] Ben Sisario, "Music Web Sites Dispute Legality of Their Closing," *New York Times*, December 19, 2010, http://www.nytimes.com/2010/12/20/business/media/20music.html: see also Mike Masnick, "If Newly Seized Domains Were Purely Dedicated To Infringement, Why Was Kanye West Using One?," *Techdirt*, November 30, 2010, http://www.techdirt.com/articles/20101130/00245312049/if-newly-seized-domains-were-purely-dedicated-to-infringement-why-was-kanye-west-using-one.shtml.

[24] Nate Anderson, "US Customs begins pre-Super Bowl online mole-whack," *Ars Technica*. February 2, 2011, http://arstechnica.com/lech-policy/news/2011/02/us-customs-begins-pre-super-bowl-mole-whacking.ars; see also Mike Masnick, "Homeland Security Seizes Spanish Domain Name that Had Already Been Declared Legal," *Techdirt*, February 1, 2011, http://www.techdirt.com/articles/20110201/10252412910/homeland-security-seizes-spanish-domain-name-that-had-already-been-declared-legal.shtml.

Under a flawed definition or one-sided process, little would prevent domain-name seizure or blocking from being used against user-generated content sites - that is, websites that enable users to store, post, and share data. This is especially true in the case of lesser-known sites that officials may not be familiar with. A judge might think twice before issuing an order against a well-known platform, but not its equally legitimate start-up competitor. Such sites have many lawful uses, but can in practice be widely used for infringement as well. There is substantial ongoing debate and litigation about whether and when such sites should bear some responsibility and/or liability for infringing activities by users. But at a minimum, that is a question that should be decided only upon a full, adversarial judicial proceeding. Short-circuiting that process would risk affecting lawful platforms for user speech.

A final reason why domain-name seizure and blocking may affect lawful speech relates to the existence of subdomains. Many web hosting services are constructed in a way such that thousands of individual sites, created and maintained by thousands of individuals, share a single domain name. For example, the service might be located at "webhost.com" and the individual sites might be joe.webhost.com and bob.webhost.com. If some infringement sites were hosted on this kind of platform, domain-name seizure or blocking would affect not just the actual offenders, but the entire platform. Moreover, the existence of additional subdomains and thus the overbroad impact might not be immediately apparent to law enforcement authorities looking at a particular infringement website. As a result, a great deal of lawful speech could be affected.

Again, the recent ICE seizures provide a cautionary tale. In early February, ICE executed seizure of ten domain names linked to sites allegedly hosting child pornography. Child pornography is a despicable crime. But in seizing one domain, "mooo.com," ICE inadvertently blocked thousands of innocent and unrelated subdomains.[25] The owner of mooo.com allows individuals to register subdomains, which they can then point to any IP address. That means the mooo.com domain name is effectively subdivided and shared among numerous, entirely independent users. The content hosted at any particular subdomain is wholly separate - hosted on different servers with different IP addresses - than the content hosted at other subdomains or at the first-level "mooo.com" domain itself. But because of illegal content allegedly present at one such subdomain, all were seized and redirected to an ICE banner announcing that the domain had been seized for violating child pornography laws.

Websites hosted at those subdomains include many personal websites that do not appear to be hosting any illegal content. In looking into the incident, CDT discovered personal blogs, discussion forums, a small business, and sites where academic researchers

---

[25] Thomas Claburn, "ICE Confirms Inadvertent Web Site Seizures," Information Week, February 18, 2011, http://www.informationweek.com/news/security/vulnerabilities/showArticle.jhtml?articleID=229218959&cid=RSSfeed_IWK_All.

shared papers and professional information.[26] During the time all mooo.com subdomains were inaccessible, these users were no doubt shocked to see as they tried to visit their sites not only that their sites were inaccessible, but that law enforcement was telling other would-be visitors that the sites had been taken down due to child pornography. This is an incredibly serious allegation that alone can damage an individual's reputation.

The experience of mooo.com users stands out as the most egregious example to date of overblocking that can result from domain-name seizure. Clearly ICE had not thoroughly ensured that the action it was taking was narrowly tailored to the criminal actors, and the result silenced protected speech and harmed the reputations of innocent parties.

The risk of overbreadth would be greatly exacerbated if legislation in this area were to include a private right of action. As noted above,[27] there is a long history of civil copyright challenges to mainstream technologies and bona fide businesses. Narrowly targeting a new enforcement tactic at true "bad actors" would be impossible if any private rightsholder could initiate an action. Borderline cases inevitably would be initiated and the unintended impact on lawful businesses and speech would be significant. Adding a private right of action to the kind of process contemplated last year's Senate bill would intensify that tactic's risks and costs.

In sum, seizing and blocking domain names would impede access to some material that is not itself infringing, but that simply shares a domain name with infringing material.

This overbreadth, in turn, raises serious constitutional questions. There is a strong argument that the tactic of domain name seizure and blocking targets an instrumentality of speech (domain names) and that it creates a prior restraint, effectively trying to censor the owner of a domain name based on his or her illegal activity in the past. Especially given how ineffective domain-name focused enforcement measures are likely be in achieving their stated goal, as discussed above, a bill that adopts the approach could be vulnerable to a First Amendment challenge.

### *C. Technical Impact and Cybersecurity*

Seizing and blocking domain names presents a number of technical challenges that could have an impact on the Internet's reliability, security, and performance.

First, for ISPs, compliance with blocking orders may come at the expense of implementing the DNS Security Extensions (DNSSEC). For over 10 years, Internet engineers have been working to develop and implement a set of standards for addressing security flaws in the domain name system. DNSSEC is finally being deployed; the Office

---

[26] See, e.g., http://greyghost.mooo.com/; http://cowbell.mooo.com/catalog/index.php.

[27] See supra note 5 and accompanying text.

of Science and Technology Policy calls it a "major milestone for Internet security."'[28] But having DNS lookup providers either pretend a site does not exist or redirect users to a site they have not requested (such as to a site saying "access to the site you were seeking is being blocked due to a court finding of copyright infringement") is flatly inconsistent with DNSSEC. The incompatibility is technical; DNSSEC uses cryptography to prevent DNS responses from being tampered with or falsified. A DNS resolver using DNSSEC simply is not able to give a cryptographically signed response that is false. DNS lookup providers could try to avoid the incompatibility by declining to respond to certain DNS requests at all, but this carries performance drawbacks that providers might prefer to avoid. Congress should avoid steps that would prevent or discourage Internet service providers from implementing this important security standard.

Second, blocking at the service provider level carries security risks for Internet users beyond the tension with DNSSEC. Most users today rely on their ISP to perform domain-name lookup functions. But as explained above with regard to ineffectiveness, switching to another lookup provider is trivial. The more ISPs and other major DNS providers are required to block lookup requests for websites that users want to reach, the more users will switch to independent, non-ISP DNS servers. And critically, they will not switch to other trustworthy U.S.-based DNS providers, but to DNS services located outside of the reach of U.S. law.

This would do more than just render service-provider-level domain-name blocking ineffective. ISPs' DNS servers offer a crucial window into network usage; migration away from these servers would undermine ISPs' ability to observe and track botnet activity and other cybersecurity threats on their networks.[29]

In addition, it would put users at the mercy of potentially unscrupulous foreign DNS servers, which could redirect user traffic for phishing or botnet purposes. Though they may be unaware of it, users place an enormous amount of trust in their DNS provider to route requests to the proper sites. ISPs have incentive to maintain that trust, but other DNS operators - especially those with an interest in evading the blocking of sites dedicated to commercial infringement - will likely not share that same incentive. By creating strong incentives to rely on potentially untrustworthy DNS providers, the widespread use of domain-name seizure and blocking would create new and very dangerous opportunities for security risks and crime online.

Finally, encouraging many residential customers to rely on out-of-country DNS servers could undermine the efforts of CDNs (content delivery networks, such as Akamai) to improve the overall speed and efficiency of the Internet as a whole. CDNs rely on the approximate location of users' DNS lookup servers (based on IP address) to

---

[28] Andrew McLaughlin, "A Major Milestone for Internet Security," White House Office of Science and Technology Policy Blog, July 22, 2010, http://www.whitehouse.gov/blog/2010/07/22/a-major-milestone-internet-security.

[29] See statement of DNS security researcher Dan Kaminsky regarding S. 3804, available at http://www.publicknowledge.org/files/docs/COICA_Kaminsky_letter.pdf.

choose the best location from which to deliver content. As users change their DNS settings to use foreign nameservers, this signal will become a less reliable proxy for a user's location. For example, a CDN might assume a Maryland user using a Russian DNS provider is in Russia, undermining the benefits of CDNs and distributed hosting and increasing Internet congestion.

These security and reliability harms flow directly from the use of domain-name remedies to address infringing content. In light of how ineffective the approach is likely to be, this should raise serious questions as to whether the approach is worth the risk.

### *D. International Implications*

From an international perspective. Congress should think twice before endorsing domain-name blocking and seizure as common tools for enforcing domestic U.S. law against foreign websites. If other countries were to follow this example, the result would be a dangerous jurisdictional scrum. Other countries, citing the U.S. example, could try to seize or block the domain names of U.S. websites that are lawful here but that are asserted to violate some foreign law. This risk is not limited to repressive regimes. The scope of protection provided by the First Amendment remains the most expansive in the world, and speech protected in the United States remains proscribable in many other democratic countries. Local access to such speech remains a frustration to governments in those countries, and they would welcome a U.S.-based precedent to justify blocking it.

To take a concrete example, in 2000, a French court ruled that a Yahoo auction site (located at the Yahoo.com domain) violated French law because it contained postings for Nazi memorabilia.[30] A U.S. court refused to enforce that judgment, because the site's activity was lawful in the United States. Taking the domain-name approach, however, in the future a foreign country with a similar complaint could try to seize or block the site's domain name. If the registrar or registry for the domain name in question has an office in that foreign country, it could be ordered to transfer control of the name.

Enshrining domain-name seizure and blocking in statute could also serve as precedent for a variety of actions that the United States would characterize as censorship. Already, some countries erect national Internet "firewalls," in an effort to suppress access to certain speech. Over forty countries (and growing) now filter the Internet to some degree, and even many liberal democracies like Australia and France are considering mandatory regimes in which the government requires ISPs to block certain websites.[31]

---

[30] *UEJF and Licra v. Yahoo! Inc. and Yahoo France*, Tribunal de Grand Instance de Paris, May 22, 2000, http://www.juriscom.net/txt/jurisfrictilyauctions20000522.htm.

[31] See Australian Department of Broadband, Communications, and the Digital Economy, "ISP Filtering," http://www.dbode.gov.au/funding_and_programs/cybersafety_plan/Internet_service_provider_isp_filtering; see also Projet de lol d'orientation et de programmation pour la performance de la sécurité intérieure (France), passed by the French Senate on February 8, 2011 and available at http://www.senat.fr/pelite-loi-ameli/2010-2011/262.html (in French: bill including a requirement that ISPs block access to Internet sites when ordered by an administrative authority).

Historically, the U.S. State Department has been the strongest global voice against such balkanization of the Internet. Indeed, Secretary of State Clinton has made the concept of a single, global Internet a cornerstone of U.S. foreign policy on Internet matters, as she reaffirmed in a major speech last month.[32] But if the United States were to set the precedent that any country can order the blocking of a domain name if some of the content at that name (wherever its physical location) violates the country's local laws, it is hard to see what credibility the United States would have as it urges other countries not to block access wherever they see fit.

To be clear, CDT does not suggest that the United States should not take action against online infringers and encourage other countries to do likewise. The concern is simply that trying to use domain names as the means for fighting infringement would signal U.S. acceptance for the proposition that countries have the right to insist on removal of content from the global Internet as a tactic for enforcing domestic laws - and nothing would limit the application of this approach to copyright infringement and counterfeiting.

In countries where rule of law is weak or entirely absent, that approach would open the door to serious misuse. Once the United States sends the green light, the use of domain-name seizures and blocking to attempt to silence other kinds of content considered unlawful in a given country - from criticism of the monarchy in Thailand to any speech that "harms the Interests of the nation" in China - would surely spread. In short, the International precedent set by codification or expansion of domain-name focused enforcement efforts would worsen the balkanization of the Internet and undermine the effort to protect the ability of Internet users, human rights defenders, and citizen journalists to speak and access content online.

### *E. Compliance Costs*

A substantial portion of the costs of domain-name-focused enforcement measures would fall on third parties - specifically, registrars, registries, or ISPs. While the expense to third parties of complying with seizure and blocking orders is not a primary focus for CDT, Congress should take account of such costs in conducting a cost-benefit analysis of such tactics. Given the minimal effectiveness of measures targeting domain names, CDT believes there is little justification for asking registrars, registries and ISPs to bear the cost of carrying out such measures on behalf of law enforcement authorities.

---

[32] Secretary of State Hillary Rodham Clinton, "Internet Rights and Wrongs: Choices & Challenges in a Networked World," Speech at George Washington University, February 15, 2011, http://www.state.gov/secretary/rm/2011/02/156619.htm.

## IV. Conclusion

Fighting online infringement is a worthy goal. The tactics policymakers choose, however, matter a great deal. Unfortunately, there is no "silver bullet" that can eliminate infringement sites entirely or make them inaccessible to Internet users. Domain-name blocking and seizures are certainly not the answer; codification and widespread use of this tactic would carry costs and risks that would far exceed its minimal impact on infringement. CDT believes it would be a serious mistake for Congress to enact legislation focused on using domain names to control infringement.

As the principles discussed above suggest, a sound policy approach regarding enforcement in this area would focus first and foremost on catching and punishing true "bad actors." In the case of non-U.S. perpetrators, this will require cooperation with foreign governments. While such cooperation undoubtedly takes some effort, it ultimately offers the most effective approach, because it is the only way to ensure that the "bad guys" and the computer servers they use are actually taken offline for good. Moreover, a recent study found that a small group of users (around 100) were responsible for the lion's share of infringing files on major BitTorrent sites.[33] This suggests that well-targeted enforcement cases could have a substantial impact and be well worth the effort.

To the extent Congress believes new enforcement tools are necessary, it should look for remedies other than domain-name blocking and seizures. Cutting off infringers' sources of financial support would be one area to explore. In addition. Congress should be careful to focus any special new enforcement mechanisms narrowly on cases in which it has been shown that current tools cannot work. Congress should take into account not just existing legal mechanisms, but other available tools as well. For example, major payment systems have established procedures that can be used to cut off payments to Infringement sites. A representative from Visa recently told a Senate Committee that "few intellectual property owners have availed themselves of Visa's procedures" and that "[other payment systems have shared similar experiences."[34] It is unclear why this potentially powerful tool is not being used more widely by rightsholders.

Finally, any enforcement measures that aim to sidestep normal judicial process would, at a minimum, need to be narrowly tailored and contain carefully crafted procedural safeguards. Without such safeguards, there would be a risk of impairing lawful websites and speech, as the experience with ICE seizures has already begun to demonstrate.

---

[33] Ruben Cuevas et al., *Is Content Publishing in BitTorrent Altruistic of Profit-Driven*?, ACM CoNEXT Conference (November 30 - December 3, 2010, Philadelphia, PA), http://conferences.sigcomm.org/co-next/2010/CoNEXT_papers/11-Cuevas.pdf See also Carlos III University of Madrid, "A research study Identifies who uploads the majority of the content to the P2P piracy networks," Press Release, http://www.uc3m.es/portal/page/portal/actualidad_cientifica/noticias/P2P_network (last visited March 7, 2011).

[34] *Hearing on Targeting Websites Dedicated to Stealing American Intellectual Property Before the Senate Comm, on the Judiciary*, 112th Cong. (February 16, 2011) (statement of Denise Yee, Visa, Inc.) at 15.

CDT appreciates the opportunity to testify today and stands ready to work with the Subcommittee on this and other important issues of Internet policy.

Mr. Goodlatte. Mr. Castro. Welcome.

## TESTIMONY OF DANIEL CASTRO, SENIOR ANALYST, INFORMATION TECHNOLOGY AND INNOVATION FOUNDATION (ITIF)

Mr. Castro. Chairman Goodlatte, Ranking Member Watt, and Members of the Subcommittee, I appreciate the opportunity to appear before you to discuss strategies for dealing with these so-called parasitic, or rogue sites, on the Internet. These websites steal American and intellectual property either through engaging in digital piracy or selling counterfeit goods.

Rogue sites stunt economic growth, eliminate American jobs, and put U.S. consumers at risk. The problem of digital piracy has become so pervasive today that one in four bits traveling on the Internet is infringing content.

With just a few clicks, Internet users can download pirated copies of full-length Hollywood movies, watch unauthorized video streams of live sports games, and illegally download software to use on their computers. Sometimes it is even easier to find pirated content on the Internet than legitimate content.

To give just one example, I recently performed a Web search for "watch Inception online," and there was not a single link to a legitimate website in the first two pages of results. Instead, I received a list of rogue sites that earned, had revenue every time a user watches the movie illegally.

Consumers shopping online are also exposed to counterfeit shoes, counterfeit goods, including prescription drugs, cosmetics, handbags and shoes. Not only are these goods, counterfeit goods, often of poor quality, many counterfeit items such as infant formula or baby shampoo have been found to be harmful to human health.

Here, too, the problem is substantial. A recent study found that traffic to 48 sites selling counterfeit goods averaged almost a quarter of a million visits per day. This translates into serious consequences for our economy. One group estimates the counterfeiting has directly resulted in the loss of more than 750,000 jobs.

Currently rogue sites operate in a low risk, high reward environment. Site operators, especially those outside of the United States, face few personal risks from law enforcement and encounter few, if any, barriers to distributing illegal content online. We need to change the equation.

More can be done to help reduce online infringement, including the following, create a process by which the Federal Government, with the help of third parties, can identify websites around the world that are systematically engaged in piracy or counterfeiting;

enlist ISPs to combat rogue sites by blocking them, implement notice and response systems for repeated infringers and impose data caps where necessary; enlist search engines to combat IP theft by removing rogue sites from the search results; Require ad networks and financial service providers to stop doing business with websites supporting IT theft; create a process so that the private sector can consult with government regulators on proposed uses of anti-piracy or any counterfeiting technology; use NSF or NIST to fund anti-pi-racy and anti-counterfeiting technology R&D; and, finally, pursue global framework to protect IP internationally, and impose significant pressure and penalties on countries that steal from the United States.

The purpose of these actions should not be to target minor violations of the law, but rather to target websites primarily designed to steal intellectual property. New tools are especially needed for foreign rogue sites such as the Pirate Bay, a Swedish site dedicated to stealing software, movies, music, video games, books and other digital content.

One way to address these sites is to block them at the DNS level. DNS is like the global phone book for the Internet where providers use the number that—provide users the number that corresponds to each name. Using DNS to block rogue sites is certainly straightforward.

DNS servers can be instructed to no longer resolve an IP address when users look up the domain of a known rogue site. Without this IP address, users would not be able to go on and visit these sites. Basically this would be like taking a list of criminal organizations out of the phone book.

Some opponents of better enforcement of IP claim this will disrupt the Internet. I am here to tell you this claim is 100 percent false. The simple fact is that using DNS to block access to websites or servers is not particularly new or challenging. DNS redirection has been used for many years to block spam and hot nets and to protect users from malware. It is also widely used to provide parental control filters, correct typos in URLs and to provide improved search results.

Another objection some critics make is that blocking rogue sites contradicts the idea of a free and open Internet. However, websites that egregiously violate the law at the expense of American consumers and American workers have no place on the Internet. Democratic nations are well within their rights to use clear and transparent legal means to enforce IP rights online.

The responsibility for maintaining the Internet falls upon each user, each service provider and each business and institution that uses it, operates it and profits by it. I encourage you to put in place the frameworks and policies needed to facilitate and encourage all actors within the Internet ecosystem to take some measure of responsibility for maintaining its integrity and protecting consumers.

Thank you. Mr. Goodlatte. Thank you, Mr. Castro.

[The prepared statement of Mr. Castro follows:]

## Daniel Castro, Senior Analyst, Information Technology and Innovation Foundation (ITIF), "Promoting Investment and Protect Commerce Online: Legitimate Sites vs. Parasites, Part I," before the Committee on the Committee on Judiciary, Subcommittee on Intellectual Property, Competition, and the Internet U S. House of Representatives, March 14, 2011

Mr. Charmian and members of the Committee, 1 appreciate the opportunity to appear before you to discuss how to promote investment and protect commerce online by creating new enforcement mechanisms to restrict the impact of parasitic websites. These websites are an economic leech on the Internet economy. My name is Daniel Castro. I am a senior analyst at the Information Technology and Innovation Foundation (ITIF). ITIF is a nonpartisan research and educational institute whose mission is to formulate and promote public policies to advance technological innovation and productivity.

The Internet is a tremendous enterprise of user empowerment, free speech, and innovation, but it facilitates unlawful acts just as much as lawful ones. The proliferation of parasitic or rogue sites—websites enabling online piracy and the trade of counterfeit goods at the expense of legitimate businesses—is a pervasive problem that hurts American consumers and costs Americans jobs. Unchecked these rogue sites are a threat to the economic welfare of the United States.

While there is no silver bullet for stopping these rogue sites, we have an arsenal of "lead bullets" that collectively can significantly reduce their impact and sustainability. As with any law enforcement initiative, efforts at reducing digital piracy and online counterfeiting involve balancing costs and benefits. For example, while street crime could be reduced by doubling the number of police officers, communities seek an equilibrium where the marginal cost of an additional police officer does not outweigh the corresponding reduction in crime. With regard to rogue sites, it is hard to argue that this equilibrium has been reached—that society would not be better off with greater efforts to stop these sites. The extent of online copyright infringement is so large, and the costs of additional enforcement are so reasonable, that it is clearly in the public interest to take more aggressive steps to curb it.

Critics of stronger online intellectual property (IP) enforcement claim that such efforts will negatively impact the Internet ecosystem. This claim seems to assume that piracy is the bedrock of the Internet economy, an assertion not backed up by any evidence. Rather than limiting Internet innovation, as some assert, protecting copyrighted works online is necessary for innovation to continue to thrive on the Internet, While some anti-piracy proposals impose too much of a burden on businesses and consumers, many anti-piracy efforts do not negatively impact the Internet ecosystem. The goal of policymakers should be to identify and encourage as many of these tools and techniques as possible.

While the Internet is a vast, distributed system that has no central point of control, it should not be without any control whatsoever. Rather, the responsibility for maintaining the Internet falls upon each user, each service provider, and each business and institution that uses it, operates it, and benefits from it. Not every effort targeted at rouge sites should be embraced. But there are many cost-effective technologies available to confront rogue sites that only impinge on the "freedom" to steal. The U.S. government needs to put in place a framework that facilitates and encourages responsible control by all. Much more can and should be done. We need to make sure that all stakeholders, including government, content owners, website operators, financial service providers, ad networks, search engines, ISPs and other intermediaries, work together to form a comprehensive response to rogue sites.

## Rogues Sites Remain a Significant Problem for the United States

Rogue sites—websites engaged in digital piracy or selling counterfeit goods—steal U.S. intellectual property and stunt economic growth, eliminate American jobs, and put U.S. consumers at risk. As documented here and elsewhere, intellectual property (IP) makes substantial contributions to the U.S. economy. IP enforcement is an increasingly urgent matter for the United States because IP is a large component of what the United States produces and because this content is increasingly vulnerable in the global, knowledge-based economy. While U.S. firms increasingly manufacture overseas, an estimated 45 percent of the U.S. GDP comes from the proprietary ideas inside a product rather than the assembly of products.[35] The United States is a net exporter of IP, with IP contributing $37 billion to our trade balance in 2006.[36] IP industries also contribute to the U.S. trade balance through royalties and licensing fees. In 2006, U.S. receipts from cross-border trade in royalties and license fees (including patents, trademark, copyright, and other intangible rights) amounted to $63.4 billion and payments totaled $26.4 billion.[37]

The costs imposed on businesses by digital copyright infringement and counterfeiting restrict the ability of innovators to recover the expenses they incur to develop new products and services or produce new content. These activities reduce investment in research and development for new technology, lower U.S. economic growth, and ultimately result in a less robust innovation economy.

---

[35] Robert D. Atkinson, 'Comments on the Coordination and Strategic Planning of Federal Efforts Against Intellectual Property Infringement" Information Technology and Innovation Formation, 2010.

[36] Shayerah Ilias and Ian F. Fergusson. "Intellectual Property Rights and International Trade." *Congressional Research Service*, December 2007.

[37] Shayerah Ilias and Ian Fergusson, "Intellectual Property Rights and International Trade," *Congressional Research Service*, February 5. 2009.

## Online Piracy

Of all the industries that have been revolutionized by the rise of digital technology and the global Internet, few have been hit as hard as the industries that produce creative works—the producers of software, music, movies, television programs, video games, books, photos, and other media. The Internet has made global distribution of content easier than ever, with the ultimate promise of slashing costs by reducing the role of middlemen who produce, distribute, and sell the physical copies. Many users go online and pay for digital content or applications through sites like Amazon, iTunes or Netflix. Unfortunately, the digital era also has a serious downside for content producers and others in the industry as it has made it easier than ever for consumers to get access to content without authorization or without paying for it. Many Internet users around the world still choose to download pirated digital content from illegal sites or peer-to-peer (P2P) networks. The problem has become so pervasive that one in four bits of traffic traveling on the Internet today is infringing content.[38]

Much of the illegal exchange of content has been facilitated by digital tools that facilitate file sharing between users, including peer-to-peer (P2P) file sharing networks, hosted online file shares and online streaming services. P2P-based and unicast streaming services such as TV Ants and SopCast are widely used for re-transmission of live sports games and other events.[39] While all of these technologies have legitimate uses, the technologies have also been used for the unauthorized distribution of digital content on a global scale. In some cases, such as with some P2P file sharing networks, this has even become the principal use of the technology, although some P2P networks are focused on distributing legal content.[40] Websites like the Pirate Bay, isoHunt, and Btjunkie routinely rank among the most popular websites on the Internet and offer the ability to illegally download virtually all popular TV series, movies, recently released songs, software and games.[41] Unauthorized file sharing has been exacerbated by the growth of Web 2.0, or websites that cater to user-generated content, as many Internet users make no distinction when uploading between content they are authorized to upload and content they are not.

ITIF has previously documented how Internet users can easily go online and, with just a few clicks, download pirated copies of full-length Hollywood movies, watch unauthorized live video streams of sports programming online for free, or illegally

---

[38] David Price, "An Estimate of Infringing Use of The Internet," Envisional (2011), http://documents.envisional.com/docs/Envisional-Internet_Usage-Jan2011.pdf.

[39] "Background Report on Digital Piracy of Sporting Events," Envisional and NetResult. 2008.

[40] While P2P file sharing is dominated by copyright content, some people mistakenly associate P2P only with file sharing networks. However, P2P technology encompasses many types of applications and services from the Skype-to-Skype dialing procedure to video streaming on mainstream websites like CNN. (Note: Skype is not only a P2P application; it only does session initiation by P2P, the rest is a straight UDP session).

[41] As of November 2009, the Pirate Bay was ranked as 109th and isoHunt was ranked as 187th. "Alexa Top 500 Global Web Sites." web page, ND. http://www.alexa.com/topsites/global (accessed Nov. 28, 2009).

download software programs to use on their computers.[42] To give just one example, a recent web search for "Watch Inception Online" did not yield a single link to a legitimate website in the first two pages of results, but instead produced links to rogue sites to watch or download the movie.[43] Many of these sites earn advertising dollars from major companies. In ITIF's 2009 review of the websites The Pirate Bay and isoHunt, we found these sites displaying ads for brands such as Amazon.com, Blockbuster, British Airways, and Sprint.[44]

Some argue that online piracy is not really a problem, and that it only hurts large, profitable multinational companies, and even helps consumers by enabling them to obtain content at no cost. But this is fundamentally wrong. Online piracy harms the artists, both the famous and struggling, who create content, as well as the technicians—sound engineers, editors, set designers, software and game programmers—who produce it. And it also hurts law-abiding consumers who must pay higher prices for content, enjoy less content or relatively lower quality content, or pay higher prices for Internet access to compensate for the costs of piracy. Moreover, digital piracy not only results in the unauthorized distribution of content, it hurts the ability of content producers to create legitimate business models for selling digital content. As the saying goes, "It's hard to compete with free." While many companies have rallied to the challenge and created compelling businesses to sell content legally, on the whole, illegal content still remains widely available and commonplace.

While most individuals do not shoplift DVDs out of retail stores, many people feel comfortable downloading movies without paying for them. Why do so many people knowingly choose to continue to download unauthorized content? One reason is that it is so easy to find and download copyrighted content online. If stealing cars was as easy as pointing and clicking (and no one could tell if the car you are driving is stolen), the rate of motor vehicle theft would probably be much higher. A Pew Report found that "75% of teen music downloaders ages 12-17 agree that 'tile-sharing is so easy to do, it's unrealistic to expect people not to do it.'"[45] This survey also reflects the mentality of many people who think that "everybody is doing it" or that piracy is just "a function of the Internet."[46] Moreover, the Internet gives users a sense of anonymity where the risk of getting caught is relatively low and that of punishment even lower.

---

[42] Daniel Castro, Richard Bennett, and Scott Andes. "Steal These Policies: Strategies for Reducing Digital Piracy." Information Technology and Innovation Foundation (Washington DC: 2009), http://www.itif.org/files/2009-digital-piracy.pdf.

[43] Result of author's tests on March 10, 2011.

[44] Daniel Castro, Richard Bennett, and Scott Andes. "Steal These Policies: Strategies for Reducing Digital Piracy." Information Technology and Innovation Foundation (Washington DC: 2009), http://www.itif.org/files/2009-digital-piracy.pdf.

[45] Mary Madden. "The State of Music Online: Ten Tears After Napster," Pew Internet & American Life Project. 2009, http://www.pewinternet.org/Reports/2009/9-The-State-of-Music-Online-Ten-Years-After-Napster.aspx.

[46] Eliza Krigman, "IP Enforcement Policies Stir Censorship Debate," *Tech Daily Dose*, October 22, 2010, http://techdailydose.nationaljournal.com/2010/10/ip-enforcement-policies-stir-c.php.

Piracy has a negative effect on the U.S. economy. Because the United States is the nation that is most specialized in the production of digital goods (e.g., music, movies, software, video games, books, etc.) it also the nation that is most vulnerable to digital piracy. And much of this piracy occurs online. While the exact cost of piracy is difficult to measure, we have some good estimates of its magnitude. For example, one estimate found that the U.S. motion picture, sound recording, business software, and entertainment software/video game industries lost over $20 billion dollars in 2005 due to piracy, and retailers lost another $2 billion, for a combined loss of over $22 billion.[47] In 2006, another study found that the U.S. recording industry and related industries lost over $3.5 billion to online piracy and approximately $1.5 billion in physical piracy.[48] The recording industry has been particularly hurt by online theft because digital music files are small enough to transmit quickly, even over relatively slow Internet connections. The International Federation of the Phonographic Industry (IFPI) estimates that for every purchased track there are as many as 20 illegally downloaded songs.[49] In 2005, music piracy was associated with the loss or lack of realization of over 12,000 jobs in the sound recording industry in the United States.[50]

Other content industries have been impacted by piracy as well. The motion picture industry has lost significant amounts of money to pirated movies both online and on DVD. According to a report published by LEK Consulting, the U.S. motion picture industry lost $6.1 billion to piracy in 2005, which one report argues eliminated or prevented the creation of 46,597 jobs in the motion picture industry.[51] Neither are software companies immune from piracy. With pirated software equaling 20 percent of legitimate sales, the total value of pirated software is estimated to be over $9 billion in the United States.[52] Moreover, although piracy rates have hovered around 20 percent for the last several years, total software piracy has steadily increased in line with the growth in software sales.

Online piracy of sporting events, either through distributing illegal recordings or retransmission of live events, is another pervasive problem. A 2008 study found that the audience for unauthorized live streams of sporting events, such as NBA, NFL and MLB games, exceeded one million viewers and users can often find numerous unauthorized live streams for popular events.[53] Sites streaming this content generate revenue either through ads or subscriptions. The impact of unauthorized transmissions is growing. For

---

[47] Stephen Siwek, "The True Cost of Copyright Industry Piracy to the U.S. Economy." Policy Report 189, The *Institute for Policy Innovation*, September 2007.

[48] Ibid.

[49] IFPI. IFPI 2008 Digital Music Report. IFPI, 2008. 8. http://www.ifpi.org/content/library/dmr2008.pdf.

[50] These figures are for direct losses. Stephen Siwek, "The True Cost of Sound Recording Piracy to the U.S. Economy," *Policy Report 188*, The Institute for Policy Innovation, September 2007.

[51] Stephen Siwek. "The True Cost of Motion Picture Piracy to the U.S. Economy," Policy Report 186. The *Institute for Policy Innovation*. September 2006.

[52] Business Software Alliance, Sixth Annual BSA-IDC Global Software 08 Piracy Study, BSA, May 2009, http://global.bsa.org/globalpiracy2008/studies/globalpiracy2008.pdf.

[53] "Background Report on Digital Piracy of Sporting Events," Envisional and NetResult. 2008.

example, between 2007 and 2008 illegal distribution of Major League Baseball content increased by 25 percent.[54]

Videogame piracy is a growing problem worldwide. In 2008 the Entertainment Software Alliance detected more than 700,000 copyright infringements a month across more than 100 countries and sent out 6 million copyright infringement notifications. According to a report by the International Intellectual Property Alliance, in December 2008, 13 titles were illegally downloaded 6.4 million times. The top two titles alone accounted for nearly three-fourths of illegal downloads. The report, which evaluated piracy in 219 countries, found that two P2P networks, BitTorrent and eDonkey, were the largest sources of gaming piracy.[55]

Although not as common as music, movie, software, or videogame piracy, e-book piracy is growing, particularly as more content is sold in digital format. While hard data on book piracy is scarce, many publishing industry analysts see evidence of an alarming increase in piracy, due in part to the advent of the e-book reader. For example, John Wiley & Sons (publisher of the Dummies series) reports that in April 2009 it sent out 5,000 notices of online copyright violation—more than double the number of notices sent in the previous year.[56] In addition, e-book piracy appears to be more concentrated on certain websites than music, software, or motion picture piracy. Indeed, some industry observers estimated that as of 2009 as much as half of e-book piracy was housed on RapidShare, a Switzerland-based file hosting company that has advertised more than 10 petabytes of user uploaded files.[57]

## Counterfeit Goods Online

Rogue sites are also used to sell counterfeit goods. Counterfeit goods are widely available online through retail websites and online auctions. A recent study found that traffic to 48 sites selling counterfeit goods averaged more than 240,000 visits per day or more than 87 million visits per year.[58] Consumers shopping online are exposed to counterfeit goods, especially luxury goods such as jewelry, cosmetics, handbags, garments and shoes. Often these products are sold on sites that appear legitimate, charge reasonable prices, and may even link to the customer service of the brand owner. These counterfeit goods are often of poor quality. Counterfeiters also produce non-luxury goods. For example, counterfeit products such as infant formula or baby shampoo have

---

[54] Ibid.

[55] International Intellectual Property Alliance, Special Report 301, February, 2009.

[56] Motoko Rich, "Print Books Are Target of Piracy on the Web," *New York Times*, May 11, 2009, http://www.nytimes.com/2009/05/12/technology/internet/12digital.html.

[57] Randall Stress, "Will Books Be Napsterized?" *New York Times*, October 3, 2009, http://www.nytimes.com/2009/10/04/business/04digi.html.

[58] "Traffic Report: Online Piracy and Counterfeiting," *MarkMonitor*. January 2011.

also been discovered that pose health risks to young children. Illegal online pharmacies sell counterfeit prescription and non-prescription drugs to consumers for a variety of health conditions. As best, these drugs may simply be ineffective; at worst, they can be harmful, even lethal, to human health. Statistics about the exact size of the global market for counterfeit drugs vary, but most experts agree the problem is serious.[59] A 2011 report found that the combined traffic to 26 sites selling counterfeit prescription drugs averaged 141,000 visits per day or more than 51 million visits per year.[60]

Counterfeiting hurts American consumers. First, consumers face financial losses. Consumers who unknowingly purchase counterfeit goods waste their money on inferior products. In addition, all consumers pay higher prices for goods as businesses must charge higher prices to recoup losses from the trade in counterfeit goods. Second, consumers risk physical harm. Counterfeit products can be unsafe, unmonitored for quality assurance, and pose a threat to human health. Injury and even death has been reported as a result of counterfeit baby formula, drugs, cosmetics and toiletries.[61]

Counterfeiting also hurts American companies. First, companies face direct losses from counterfeit goods that erode their sales. Second, consumers who unknowingly purchase low-quality counterfeit goods may mistakenly attribute the defects to the brand owner and no longer purchase products from that company. Companies must also allocate resources to responding to complaints from these "customers" who call to report defects or ask for service under an illegitimate warranty.[62]

Counterfeit goods account for approximately 7 percent of global trade.[63] The worldwide market for counterfeit goods exceeded $500 billion in 2006 of which $250 billion was for U.S. goods.[64] The impact of these losses is substantial. The International Anti-Counterfeiting Coalition estimates that counterfeit merchandise directly results in the loss of more than 750,000 American jobs.[65]

---

[59] See Carl Bialik. "Dubious Origins for Drugs, and Stats About Them," *Wall Street Journal*. September 10, 2010, http://blogs.wsj.com/numbersguy/dubious-origins-for-drugs-and-stats-about-them-990/ and Randall W. Lutter, "Counterfeit Drugs," Testimony before the House Committee on Government Reform, Subcommittee on Criminal Justice, Drug Policy, and Human Resources, November 1, 2005, http://www.fda.gov/NewsEvents/Testimony/ucm112670.htm.

[60] "Traffic Report: Online Piracy and Counterfeiting." MarkMonitor. January 2011.

[61] Kevin Lewis, "The Fake and the Fatal: The Consequences of Counterfeits," *The Park Place Economists*: Vol. 17, 2009, http://digitalcommons.iwu.edu/parkplace/vol7/iss1/14.

[62] Ibid.

[63] Joint Teresko "Fighting the LP Wars," *IndustryWeek.com*, February 1, 2008. http://www.industryweek.com/articles/fighting_the_ip_wars_15605.aspx.

[64] Shayerah Ilias and Ian F. Ferguson, "Intellectual Property Rights and International Trade," Congressional Research Service, December 2007.

[65] "The Truth About Counterfeiting." International Anti-Counterfeiting Coalition. n.d. http://www.iacc.org/about-counterfeiting/the-truth-about-counterfeiting.php) (accessed March 10, 2011).

## Potential Legislative Responses

While the existing notice and takedown regime has provided an initial step towards combating piracy, clearly more can and needs to be done. Currently rogue sites operate in a low risk, high reward environment. Site operators, especially those outside of the United States, face few personal risks from law enforcement and encounter few barriers to distributing illegal content online. We need to change the equation. In December 2009, ITIF proposed a number of policies to help reduce online copyright infringement, especially in countries that turn a blind eye to copyright enforcement.[66] The purpose of these policies is to establish a robust enforcement mechanism to combat IP theft online. These recommendations include the following:

- Create a process by which the federal government, with the help of third parties, can identify websites around the world that are systemically engaged in piracy
- Enlist ISPs to combat piracy by blocking websites that offer pirated content, allowing pricing structures and usage caps that discourage online piracy, and implementing notice and response systems
- Enlist search engines to combat piracy by removing websites that link to infringing content from their search results
- Require ad networks and financial service providers to stop doing business with websites providing access to pirated content
- Create a process so that the private sector can consult with government regulators on proposed uses of anti-piracy technology
- Fund anti-piracy technology research, such as content identification technology
- Pursue international frameworks to protect intellectual property and impose significant pressure and penalties on countries that flout copyright law

Many of these recommendations have been considered in recent legislation, such as the Combating Online Infringement and Counterfeits Act (COICA), introduced by Senators Patrick Leahy (D-VT) and Orrin Hatch (R-UT) in 2010. COICA would provide important new tools to crack down on online infringement of intellectual property. The legislation would not target minor violations of copyright, but rather would target "Internet sites dedicated to infringing activities" which it defines as a site that is "primarily designed, has no demonstrable, commercially significant purpose or use other than, or is marketed by its operator... to offer" unauthorized access to copyright-protected content. Many of these "Internet sites dedicated to infringing" are well-known foreign

[66] For more details, please see Daniel Castro, Richard Bennett, and Scott Andes. "Steal These Policies: Strategies for Reducing Digital Piracy." Information Technology and Innovation Foundation (Washington DC: 2009), http://www.itif.org/files/2009-digital-piracy.pdf.

websites in countries including Russia, Sweden and the Ukraine, such as the Pirate Bay and others identified in the USTR's "Out-Of Cycle Review of Notorious Markets."

## Response to Criticism of Legislation

Critics of implementing these enforcement mechanisms make three general objections: 1) that these proposals would restrict free speech; 2) that these proposals would encourage censorship in foreign countries; and 3) that these proposals would cripple the technological infrastructure on which the Internet runs. All of these objections are unfounded.

## Freedom of Speech

First, some critics oppose COICA and similar proposals on the grounds that it would hurt free speech, a groundless accusation. Not all free speech is protected. As Justice Holmes in *Schenck V. U.S.* famously argued, freedom of speech does not include the freedom to falsely yell "Fire" in a crowded theater (or more recently "Bomb!" on an airplane).[67] Nor does it entail the freedom to establish a website for the sole purpose of enabling online piracy, even if the site posts a few statements expressing the owners' political views or some other authorized content.

Neither does the idea of a "free and open" Internet mean that every website has the right to exist. Certainly, most people would agree that some websites should not be permitted to remain online, such as sites devoted to hosting child pornography or illegal scams. The purpose of this legislation is not to shut down a personal website that accidentally links to a copyrighted image or websites that use material protected by fair use, but to shut down websites whose principal purpose is to engage in egregious infringement of intellectual property.

There is no legitimate reason for parasitic websites, whose sole purpose is to leech off of the IP created by others, to exist. Russian piracy websites, like LegalSounds or other clones of the now defunct Russian website "allofmp3," add nothing of value to the Internet economy and instead weaken it for all legitimate consumers and stakeholders. The Internet was not meant to be a gigantic piracy machine. It was not designed or built for the primary (or even secondary) purpose of facilitating unlawful transactions, and it is shameful for proponents of piracy to hide behind the excuse that filtering or blocking

---

[67] "The man who said 'bomb' on an airplane." *San Francisco Chronicle*. August 6, 2010, http://www.sfgate.com/cgi-bin/blogs/crime/detail?entry_id=69558 and "Woman accused of airport bomb threats," United Press International, April 21, 2008, http://www.upi.com/Top_News/2008/04/21/Woman-accused-of-airport-bomb-threats/UPI-38521208794796/.

access to unlawful conduct is in some way analogous to the suppression of dissent in authoritarian dictatorships. There is clearly an enormous difference between the actions of an undemocratic government and the legitimate desire of liberal democracies to limit the ill-gotten gains of piracy promoters, advertisers, and service providers. The time has come for the law to catch up with technology by adopting a reasonable set of enforcement measures to make piracy less prevalent and less blatant on the Internet.

Yet critics of COICA, such as the Electronic Frontier Foundation (EFF), complain that free speech will be hurt if the government blocks "a whole domain, and not just the infringing part of the site."[68] While certainly most infringing sites will contain at least some non-infringing content, it is not an injustice to block the entire site. As noted, COICA only applies to sites where the principal purpose of the site is to engage in digital piracy. Such frivolous complaints are equivalent to arguing that it would be unfair for the justice system to shut down a bar found to be repeatedly serving alcohol to minors even if some of its customers were of legal age or a pawn shop that serves as a front for moving stolen goods even if a few of its items were acquired legally.

Others present a similar criticism of proposed legislative solutions under the guise of protecting free speech when their objection is really to an expansion of government authority. This mentality is exemplified by Bruce Schneier who as a matter of course argues against virtually any action by government to police abuses on the Internet.[69] These kinds of objections come from a purely anti-government ideology that rejects any attempt to give government more power, even if that is appropriate power to enforce laws against criminals.

## Foreign Censorship

Critics also claim that the policies in COICA would set a negative precedent and harm the United States internationally by giving political cover to the "totalitarian, profoundly anti-democratic regimes that keep their citizens from seeing the whole Internet."[70] Critics, such as the 87 Internet engineers who signed EFF's letter to the Judiciary Committee, argue that COICA would seriously harm the credibility of the United States in its role as a steward of key Internet infrastructure." Others, including groups like the American Library Association, Consumer Electronics Association, NetCoalition and Public Knowledge, argue that "COICA's blacklist may be used to

---

[68] Richard Esguerra, "Censorship of the Internet Takes Center Stage in 'Online Infringement' Bill," Electronic Frontier Foundation, September 21, 2010, http://www.eff.org/deeplinks/2010/09/censorship-internet-takes-center-stage-online.

[69] For example, with regards to the Obama Administration's plans to expand wiretapping online Schneier writes, "it's bad civic hygiene to build technologies that could someday be used to facilitate a police state." Bruce Schneier, "Web snooping is a dangerous move," CNN.com, September 29. 2010. http://www.cnn.com/2010/OPINION/09/29/schneier.web.surveillance/index.html.

[70] Esguerra, "Censorship of the Internet Takes Center Stage in 'Online Infringement' Bill."

justify foreign blacklists of websites that criticize governments or royalty, or that contain other 'unlawful' or 'subversive' speech.[71] Again, these criticisms do not stand up to a serious analysis. This is equivalent to arguing that the United States should not put rioters who engage in wholesale property destruction and violence in jail because it encourages totalitarian governments to use their police to suppress their citizens.

More narrowly, some critics, such as Wendy Seltzer at Princeton University's Center for Information Technology Policy, argue that other countries would use anti-piracy efforts as a ruse for cracking down on political dissidents.[72] Such activities are not without precedent—Russian police have raided advocacy groups and opposition newspapers that have spoken out against the government in the name of searching for pirated software.[73] Yet while certainly some unscrupulous countries might claim their actions are equivalent to that of the United States, it would be demonstrably untrue. There is simply no comparison between a country using clear and transparent legal means to enforce intellectual property rights online and a country censoring political speech online, even under the guise of protecting copyrights. Moreover, to argue that abusive regimes operating without the rule of law would somehow act more abusively because the United States cracks down on cybercrime is a stretch at best. If this were the case, we should have seen a dramatic increase in Internet censorship after nations like France and the U.K recently passed laws to crack down on online copyright theft.

In fact, if this law would have any effect on foreign nations it would be to embolden them to take stronger steps to crack down on digital piracy, a problem that is even worse in many foreign nations and one that contributes to a deteriorating balance of trade for the United States as foreign consumers steal U.S. software, music, video games, movies, books, photos, and other digital content.

## Weaken the Internet

Finally, some opponents of stricter online IP enforcement argue that this legislation "will risk fragmenting the Internet's global domain name system (DNS)."[74] To understand the debate, you must understand how DNS works. DNS is like a global phonebook for the Internet providing users a number that corresponds to each name. Before a user can visit a domain name (e.g., www.itif org), his or her computer must first discover the IP

[71] Letter from Public Knowledge et al. on "S. 3804, Combating Online Infringement and Counterfeits Act (COICA). September 27, 2010. http://www.publicknowledge.org/files/docs/JointLetterCOICA20100929.pdf.

[72] Wendy Seltzer. "Copyright. Censorship, and Domain Name Blacklists at Home in the U.S." Freedom to Tinker, September 21, 2010. http://www.freedom-to-tinker.com/blog/wseltzer/copyright-censorship-and-domain-name-blacklists-home-us.

[73] Clifford Levy, "Russia Uses Microsoft to Suppress Dissent," New York Times, September 11, 2010, http://www.nytimes.com/2010/09/12/world/europe/12raids.html.

[74] Peter Eckersley. "An Open Letter From Internet Engineers to the Senate Judiciary Committee." Electronic Frontier Foundation, September 29, 2010, http://www.eff.org/deeplinks/2010/09/open-letter.

address associated with that web address (e.g., 69.65.119.60). DNS servers provide this service to users by translating domain names into IP addresses through a recursive process. Most users rely on the DNS servers of their local ISP for this service and it is these DNS servers that are the principle target of COICA. If the DNS server knows that a given domain name is for a rogue site, e.g., www.watch-pirated-videos.tv, then the DNS servers could be instructed to no longer resolve an IP address for that domain. And without this IP address, users would not be able to visit these infringing websites.

Groups like EFF claim this will “undermine basic Internet infrastructure” and lament that it will keep ISPs from “telling you the truth about a website's location.”[75] While such fiction may be useful in generating fear about the policies in COICA, the simple fact is that using DNS to block access to websites or servers is not new or particularly challenging— DNS redirection has been used for blocking spam and botnets and protecting users from malware, for example, for many years. In addition, many DNS resolvers routinely return different answers to users as part of a service, such as to provide parental control filters, correct typos in URLs, or to provide search results in lieu of a basic “domain not found” error.[76]

Other critics, such as the Center for Democracy and Technology, argue that COICA will set a precedent where ISPs will be required to block other “illegal or unsavory contend’ creating “a controlled, ISP-policed medium.”[77] Such an end result is antithetical to the worldview of CDT (and other opponents of this legislation) that the Internet should be free of private-sector control regardless of the consequences. This “slippery slope” argument is fundamentally illogical. The analogy would be like saying that if we pass laws against a person committing physical assault on another person, then it is only a matter of time before we pass laws against people bumping into each other rudely on the street. Such stubborn and entrenched views do not reflect the kind of flexible policymaking that most people agree is necessary for the fast-paced world of the evolving Internet. Rather than relying on tradition to justify Internet policy, a better approach would be to look at the practical implications of specific policy proposals in the present.

Finally, some critics lament that by preventing DNS servers from responding with “the truth, the whole truth, and nothing but the truth” COICA will sabotage DNS Security Extensions (DNSSEC), a recent upgrade to DNS that seeks to improve the security of the DNS system. Part of the problem is that the current DNS standard does not provide a mechanism by which a DNS server can tell the requester “the site may exist, but it is illegal so I am not going to find the answer for you.” Instead, the server must choose a

---

[75] Esguerra, "Censorship of the Internet Takes Center Stage in ‘Online Infringement’ Bill."

[76] For a more detailed rebuttal of some of the technical fears about COICA, see Daniel Castro, “No, COICA Will Not Break the Internet,” Innovation Policy Blog (2011), http://www.innovationpolicy.org/no-coica-will-not-break-the-internet.

[77] "The Dangers of S. 3804: Domain Name Seizures and Blocking Pose Threats to Free Expression, Global Internet Freedom, and the Internet’s Open Architecture,” Center for Democracy and Technology, September 28, 2010, http://cdt.org/files/pdfs/Leahy_bill_memo.pdf.

less eloquent response, such as not replying (a bad idea since the user will just keep asking), replying that the domain does not exist, or replying with an incorrect address.

However, this problem appears to be the result of a deficiency in the current DNS protocol rather than any true technical limitation. It could be easily addressed by modifying the standard to support these additional types of responses. Indeed, one such modification has already been developed and proposed by a key architect of DNS.[78]

Other critics claim that DNS blocking will provoke a mass exodus of users from US.-based DNS servers to foreign DNS servers outside of the jurisdiction of U.S. lawmakers and, as a result, be ineffective. However, this argument is flawed. While switching DNS servers may be easy for some users, it is still beyond the comfort level of many, if not most, Internet users. Moreover, users who switch to foreign DNS servers would expose themselves to many security risks if they cannot trust the responses from these servers. For example, while the name servers may reliably return the correct IP address for a Russian MP3 site, they might not return the correct address for Bank of America. How many users are willing to risk their identity and financial information just to download a few songs? Similarly, the DNS server that a person uses can collect a fairly detailed record of an individual's browsing history which presents obvious privacy risks. Would most users trust their entire browsing history to an unregulated, foreign company?

Using a foreign DNS server also could result in substantial decreases in performance for many users. People usually get what they pay for (except with piracy!), and a free foreign DNS service is likely to be substantially slower than the DNS servers offered by local ISPs. How many users would tolerate a few extra seconds of delay every time they click a link? In addition, users of foreign DNS servers would likely see another performance hit when accessing websites using content distribution networks like Akamai because foreign DNS servers would point them to the CDN content servers closest to the overseas DNS server not the user.

Aside from practical matters there is also the obvious question of who would be willing to provide such a service. If, as opponents of these policies argue, virtually every American user leaves their local DNS server, who would provide all of the computing power necessary to process these DNS requests? And more importantly, who would pay for it? Moreover, these opponents miss the point that these policies can be extremely effective even if some users evade the restrictions. Many users visit these sites out of ignorance or complacency. A warning that lets them know that the site they are trying to access is illegitimate will help direct consumers to legitimate websites for legal goods.

[78] Sec Paul Vixic, "Taking Back the DNS," CircleID, June 30, 2010, http://www.circleid.com/posts/20100728_taking_back_the_dns/.

## Why the Criticism?

So what's really behind these criticisms'' Most reflect these groups' and individuals' overarching view of the Internet as a medium whose chief function is to liberate individuals from control by, or dependence on, big organizations. For these groups, the Internet is first and foremost about individual freedom, not about collective responsibility. They see the Internet as a special place, above and beyond the reach of the kinds of rules that govern the offline world. Yet, for most of the rest of us, the Internet is no different than the rest of society where we have rights and responsibilities and where laws against certain behaviors exist. We play by the rules and we expect others to do the same, and when they do not, we expect society (through the actions of democratically elected governments) to step in and punish those who commit crimes. All of these objections listed here reflect this fundamental Internet exceptionalist ideology, and as such are largely attacks not so much on this particular legislation, but on any legislation that would put limits on Internet freedom, even if it's the freedom to falsely yell "fire!" in a crowded theatre.

Because of their overriding focus on individual freedom and not on collective benefit, critics of COICA or similar proposals fail to understand that stronger enforcement of intellectual property would be beneficial to the American economy as it faces growing international competition. It is one thing for U.S. companies and workers to compete against companies and workers in other nations that play by the rules. It is quite another thing to compete against other nations that systematically cheat and steal U.S. intellectual property.

## Conclusion

Stronger enforcement mechanisms are necessary. Online piracy is no longer a hobby among college students trading files in their dorm room, but instead it has grown in to a multi-million dollar international business that is leeching jobs and investment out of the American economy. Sites hosting pirated content or linking to pirated content can generate a significant amount of revenue from online advertising and sales and easily cover their expenses. The policies that we recommend would provide a mechanism to not only cut off access to these sites and impose operational barriers, but also cut off their funding mechanisms to make operating online piracy sites unprofitable.

Should we throw out freedom of speech and long-held legal protections like due process just to protect intellectual property online? Of course not. But neither should we abandon the Constitutional provisions which support protecting intellectual property. Some issues related to online infringement are complex and will require more complex solutions. But some of these issues are clearly right or wrong. Websites that egregiously violate the law at the expense of American consumers and American workers have no place on the Internet. The responsibility for maintaining the Internet falls upon each user, each service provider, and each business and institution that uses it, operates it, and profits by it. The cost of doing nothing or doing too little is high. 1 encourage you to put in place the frameworks and policies needed to facilitate and encourage all actors within the Internet ecosystem to take some measure of responsibility for maintaining its integrity and protecting consumers.

Mr. Goodlatte. Mr. Huntsberry, welcome.

## TESTIMONY OF FREDERICK HUNTSBERRY, CHIEF OPERATING OFFICER, PARAMOUNT PICTURES

Mr. Huntsberry. Thank you, Chairman Goodlatte, Ranking Member Watt, and the Members of the Subcommittee for holding this important hearing. I am Frederick Huntsberry, Chief Operating Officer at Paramount Pictures, and I appreciate the opportunity to appear before you today.

I am here to discuss the theft of motion pictures and other American-made products via the Internet, the devastating impact the business of theft has on the U.S. economy, and the need for legislation to enforce the rule of law on the Internet.

An online shadow economy has emerged that operates in parallel to our legitimate economy. In this online shadow economy, every single film we distribute is stolen and then illegally made available online. Other forms of content like TV shows, music, games, books and software are also illegally distributed for profit.

The U.S. film industry creates jobs and tax revenue across America ranging from advertising expenditures to employment at movie theatres to retail jobs selling DVDs. But it is often overlooked that motion pictures are shot in all 50 States, creating local jobs, supporting local small businesses and generating significant revenue and tax dollars all across the country.

A typical Paramount motion picture will employ anywhere between a few hundred to many thousand American workers. We also spend money in States across the country. Last year “True Grit” was shot in Texas and New Mexico, adding an estimated $16 million to those local economies. “The Last Airbender” was shot in Pennsylvania, adding an estimated $72 million to the local economy.

Paramount embraces technology, and we believe that consumers will increasingly choose to view our films via authorized Internet distributors like Netflix and iTunes. Already today, we license our films to more than 200 online digital distribution platforms across more than 70 countries covering more than 750 films in more than 25 languages.

The online illegal shadow economy does not create any American jobs. It does not reinvest any revenue in the creation of new films or goods. It does not pay taxes and it does not contribute to the U.S. economy. Instead, it steals from the U.S. economy and enriches thieves.

Today an online search for movies leads consumers away from legitimate services by providing results for numerous sites that lead the consumer to stolen content. It is so simple and convenient that consumers may never know the difference. Some of these websites look like legitimate sites, accepting credit cards and displaying ads for well-known products. Further examples of these are in my written testimony.

Let me draw your attention to the screens in the room. Just to give you an example how simple it is for a consumer who is looking for legitimate ways to stream content online to find illegal content. So you can go to Google and type in "stream," just the word "stream," and you will get an autofill from Google that says "stream movies" or "stream TV shows," as well as a list of websites ranked in popularity.

It turns out all of the websites highlighted in yellow are actually pirated websites. We are going to select the first one, solarmovie.com. This brings us now to a site that is a search engine called solarmovie.com, and this search engine finds pirated content on the Internet.

We can see here movies that have been released over the last few weeks, as well as "Grease." We are going to select now "The Adjustment Bureau," which was released by Universal last week, and then we are brought to a screen where we can see all the cyberlockers, meaning the storage websites, where the film is located. We are going to select videoBB.com, and two more clicks later, we are actually streaming the movie.

Within 6 months after Paramount released "Iron Man 2" in theatres, a camcorded copy was available in 12 languages. There have been more than 15 million peer-to-peer downloads, and more than 153,000 Internet links were made available for download or streaming. Twenty Internet storage sites, also known as cyberlockers, account for 96 percent of all infringing copies of Paramount films found on cyberlocker sites.

These 20 cyberlockers received a total of 177 million unique monthly visitors in February of this year. They use incentive programs to encourage the uploading of stolen copies of motion pictures. These programs pay cash to the person who uploaded the content every time their content is downloaded or streamed. Enormous profits can be made in trafficking and stolen motion pictures.

We estimate that Megaupload, for example, earns an annual profit of $40 to $300 million. We have reached the limits of self-help. Last year. Paramount sent over 40 million infringement notices, yet the same content is still a few clicks away.

Legislation focusing on rogue online services is profoundly needed to establish the rule of law on the Internet. Doing so will not only benefit the countless American jobs and millions of dollars in tax revenue that are currently being lost, but it will also allow the Internet to fulfill its full commercial promise.

Thank you again for affording me the opportunity to present my views here today.

Mr. Goodlatte. Thank you, Mr. Huntsberry.

[The prepared statement of Mr. Huntsberry follows:]

## WRITTEN TESTIMONY SUBMITTED FOR THE RECORD OF FREDERICK HUNTSBERRY, CHIEF OPERATING OFFICER, PARAMOUNT PICTURES CORPORATION ON "PROMOTING INVESTMENT AND PROTECTING COMMERCE ONLINE: LEGITIMATE SITES V. PARASITES, PART I," BEFORE THE HOUSE COMMITTEE ON THE JUDICIARY, SUBCOMMITTEE ON INTELLECTUAL PROPERTY, COMPETITION AND THE INTERNET U.S. HOUSE OF REPRESENTATIVES, MARCH 14, 2011

Thank you Chairman Goodlatte, Ranking Member Watt, and the Members of the Subcommittee for holding this important hearing.

Authorized online distribution of motion pictures via the internet has the potential to be the future of entertainment. But if the rule of law is not effectively applied to the internet, the internet also holds the potential to decimate the business of producing and distributing motion pictures, in the process destroying jobs across all fifty states, eliminating outlets for the expression of creativity, reducing American tax revenues, depleting American workers' retirement and health plans, and damaging the U.S. balance of trade.

I am Frederick Huntsberry, Chief Operating Officer at Paramount Pictures Corporation, a division of Viacom Inc., and I appreciate the opportunity to appear before you to discuss this issue. As COO, I am responsible for our operating divisions, which include Finance, Human Resources, Labor Relations,

Studio Operations, Information Technology, Sourcing, Business Development, Paramount's Community and State Government Relations, Legal, and, of course. Content Protection. Every day I deal with the impact that rampant online theft of our content has on Paramount.

Paramount Pictures is a global creator and distributor of filmed entertainment, with multi-faceted divisions including digital, DVD, broadcast and cable television distribution, studio operations, and consumer products and recreation. In addition to producing films that are initially released theatrically, we also produce content directly for DVD distribution and directly for online distribution.

Paramount's legendary history dates back to Cecil B. DeMille's silent film *The Squaw Man*, which was the first studio film ever shot in Hollywood, In 1927, Paramount received the very first Academy Award for Best Picture, awarded to the World War I drama *Wings*-the only silent film to win that coveted award. Paramount was, for many years, the home of Mae West, the Marx Brothers, Jerry Lewis, Bob Hope, and Alfred Hitchcock.

Over the decades Paramount has created such memorable films as *The Godfather, Chinatown, Love Story, Breakfast at Tiffany's, White Christmas, Grease, Saturday Night Fever*, the *Indiana Jones* series, *Star Trek, Ferris Bueller's Day Off, Top Gun, Airplane!, Forrest Gump, Braveheart, Saving Private Ryan, The Truman Show, Titanic* (with 20th Century Fox), and many more.

Today, Paramount works with the finest in motion picture talent, including JJ Abrams, Michael Bay, the Coen brothers, Steven Spielberg, Martin Scorcese, and many more. We launched the hugely entertaining *Transformers* series of films, scared audiences with *Paranormal Activity*, revitalized the *Star Trek* adventures, brought Justin Bieber to 3D screens, and left George Clooney *Up in the Air*.

Films produced or distributed by Paramount this year received more Academy Award nominations than any other studio, including ten nominations for *True Grit* and Best Supporting Actor and Actress awards for *The Fighter*.

In addition to our own films, we distribute the wonderfully creative films of Dreamworks Animation, including *How to Train Your Dragon, Kung Fu Panda, Madagascar*, and the saga of *Shrek*. We also distribute Marvel's Iron Man and the upcoming *Thor* and *Captain America*.

The distribution of our films creates jobs and tax revenue in all fifty states - ranging from substantial marketing expenditures to employment at movie theaters (including food and beverage sales jobs and revenue) to retail jobs involved in the distribution and retail sales of DVDs.

But it is often overlooked that motion pictures are shot in locations from coast to coast, creating jobs, supporting small businesses and generating significant revenue and tax dollars all across the country.

*True Grit* was shot in Texas and New Mexico, adding an estimated $16.3 million to those local economies; *The Last Airbender* was shot in Pennsylvania, adding an estimated $72 million to the local economy.[79]

Those are just two examples. A new version of *Footloose* has just been filmed in Georgia, *The Fighter* and *Shutter Island* were both filmed in Massachusetts, *She's Out of My League* was filmed in Pennsylvania, *Benjamin Button* was filmed in Louisiana (as was much of *Forrest Gump*); *Up In The Air* was filmed in St. Louis with additional filming days in Detroit, Miami and Las Vegas; *Tropic Thunder* was filmed in Hawaii.

---

[79] Those figures include hotel room nights, local crew, local actors and extras, per diem paid to nonlocals, location fees, stage expenses, office rentals and supplies, security expenses, communications expenses, equipment rentals, vehicle rentals and transportation expenses, catering and food expenses, art department and wardrobe expenditures, construction costs, state and local sales and use tax, city wage taxes (Philadelphia), hotel tax, state withholding taxes on resident hires and nonresident hires, and miscellaneous (such as prop expenses, shipping expenses, location scouting, local publicity, and hair and makeup expenses, among others).

The production of a single Paramount motion picture can employ from 100 to 5,000 workers, not including extras. [See Attachment 1] For example, a small-budget film like *She's Out of My League* employed 440 workers; a mid-budget film like *Shutter Island* employed 1,573 workers; a big-budget film like *Transformers* employed 4,654 workers. These numbers reflect only the individuals hired specifically to work on the film and do not include the many regular full-time Paramount employees who also work on the films, including production employees, post-production employees, accountants, lawyers, human resources, and support staff.

## The Promise of Technology; Fulfilled or Unfulfilled?

The motion picture industry is exploring and implementing many new ways to get our content to consumers via new media platforms that satisfy consumer desires. We embrace the ultimate transition from a hard goods era to a digital delivery era. With that transition comes enormous legitimate business risk, but we are not risk adverse. We take a multi-million dollar risk every time we greenlight a movie. Online piracy, however, adds an additional layer of threat which makes that transition extremely difficult to manage.

At Paramount Pictures, we believe in coming years consumers will increasingly choose to view our motion pictures via authorized online and mobile distribution.

Paramount currently licenses more than 200 online digital distribution platforms across more than 70 countries covering more than 750 films in more than 25 languages. [See Attachment 2] And we are not alone in making our content available to consumers across a wide array of online platforms; consumers can now access television shows, music, and books in a variety of exciting new ways.[80]

But none of these innovative initiatives can succeed, and the motion industry cannot survive, if the current situation is permitted to continue. This is a situation in which stolen copies of every current film are available online, in most cases commencing during the very same week in which the film opens in theatres. And those stolen copies are often distributed on a revenue-generating basis, diverting consumer spending from the creators and legitimate distributors of the content into the hands of criminals - often outside the United States - who do not create American jobs, do not reinvest that money in creating new productions, and do not pay U.S. taxes on that money.

I refer to this as the "online shadow economy."

---

[80] We are engaged in a collaborative effort with other content producers, software companies, and equipment manufacturers on a project called Ultraviolet, which will enable consumers to enjoy the content they purchase across a variety of devices and locations without the need for making multiple purchases, http://www.uvvu.com/

The same technology that will enable consumers to enjoy motion pictures and other forms of copyrighted content in new and exciting ways is being used in the online shadow economy to steal that content. Unless the rule of law is effectively applied to online distribution platforms - and it currently is not - that technology will not reach its promised potential. The result will be a substantial decrease in the number of motion pictures that are produced, which in turn means fewer American jobs, smaller tax revenues, a decrease in the positive contribution of film exports to the U.S. balance of trade, and a substantial narrowing in the type of motion pictures that will be produced.

## The Rise of the Online Shadow Economy, Its Effect on Jobs, and Its Economic Impact

Paramount and the other studios' ability to continue creating memorable films is now being jeopardized by the alarming rise of a profound online shadow economy.

This alternative economy is an illegal parallel economy that has developed alongside the legitimate economy for the online distribution of our motion pictures. This activity is not limited to feature films -it blankets all forms of Intellectual property, including television productions, music, books, games, software, and educational testing materials. And it applies as well to hard goods including apparel, handbags, toothpaste, car parts, airline parts, and fake and substandard pharmaceuticals to name a few.

In this online shadow economy, every single film we distribute is promptly stolen and then illegally made available online without creating any jobs, without reinvesting any revenue in the creation of new films, without paying taxes, and without contributing to the U.S. economy. Instead, much of that stolen revenue merely enriches foreign nationals.

Until recently, a simple technological barrier provided some degree of insulation for creators and distributors of motion pictures from the economic ravages created by the illegal economy: consumers could not easily watch stolen content on their living room TV the way they could with DVDs.

That barrier is now disappearing. New television sets can offer built-in internet access, and internet access can be added to all other television sets with a simple and inexpensive plug-and-play interface device. [See Attachment 3] Consumers are no longer limited to watching stolen films on computer screens. Now, with the wave of a remote control, everyone can have direct access to illegal content on their living room television. Moreover, the rise of iPad-style applications will make it even easier to bring the iPad experience to your television set. [See Attachment 4a-b]

We are excited about and embrace the new legitimate distribution models that technology is opening up, but we also recognize that those who profit from the online shadow economy will siphon away those opportunities if left unchecked.

While it may be popular In some quarters to blame the victim, claiming that the rise of this parallel economy is the fault of content owners because of pricing or distribution patterns, the truth is that no business, no matter how Innovative, nimble, or creative, can compete with a shadow economy that offers consumers high-quality distribution of the exact same goods at no cost or nominal cost.

The harm caused by the shadow economy Inflicts severe damage on the U.S. economy during a time at which the country can least afford to bear that harm. Research has indicated that industries nurtured and supported by copyright represent approximately 6% of America's GDP - that's nearly $1 trillion a year in business and 5.6 million jobs. When supportive industries are included, that number rises to more than $1.5 trillion, which was 11% of GDP in 2006-2007.[81]

Certainly those numbers are staggering and I would like to share with you the perspective that I see on an operational level at Paramount.

While box office revenues remain strong - which indicate that we are still creating movies people want to see - DVD and other forms of home entertainment sales are declining. Why pay to buy a DVD when any film can be streamed online at any time at no cost or nominal cost? And the negative impact is clear. Theatrical exhibition contributes roughly 25% of the total revenue of a typical film; DVD contributes 50% and television distribution (subscription TV, pay-per-view, and free TV) and online distribution contribute 25%. [See Attachment 5] As DVD sales constitute a smaller share of the total revenue of a typical picture, the break-even point on the typical picture becomes more remote. Simply put, this means that the multi-million dollar investment that studios make in producing and developing films cannot be recouped, if ever, until further and further into the distribution chain. [See Attachment 6]

The number of films being produced has shrunk significantly, particularly with regards to mid-budget and independent films. [See Attachment 7] Fewer films means fewer jobs across all 50 states in production and in distribution, less tax revenues, and less contributions to workers' health and retirement plans.[82] And It means less variety in the types of films that get made - as the studios aim to mitigate their losses from piracy, we will see a continued trend towards big-event tent pole and low-budget films, but far fewer mid-range budget films will be offered to audiences because those films will have the smallest odds for breaking even in a world of diminished non-theatrical revenue.

It is easy to see how even if only a portion of that online shadow economy was returned to the legitimate economy, the positive economic impact would be enormous.

---

[81] International Intellectual Property Alliance (IIPA) study, June 2009.

[82] The heath care and pension plans for actors, directors, electricians, painters, plasterers, laborers and writers are funded in part from residuals paid by the studios based on DVD sales. As those sales continue to lose ground, the impact on those plans will be devastating.

## The Chronology of a Pirated Film

With very few exceptions, films enter the illegal economy when they are camcorded in movie theaters -often during the opening week of the film.

A few years ago, a camcord copy was a shaky, out-of-focus product with a soundtrack obscured by rustling popcorn boxes and other crowd noise. Today, In the era of digital camcorders with image stabilization and audio tracks copied from the hearing-impaired audio systems present in most theaters, camcorded copies are now of extremely high quality.

Once even a single camcorded copy of a film appears on the Internet, it is soon coupled with audio tracks in a myriad of languages.

A few months later when the film is scheduled for release on DVD, a perfect digital copy is ripped from the DVD and uploaded onto the internet, replacing the earlier camcorded copies.[83]

Once a single stolen copy appears online, it rapidly becomes entrenched throughout the illegal ecosystem. For example, within six months after IRON MAN 2 was first camcorded in a theater, it was available in 12 languages, there had been more than 15 million peer-to-peer downloads, and more than 153,000 links were available in cyberlockers[84] for download or streaming.

This problem is not limited to recent releases; most major library titles from all of the studios are also readily available online in perfect digital via copies from DVDs.

The motion picture studios are taking a broad array of actions in response to illegal online trafficking in our films. We deploy technologies which allow responsible online services to filter out illegal content. We send take-down notices to responsible online services. We release our films on a wide variety of consumer platforms including many legitimate online services.

But when it comes to rogue services, we lack the tools that could make a difference. The PirateBay website is one of the most notorious traffickers in stolen content. Not only do they refuse to filter out stolen content, they outright reject - in writing - requests that infringing content be taken down from the service. [See Attachment 8.]

---

[83] The ripping occurs weeks prior to the public release date, taking place as soon as we ship the DVDs into the supply chain for distribution to retail outlets.

[84] Cyberlockers are data storage facilities — equivalent to the hard drive on your computer but accessed through an online connection. There are many legitimate uses for cyberlockers - including backing-up computer hard drives and facilitating the sharing of large data files. Unfortunately cyberlockers are also used for the storage and distribution of stolen copies of motion pictures, music, books, games, and software. A motion picture which is stored on a cyberlocker can either be downloaded or streamed.

## Access to Stolen Films Is Now Just a Few Clicks Away

In the past, accessing a stolen copy of a motion picture required a certain degree of technical savvy and often required downloading specialized software. In the past, consumers were fully aware that they were accessing unauthorized infringing material.

Today, an online search for movies leads consumers not to one of the many legitimate online services but instead leads them directly to a streaming copy of the stolen film. And, with the widespread acceptance of credit cards and PayPal payments, coupled with the widespread presence of advertisements for well-known products, consumers may not know the difference and may not realize that they are watching stolen content.

For example, if you type "watch" into Google, as soon as you type "wat" (which could be a search for "water") Google auto-fills the search term "watch movies." That search brings up a list of sites trafficking in stolen content. [See Attachment 9] The same happens if you type in "stream" (which could be a search for "stream of consciousness"): Google suggests the search term "stream movies" and then returns a long list of sites trafficking in stolen content. [See Attachment 10]

If you click click) on the first site suggested by Google, it brings you to a linking site which looks as legitimate as iTunes or Netflix. [See Attachment 11a] When you click on a movie (2nd click) it brings up a list of stolen copies of the film accompanied by users' ratings of the quality of the stolen copy. [See Attachment 11b] With another click (3rd click), you are then taken to a landing page [See Attachment 11c]; with another click (4th click) you are taken to the film itself. When you click on the film (5th click) the movie begins to stream. [See Attachment 11d]

With just five clicks following a basic Google search, anyone can be streaming a stolen copy of almost any film. And it should be noted that the search term used in Google was not "watch stolen movies," "watch pirated movies," "watch free movies." It was merely "watch movies" or "stream movies" -searches which should have returned results for iTunes, Netflix, Amazon, or one of the many legally authorized online distribution services.[85] Instead the search results usher consumers - including consumers who are looking to pay for content-into the shadow economy.

## Traffickers in Stolen Content Are Diverting Millions of Dollars from the Legitimate Economy

Trafficking in stolen content has become big business for criminals.

[85] See Attachment 2 for a sample of those authorized online distribution platforms.

Twenty cyberlockers account for 96% of all infringing copies of Paramount films found on all cyberlockers. These twenty cyberlockers receive a total of 177 million unique monthly visitors.

To give an idea of the popularity of these twenty cyberlockers, one (MegaUpload) is currently ranked as the 51$^{st}$ most popular website by the Alexa popularity rankings.[86] By comparison, MySpace is 70$^{th}$ ESPN is 77$^{th}$ the New York Times is 84$^{th}$. Even more telling, Netflix is 94$^{th}$.

All twenty cyberlockers have used Incentive programs to encourage the uploading of stolen copies of motion pictures. [See Attachment 12] When one of the twenty discontinued its incentive program in response to legal pressure in Germany, its traffic dropped by 30% at the same time the traffic to the other nineteen increased by 65%. [See Attachment 13]

None of the twenty implement the necessary simple technological steps that can be used to filter out the distribution of stolen motion pictures.

The reason is obvious: enormous profits can be made trafficking in stolen motion pictures. A business analysis of one of those cyberlockers estimates a minimum annual profit of $41 million to $304 million.[87]

That is millions of dollars siphoned off from the creators and legitimate distributors of the content, siphoned away from employment for American workers. That is millions of dollars on which no U.S. taxes are paid, and which undermine the positive U.S. balance of trade in copyrighted content.

## The Peril to Consumers

In addition to the loss of American jobs, loss of American tax revenues, and negative impact on the U.S. balance of trade, the lack of effective rule of law on the internet poses a threat to consumers.

Many of the online services that traffic in stolen content can appear indistinguishable from legitimate services. [See Attachment 15a-d] The illegal services often accept major credit cards and PayPal [See Attachment 16a-c] and show advertising from major well-known brands. [See Attachment 17a-b] This creates a four-fold problem: it provides the revenue necessary for the traffickers to continue their activity, it leads consumers to

---

86 The Alexa rankings are a form of Neilsen-type rankings for websites based on the number of unique visitors to the site.

87 We arrived at this estimate by assuming that the cyberlocker has merely a 1% to 5% subscription rate (the cyberlocker offers a tightly limited free sample of usage beyond which a subscription is necessary), with a $6 average subscription fee and 83 million monthly unique visitors. We used an estimate of 32 million daily ad impressions at $1 - $3 cost-per-thousand-viewers. On the cost side we estimated $20 million for bandwidth charges plus $7 million for storage (the two things the cyberlockers cannot steal) and $3 million for overhead. At a 1% subscription rate the resulting profit is $41 million; at a mere 5% subscription rate the profit is $304 million. [See Attachment 14].

believe that the service is legal, it exposes consumers to credit theft, and it deprives content owners and legitimate distribution platforms - including Netflix, iTunes, and Amazon - of revenue from consumers who are paying for online access to content.

Consumers are further lured into entering in financial transactions with trafficking online services through the unauthorized use of consumer protection logos such as McAfee Secure. [See Attachment 18]

In addition to being exposed to credit theft, consumers who engage in transactions with trafficking services unknowingly expose their computers to harm from spyware, malware and viruses. The threats arise both from downloading and from streaming, despite a perception that streaming is safer. [See Attachment 19]

## The Absence of the Rule of Law

The Digital Millennium Copyright Act (DMCA) established an effective regime for notice and take-down of individual infringing files. However a growing number of illegal sites merely replace removed files with new files of the same film, often automatically.

With any of the trafficking cyberlockers, individual files may come and go, but there is never a moment that stolen copies of *TRUE GRIT* are not accessible.

This same problem applies to search engines: they will take down tens of thousands of links to individual copies of stolen films ("torrents") on the piratebay.org, while continuing to direct traffic to the PIRATEBAY.ORG website, which provides access to that never-ending avalanche of stolen files.

Legislation focusing on rogue online services is desperately needed to establish the rule of law on the internet. This is particularly true where rogue services force content owners into an endless process of whack-a-mole in fruitless efforts to remove Illegal content. Foreign sites often pose an even greater challenge because they refuse to comply with obligations under the DMCA and it can be difficult or impossible to achieve jurisdiction over them in U.S. courts or in an effective foreign court system.

In the same way that department stores must cope with losses due to shoplifting, the motion picture industry will always be coping with losses due to online theft. But we need the necessary tools to address the fact that our all of our films are continually being offered online in the shadow economy. And we need search engines, credit providers, ad brokers, and ISPs to shift from an enabling mode to a mode of cooperating in thwarting theft. Among those players, we have had varying degrees of cooperation, with MasterCard stepping forward with the most positive and aggressive action. It appears that it may take legislation to shift many of the other facilitators away from a position of enabling online theft.

From the 1909 Copyright Act to the 1976 Copyright to the DMCA, other countries have looked to the U.S. for leadership in innovative copyright legislation that fosters creativity and development while protecting content and permitting creators of content to benefit financially from their creations.

We at Paramount Pictures are constantly being asked in other countries what the U.S. is doing to address this problem - particularly in light of the fact that the content industry is so enormously vital to U.S. jobs and the U.S. economy. Spain, for example, has recently passed legislation providing for the expedited blocking of sites that refuse to remove infringing content. Similar provisions are being proposed by Italian regulators, and the UK government is exploring site blocking options. At the EU level, the European Commission's review of the EU Enforcement Directive is likely to consider an EU-wide requirement on member states to adopt measures to counter online piracy. Rogue service legislation would provide an opportunity for the U.S. to add its leading voice in reasserting the rule of law on the internet in order to protect content and consumers and to encourage the growth and development of both content creation and new delivery systems for online and mobile distribution of content.

## Conclusion

The Copyright Clause of the Constitution (Article I, Section 8) empowers Congress to secure to authors and inventors the exclusive rights to their writings and discoveries. Today, those rights are anything but secure.

It is incumbent on Congress to find ways to restrict the online shadow economy and to once again level the commercial playing field and secure those rights.

Doing so will not only benefit the thousands of American jobs and millions of dollars in tax revenue that are currently being lost, but it will also allow the internet to fulfill its full commercial promise.

An apt analogy has been drawn to an earlier moment of transformation in American society. In the 1950's, the Eisenhower Administration undertook one of the most massive infrastructure projects in our nation's history - the creation of the interstate highway system.

The advent of the interstate highway system transformed how we did business, traveled, and conducted our daily lives. But unlike the internet of today, the highways were built and operated with a set of rational guidelines for users. Speed limits saved lives, weight limits saved maintenance costs. New forms of law enforcement, such as the Highway Patrol, were created to ensure that the rules were obeyed.

The FBI and other law enforcement agencies stepped up efforts to deal with interstate crime. As a result, as interstates flourished, so did the economy. Over the course of its first four decades of existence, the interstate highway system is reported to have been responsible for fully one-quarter of America's productivity growth.

The internet will not reach its potential for being a vehicle for creativity, for job creation or for revenue generation, if the rule of law is not effectively applied. We are at a decision point: are we going to allow the illegal economy to flourish, destroy American Jobs, gut American tax revenues, undermine the health and pension plans of American workers, and restrict creativity? Or are we going to take steps to curtail the shadow economy and thereby enable the legitimate economy to compete and thrive on a level playing field?

The internet has the potential to be the future for the motion picture industry or the undoing of that future. This is why it is so important that Congress take action now - before irreparable harm is done-to enable legitimate businesses to flourish in the online world creating American jobs and tax revenue and expanding choices for consumers.

ATTACHMENT

Attachment 1. (Reference on page 62)

Sample of the broad array of online distribution platforms offering Paramount's films

Attachment 2. (Reference on page 62)

Any television set can be Internet enabled with a set-top-box, bringing pirated movies directly into your television set

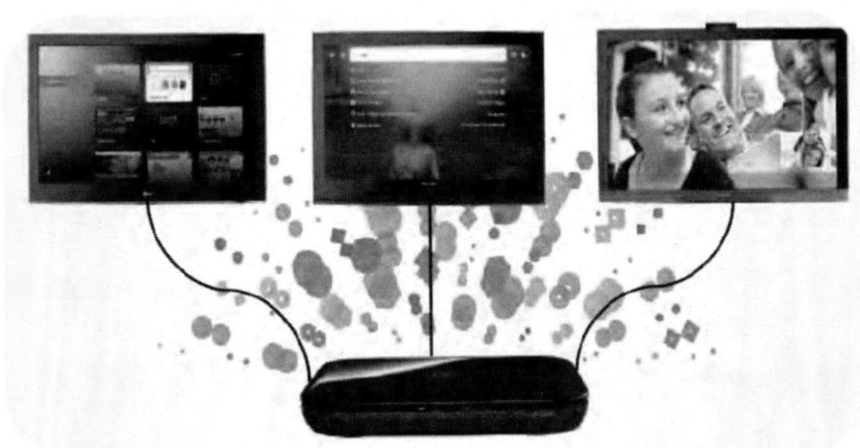

Attachment 3. (Reference on page 63)

## The future is applications

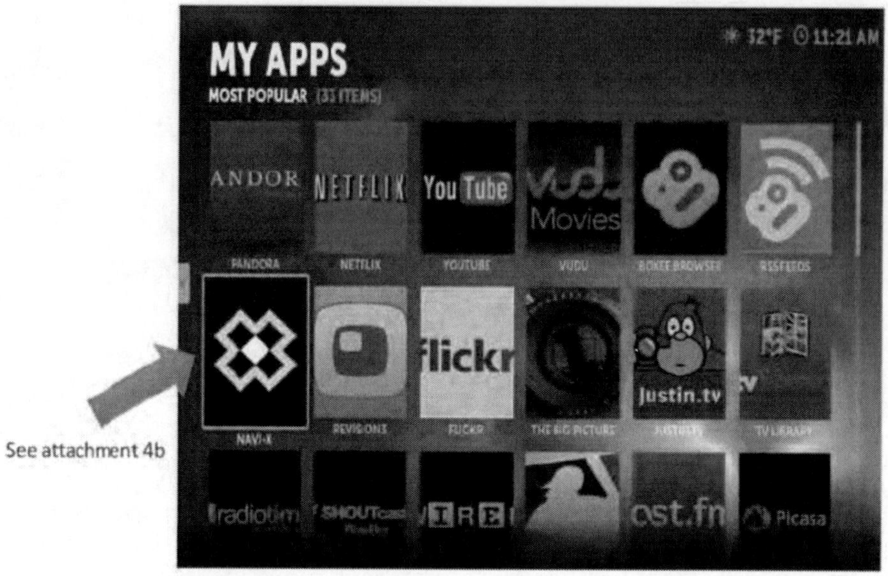


Attachment 4a. (Reference on page 63)

## Some applications offer pay-per-view without the "pay"

Attachment 4b. (Reference on page 63)

## The ancillary revenue streams on which the film industry depends are rapidly declining

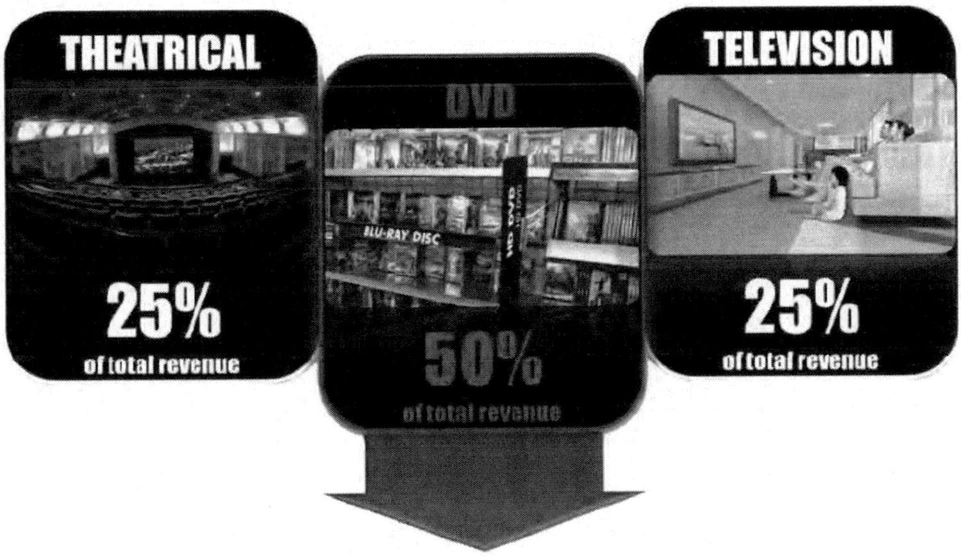


Attachment 5. (Reference on page 64)

## Cash flow timing for a typical film

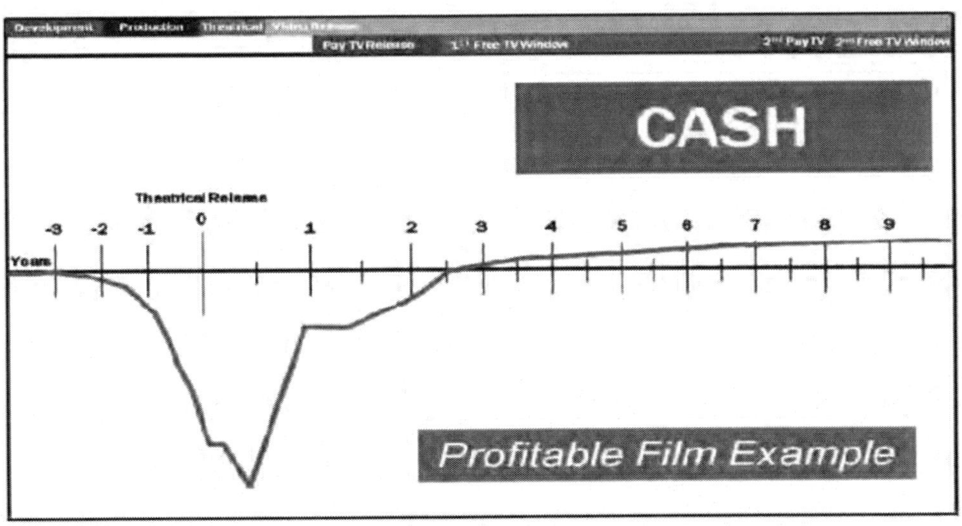


Attachment 6. (Reference on page 64)

Film production is down as studios release fewer films and smaller labels are closed or restructured

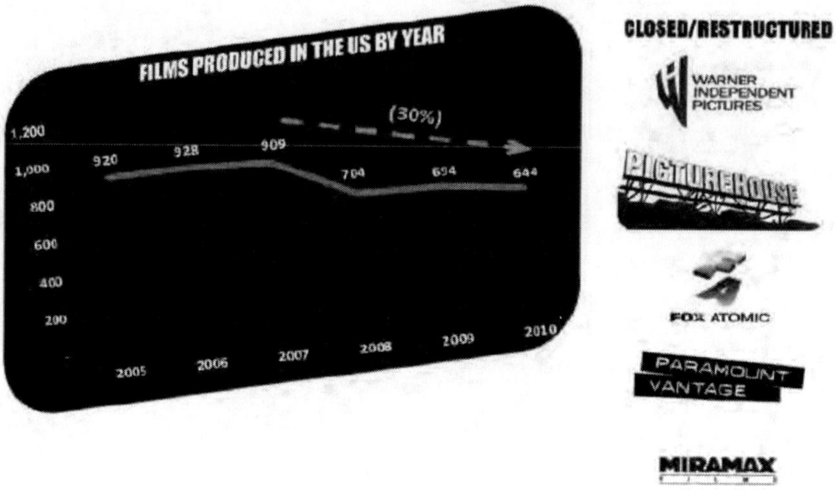


Attachment 7. (Reference on page 63)

Piratebay's refusal to comply with DMCA takedown request

As you may or may not be aware, Sweden is not a state in the United States of America. Sweden is a country in northern Europe.
Unless you figured it out by now, US law does not apply here.
For your information, no Swedish law is being violated.

Please be assured that any further contact with us, regardless of medium, will result in
a) a suit being filed for harassment
b) a formal complaint lodged with the bar of your legal counsel, for sending frivolous legal threats.

It is the opinion of us and our lawyers that you are ....... morons, and that you should please go sodomize yourself with retractable batons.

Please also note that your e-mail and letter will be published in full on http://www.thepiratebay.org.

Go f ---* yourself.

Polite as usual,
anakata

The Pirate Bay

* Word deleted by Paramount

Attachment 8. (Reference on page 65)

A Google search of "wat" auto-fills "watch movies" and top results are mostly illegal pirate sites

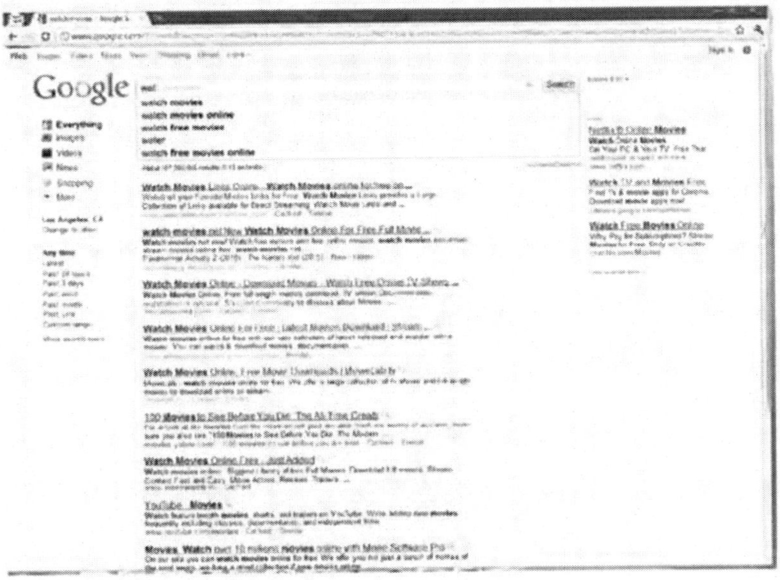


Attachment 9. (Reference on page 66)

A Google search of "stream" auto-fills "stream movies" and top results are mostly illegal pirate sites.

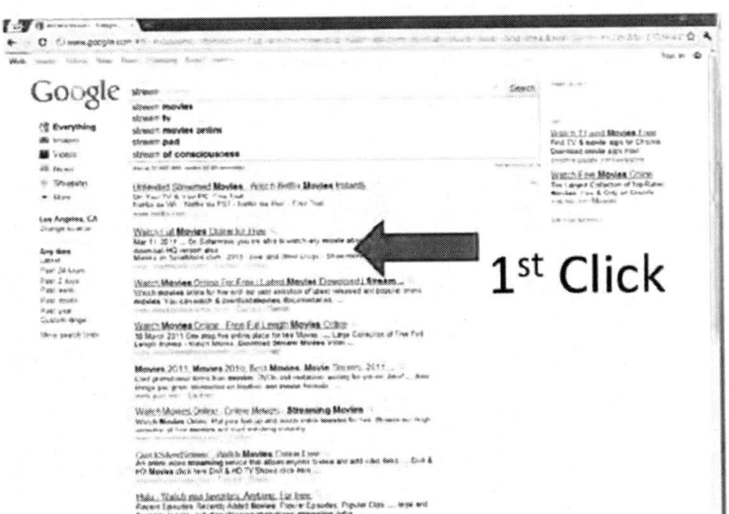


Attachment 10. (Reference on page 66)

# Click #2

Attachment 11a. (Reference on page 66)

# Click #3

Attachment 11b. (Reference on page 66)

# Click #4

Attachment 11c. (Reference on page 66)

# Click #5

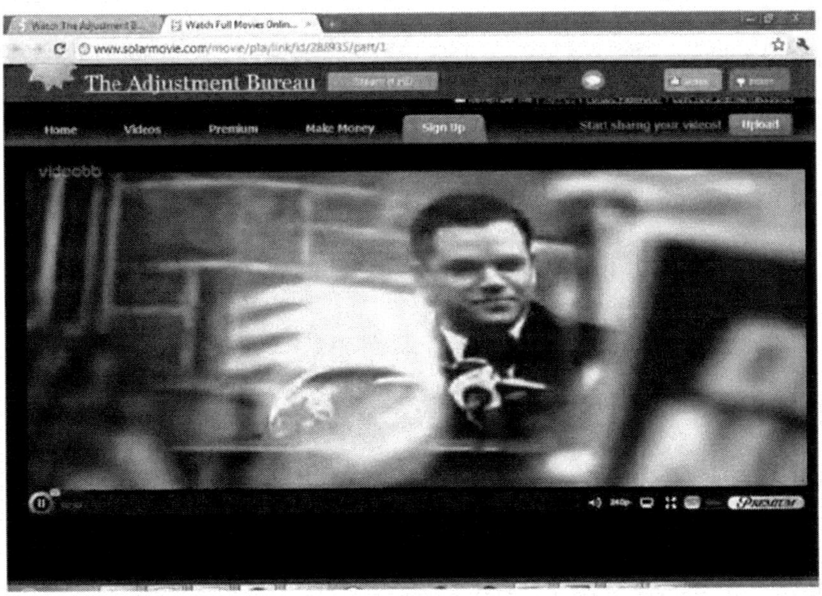


Attachment 11d. (Reference on page 66)

Rewards programs promise money for "uploading popular content"

Attachment 12. (Reference on page 67)

Cyberlockers with rewards gain tremendous market share while Rapidshare declines after discontinuing rewards

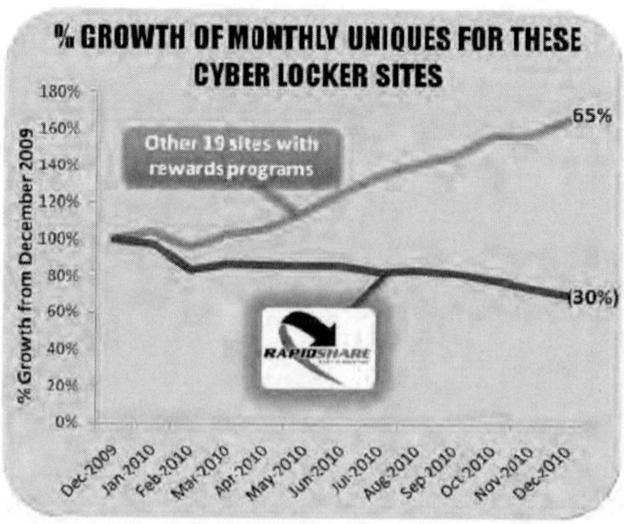


Attachment 13. (Reference on page 67)

We arrived at this estimate by assuming that the cyberlocker has merely a 1% to 5% subscription rate (the cyberlocker offers a tightly limited free sample of usage beyond which a subscription is necessary), with a $6 average subscription fee and 83 million monthly unique visitors. We used an estimate of 32 million daily ad impressions at $1 - $3 CPM. On the cost side we estimated $20 million for bandwidth charges plus $7 million for storage (the two things the cyberlockers cannot steal) and $3 million for overhead. At a 1% subscription rate the resulting profit is $41 million; at a mere 5% subscription rate the profit is $304 million.

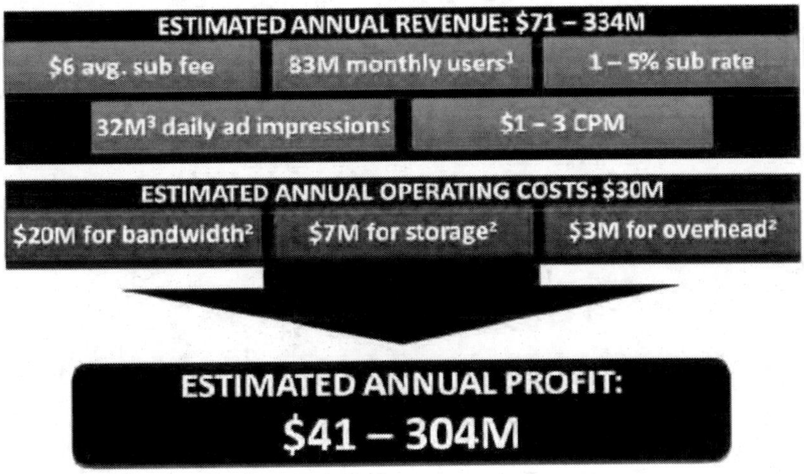


Attachment 14. (Reference on page 67)

## Sophisticated looking sites offering stolen content

Attachment 15a. (Reference on page 67)

## Sophisticated looking sites offering stolen content

Attachment 15b. (Reference on page 67)

## These sites offer multiple viewing formats

Attachment 15c. (Reference on page 67)

## The websites for the iTunes and Netflix distribution services

Attachment 15d. (Reference on page 67)

## Examples of major credit cards used for payment of illegal copies on trafficking web sites

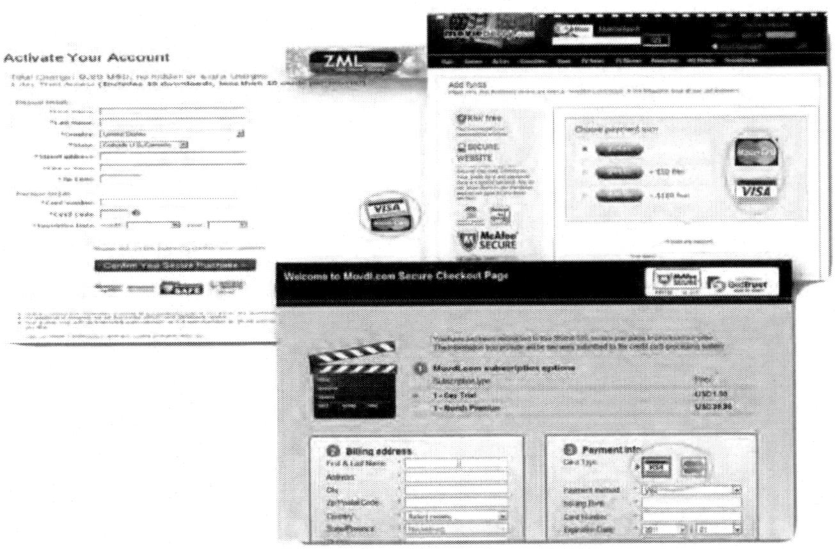


Attachment 16a. (Reference on page 67)

## PayPal is also widely accepted

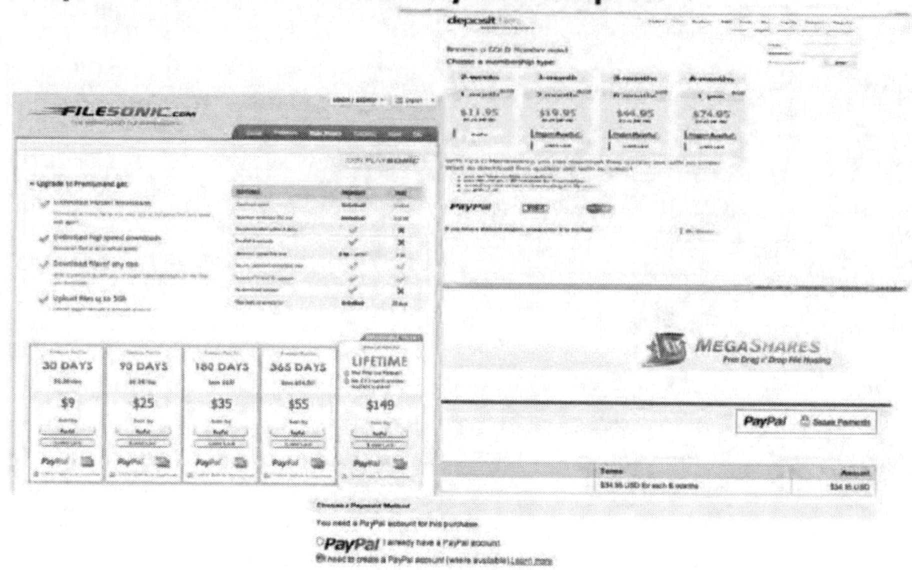


Attachment 16b. (Reference on page 67)

## The flow of customers to PayPal from cyberlockers outpaces that from major American businesses

Attachment 16c. (Reference on page 67)

## Major advertisers appear on sites trafficking in illegal content

Attachment 17a. (Reference on page 67)

## Major advertisers appear on sites trafficking in illegal content

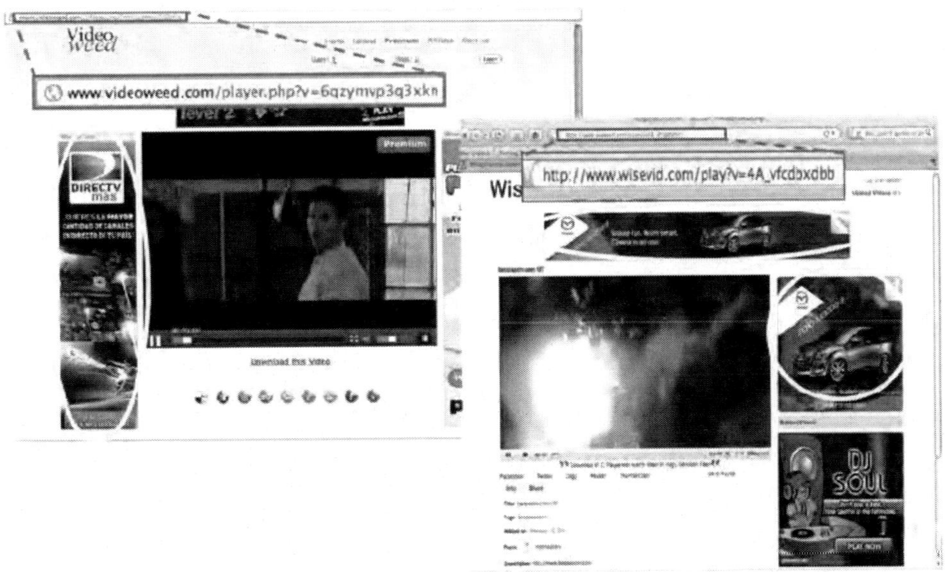


Attachment 17b. (Reference on page 67)

## Examples of unauthorized use of the McAfee Secure logo

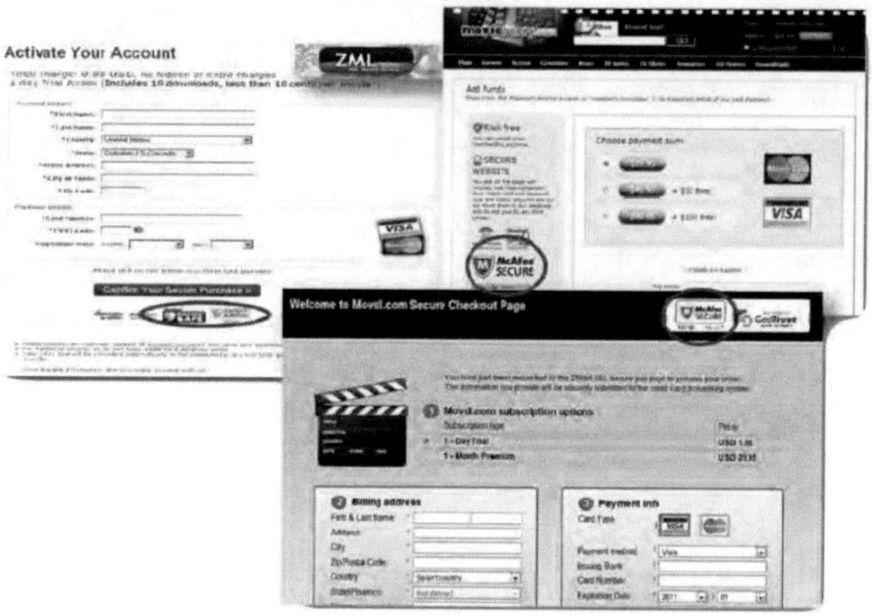


Attachment 18. (Reference on page 68)

## Consumers are exposed to the same threats whether they download or stream the content

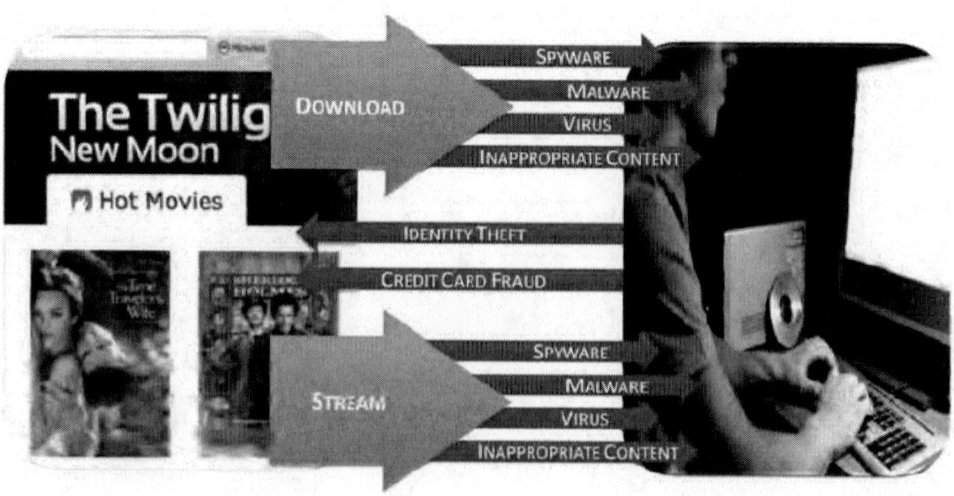


Attachment 19. (Reference on page 68)

*Chapter 3*

# LETTERS, STATEMENTS, ETC., SUBMITTED FOR THE HEARING

Mr. Goodlatte. I will begin the questioning with you and to the very point you have raised. Where do you see the motion picture industry in 5 years or so, if we don't anticipate and provide the necessary tools to ensure effective online enforcement of IP rights, at least within U.S. herders?

Mr. Huntsberry. Well, I think the future can he described as one of less volume and different type of product. If you look at the history of this industry, it has been one that was never constrained by theft or piracy and, therefore, was able to produce as many films as the market afforded, the opportunity that was created.

As a result of the theft that has been going on already over these last 5-plus years, we have seen a dramatic reduction in the number of films produced. The six major motion picture studios used to produce over 200 movies just 5 years ago; we are down now to 140 movies as of last year. And also the profile of those movies has changed, meaning that we are concentrating more and more on movies that we believe can at least withstand the pressure that piracy is putting on us.

That means that movies that are sort of in the mid-budget range, which is sort of a \$50-\$100 million range, which are dramas with a smaller audience, have a very hard time right now reaching audiences. So as I said, we are going to see lower volume going forward and we will see more changes in the profile, which means there will be less choices offered to consumers.

Mr. Goodlatte. Thank you.

Mr. Sohn, with that in mind, you stated that addressing foreign infringement activity required international cooperation. But what if the hosting country fails to act, or as in the case of the Piratebay, the service hops to another country.

Why should the U.S. be held hostage to hostile, corrupt or uncooperative foreign interests? Don't we have the right and responsibility to protect U.S. consumers who are targeted by malicious foreign actors, and shouldn't we protect U.S. creators who play by the rule?

Mr. Sohn. Sure. And I think we ought to be looking for ways to do that. I do think that, as a starting point, though, it is important to recognize that actually trying to punish and catch actual bad actors is really the way you get the most bang for the buck. If you can do that, you can actually get the problem at its source.

So we have efforts underway to improve cooperation with other countries. There is a chapter on that in ACTA. It is part of the IPEC annual report. The IPEC, I think, was here and listed a number of efforts in that area. I think it is essential to pursue that kind of international cooperation. In fact, there was a report that MarkMonitor put out in January that said that the bulk of digital piracy sites are actually based in North America and Western Europe.

So I think actually a lot can be done cooperating with our known trading partners.

For that category of sites where we can really go through the tools on the table and see that they don't work and that can actually be shown, I think it is worth thinking about whether there are narrowly targeted congressional actions that could work. The phrase I have heard several times today is "follow the money," and I think that would be a fruitful path to explore.

Mr. Goodlatte. Thank you.

Ms. Pallante, in your opinion, has U.S. copyright law kept pace with technology?

Ms. Pallante. Well, I think Congress has done a very good job over the last hundred years of catching up to technology, but we are rarely out in front of it. And the great thing about this issue is that it is a chance for us to ensure, before we go over a cliff, that there is a vibrant e-commerce environment so that there are incentives. So it is not just about going after the content that we already know is infringing, but, by providing a safe environment, we can provide incentives for commerce to flourish.

Mr. Goodlatte. You noted that operators of these parasitic websites have no real expectation of enforcement. What are the most important steps that we might take to put teeth in our enforcement measures?

Ms. Pallante. As we said, we have been talking with a lot of stakeholders who have a lot of views on this. But the theme that has emerged is that by starving them from financial ties like credit card processing and PayPal and advertising revenue, that that would go a long way toward reducing the impact. Not all of them operate with direct financial motivation, but it would help a lot to start there.

Mr. Goodlatte. Thank you.

And, finally, about a dozen years ago, I spent many, many weeks in a cramped room—warm, hot room downstairs in this building with many of the Internet service providers, many representatives of the content community, some companies that had a foot in both camps; and we negotiated some of the key provisions, particularly the notice and takedown provision of the Digital Millennium Copyright Act, which is, as you know, the principal tool copyright owners have to protect their intellectual property online. It was written at a time when relatively few people were connected to the Internet, and those who were generally had a maddeningly slow connection.

Looking forward, do you think the balance struck in the DMCA provides appropriate respect and protection for creative works, or do we need to take another look at it?

Ms. Pallante. Well, that is a big question.

Mr. Goodlatte. It is.

Ms. Pallante. I think it always helps when Congress takes a look at existing law that relates directly to technology, so we would not be afraid of that process. It is an important tool, the takedown, and a lot of good companies have built into their business practices ways to deal with those. Others don't. They ignore them. They are not set up for them. They are set up so that they have automated systems that repost the content immediately through computer software. So there is that. And in this context that we are talking about today. Chairman, the DMCA doesn't help with the offshore rogue websites.

Mr. Goodlatte. Thank you very much.

The Chair now recognizes the gentleman from North Carolina, Mr. Watt.

Mr. Watt. Thank you, Mr. Chairman.

I am not sure exactly where to start here. So many issues.

Ms. Pallante, let me be clear first, that, although your testimony is directed at copyright, are there also similar problems in trademark infringement and other areas and whether you would treat those areas the same way as you would in the copyright area?

Ms. Pallante. Thank you for the question.

Mr. Watt. Or whether there is an impediment to doing that?

Ms. Pallante. There are clearly very important trademark violations and counterfeiting problems relating to drugs, relating to toys, and relating generally to consumer products. They were not the focus of my testimony because we administer the copyright law in my office.

Mr. Watt. So my point is, whatever system we set up to deal with one industry, we probably need to set it up to deal across the board, right?

Ms. Pallante. Yes —

Mr. Watt. I am trying to cover a lot of territory here. I just want to be clear on that.

Mr. Huntsberry, you described—you gave us these visuals on a number of things that you all license, and you have pretty good information about the people who are pirating. There seems to me to be a dual track here that has to be being pursued. That is the one that is on the criminal side, and one is on the civil side. I thought you put up, identified, 18, 20 sites that were doing 80, 90 percent of the pirating. What are you all doing on the civil side to pursue those, or is there some impediment to doing that?

Mr. Huntsberry. What we do is we work through the MPAA to take action against those sites.

Mr. Watt. Why is that not an individual business imperative? I mean, given the extent of this, you are working through an association to do it, as opposed —

Mr. Huntsberry. That is right, because all studios are affected by the same sites, typically.

Mr. Watt. What is the MPAA doing to really aggressive—can they bring a lawsuit in the name of —

Mr. Huntsberry. In the name of some of the studios, that is correct.

Mr. Watt. You also put up, identified on the screen the companies that you all license to do this. Is there any way that electronically or technologically you could require before something is shown, some kind of discrete identification that would enable it to be easier to identify the rogue sites?

Mr. Huntsberry. Mmh-hmm.

Mr. Watt. You understand what I am asking?

Mr. Huntsberry. I do, and I appreciate the question. Because the problem that we run into is we find that —

Mr. Watt. Somebody would pirate that, too, right?

Mr. Huntsberry. That is exactly what happens today. In fact, McAfee, which is a well-known protective software for consumers, their logo is stolen and then used on the pages where the rogue sites are asking consumers to subscribe to the site.

Mr. Watt. There has got to be more than a logo. I am talking about some unique identifier of some kind.

Mr. Huntsberry. Yes, but, again, what happens is whatever you flash up can be copied by others. We even have an example where a rogue website was luring consumers with a well-known brand URL, www.redbox.com, which is a well-known company that licenses legally or that rents DVDs in stores; and they were using that brand name to then send consumers to a rogue website.

Mr. Watt. Maybe in California you see a lot more coverage of this, but I have seen very little coverage of any civil litigation about this. Am I missing something here? Is that being aggressively pursued?

Mr. Huntsberry. We are definitely pursuing it wherever we can. Absolutely.

Mr. Watt. It doesn't seem to be getting much coverage.

Mr. Huntsberry. Well, many of the sites you also have to remember are outside the United States; and so it becomes more difficult to go after them because there is the question about where does the management reside —

Mr. Watt. Law enforcement has them—domestic law enforcement has that same impediment going across into another country.

Mr. Huntsberry. That is part of the issue that we have here today, is that we cannot go after the foreign sites.

Mr. Watt. My time has expired all too quickly. I will go on to the next round if we have one.

Mr. Goodlatte. The gentlewoman from Florida, Mrs. Adams, is recognized for 5 minutes.

Mrs. Adams. Thank you, Mr. Chair.

Ms. Pallante, I want to thank you for coming and agreeing to meet with the stakeholders and everything to investigate this matter.

Can you give us a sense of the process you have gone through, the types of stakeholders you met with, and what themes are emerging from those discussions?

Ms. Pallante. Yes, thank you very much for the question.

In the last month, we have had over 30 meetings with probably over 50 stakeholders, really in a fact-gathering approach. We have met with everybody from representatives of small authors, book authors, for example, to corporations that are in the music or movie businesses. We have met with search engines. We have met with ISPs. We have talked to payment processors. So we have really tried to cast a wide net. We have also met with ICE, and we have met with the FCC. Because there are other government entities that come into play on this, and they have very valid perspectives that have been quite helpful to us.

So we are still vetting the issues; and, as I keep saying, they are very complex. But, in general, the complexity in the view of most stakeholders is not a reason not to approach the issue. In other words, just because these technical pirates may be so smart and may get around anything that you may enact is not a reason not to go down that road.

Most people do agree that there should be a role for all who benefit in the ecosystem, and there should be a mix of legislative and private procedures and practices that come into play to solve it. Due process is extremely important, and everybody agrees with that, and the remedies should not affect the current doctrines of copyright liability. In other words, this is really about remedies.

Mrs. Adams. Search engines, I know you noted that search engines are perhaps the most important player on the online ecosystem and stated search engines have sought algorithms that currently often provide Internet users with search results for rogue websites that technology makes—to allow search engines to block such sites from paring the search results, much as search engines have eliminated child pornography from results.

So as part of your discussions, has the Copyright Office attempted to engage the search engine community? Do you think it might he productive to discuss the adoption of voluntary agreements to address the piracy through either the removal of the illegal sites in search results and/or giving prioritization to authorize domains in search results?

Ms. Pallante. I think all voluntary cooperation is a part of this. The question is, can the suppression of searches to rogue sites be possible technically? Is it viable? Would it ruin the process that search engines engage in for good-faith customers and in their good-faith business? And we don't know the answer to the technical questions in the Copyright Office, but we think that they need to be explored.

Mrs. Adams. You do agree they do need to be explored, correct? I think we need to be looking at all avenues to try to at least discourage the rogue sites from popping up so quickly.

I am curious, and maybe anyone—but what would you see as Congress' role to the new—if they were to grant new authorities to the Federal agencies, what resources do you believe they would need?

Mr. Huntsberry. I think what we need is the ability to go after foreign rogue sites, first and foremost.

Mrs. Adams. Mr. Castro.

Ms. Castro. I would just echo what has been said here today, that it needs to be comprehensive. Too many of these recommendations are only looking at domestic solutions; and piracy, as we know, is global. So, yes, it needs to be a global solution.

Mr. Sohn. In terms of resources I would say it is especially important that law enforcement has the resources to pursue actual cases against bad actors and to do the hard work of working with other governments to try to pursue entities that are abroad as well. I think some of that can be done. I am sure it is resource intensive.

Mrs. Adams. You are grinning.

Ms. Pallante. Yes. I think our law enforcement entities have something like 400 Federal laws that they are responsible for enforcing. So, assuming they are doing the absolute best that they can, they would need very clear parameters about what they can go into court and request a court order for. So could they shut down payment processors? Could they ask ISPs to block? They would need to know exactly what the parameters of the law were before they undertook the resources to go after these kinds of sites.

Mrs. Adams. So very clear and distinction legislative laws, I would agree, coming from the law enforcement community. Thank you.

Mr. Goodlatte. I thank the gentlewoman.

The gentleman from Michigan, Mr. Conyers, is recognized.

Mr. Conyers. Thank you. Chairman Goodlatte.

This sounds like a 101 in copyright law in which everybody re-describes the problem in their own unique way. But the purpose of a hearing is for the witnesses to come to us and give us some recommendations; and, so far, I haven't gotten one concrete recommendation about what we do. You are all describing the problem.

And I am disappointed in all the witnesses. I mean, here is a trillion-dollar industry losing billions of dollars every year. The Judiciary Committee holds a hearing, and what do you four come and tell us? That this is a big, complicated problem, much of it is offshore, so we can't do anything about it. And the question comes down to, when this is all over, we are going to read through this transcript and say, what did we learn?

And I can tell you what I have learned.

Now let me take the rest of my few minutes and ask you each one specifically, starting with Paramount, what do we do in the Congress?

Mr. Huntsberry. Right. So, as I said earlier, we need to have the ability for law enforcement to pursue the owners of foreign rogue websites. That is one of our biggest hurdles today. These sites know exactly how —

Mr. Conyers. You mean you haven't—you don't have lawyers that have recommended something specific to you?

Mr. Huntsberry. Oh, sure. But therein lies —

Mr. Goodlatte. Well, why don't you tell us?

Mr. Huntsberry. Because therein lies the problem. It is today impossible to even discover who the owners are of these sites as well as where the sites are served. It becomes very complicated.

Mr. Conyers. That is an excuse. That is not answering my question.

What do you say, Mr. Expert?

Mr. Castro. There are a number of recommendations that we have that are very specific about what you can do.

Mr. Conyers. Name them.

Ms. Castor. You can block the DNS-level foreign sites and domestic sites that are systematically engaged in piracy. You can require search engines, ad networks, and financial service providers to stop doing business with these sites. You can create a process for the Federal Government to work with industry to identify these sites, create a master list of all of these sites. And then with this list, once you know where all the rogue sites are, you can work to create a culture that rejects piracy.

As you pointed out, we all know this is a big problem. If we had a list and said, here are the top thousand sites that are engaging in piracy—everyone in the Internet needs to be involved in doing this. You can use a carrot, you can use a stick, you can use a gentleman's agreement, but you can get it done if you have that list.

Mr. Sohn. I wish that I had an easy answer for you to solve the problems —

Mr. Conyers. I am not looking for an easy answer.

Mr. Sohn [continuing]. But here is what I would suggest.

Number one, I think Congress needs to continue the process it started with the PRO-IP Act of trying to improve our law enforcement capability, make sure that we are as effective as possible in our actual prosecution of bad actors. That requires the hard job of working with other countries, and I think Congress has a really important oversight role there.

I think that it is worth looking at narrowly targeted ways to address situations where we can show that that process can't work. In other words, ordinary law enforcement can't work. And the approach I would recommend that Congress look at is this follow-the-money approach that has been discussed a couple of times today. I think that trying to make sure that rogue websites can't make a profit, can't turn this into a profitable business enterprise, would be an important step.

Ms. Pallante. At this stage, our primary recommendation is exactly that, that you find a way to give enforcement agencies like ICE the authority to request a court order to ask payment processors and ad networks to cut off their financial ties to rogue sites.

Mr. Conyers. Thank you, Mr. Chairman. I can see why the industry is losing so much money.

How many times do you think this Committee is going to have hearings on this subject in the 112$^{th}$ Congress?

Well, this may be it. So I thank you. Chairman Goodlatte.

Mr. Goodlatte. I thank the gentleman; and the Chair now recognizes the gentleman from New York, Mr. Reed, for 5 minutes.

Mr. Reed. Thank you, Mr. Chairman.

I am going to go down a path here that Mr. Conyers is kind of exploring. When I have looked at this issue, I have looked at it from a traditional model of historical thinking that this is a common theft situation and we need to arm our law enforcement with the traditional means and methods of enforcing the laws and go after those offenders.

One thing that I have been asking myself recently when looking at this issue is, is there something that we are missing that the Internet presents to us in a new environment? Is there something within the Internet itself, technological protective measures or enforcement measures, we could be arming our law enforcement with to go after these offenders? By that, I mean the Chairman in the full Committee in his opening comments said something about if you are getting into an armed robbery situation you make sure you go in and cut off the offender.

Is there some way that the technology offers us to utilize to go after these offending entities that are engaged in this clearly illegal activity—we go through the courts, we get the appropriate measures, but is there something that technology can provide to us that the law enforcement would be looking for in order to go after the offending parties?

And I guess I will go to the government office to see if—does law enforcement have any ideas that could be of assistance to us?

Ms. Pallante. Thank you for the question; and, just to be clear, our office is not a law enforcement agency.

Mr. Reed. I understand, but from the government, from your dealings with the Department of Justice and whatever.

Ms. Pallante. In the greater government family, the law enforcement piece is obviously the big hammer. It has to be there or there is no real expectation of enforcement. The technology has really been a huge investment on the part of private rights holders based on everything they can do to track infringement, to bring infringement to the attention of ISPs, for example, so that they can put takedown notices out there in the hopes that people will comply.

One interesting question is what responsibility, if any, should those who host sites have in employing technology, say filtering technology, to weed out infringement as a good corporate citizen?

Mr. Reed. Okay. Any other suggestions? Any other tools that could be at our disposal that we are missing, given the nature of the Internet and its technological advancement?

Mr. Sohn. I think, at the end of the day, there are some limits to what technology can do. Information technology puts powerful tools in the hands of users, and I think in the long run the solution here is not going to be so much the users not having the technological capability to reach bad sites, but it is going to be more trying to develop some norms and some deterrents that prevent people from using it that way.

I think technology can play an important role as different entities in the ecosystem try to roll out tools to stop infringement. For example, technology can be used to make the DMCA notice and takedown processes more effective, more streamlined.

So I think there is lots of ways that individual entities within the system—within the ecosystem, I should say—can be more effective in the role they are trying to play. And that can include, for example, YouTube, which has a process right now for trying to identify infringing videos when they are uploaded and for allowing rights holders to monetize that.

So I think there are lots of ways that technology can be deployed. I think the difficulty is that it is unlikely to be a one-size-fits-all technology solution, and it would be difficult for Congress to go down the path of trying to mandate particular technologies here. This is something that different players have to explore.

Mr. Reed. I guess what I am hearing here—and I don't mean to cut you off; I am running out of time—is we really have two points of potential areas to look at this from, the money perspective and also from the structure of the Internet perspective.

Am I clearly understanding? Does anybody disagree with those two points of areas where we can step in and potentially attack this issue? Are there any other areas out there?

Mr. Huntsberry. I see it as money and technology. Those are the two.

Mr. Reed. Money and technology?

Mr. Huntsberry. That is right.

Mr. Reed. Does anybody else disagree with that? Okay.

When we deal with the size of the enforcement mechanisms we need, are there any limits that we should be considering on the size of the penalties or tools that are at our disposal or should we just be fully unlimited?

Anyone? Ms. Pallante.

Ms. Pallante. Well, one question that has been raised in the stakeholder discussions that we have had is whether there will ever be enough government resources for the government to pursue this as a priority, this being infringement or counterfeiting, for example. So even if the law were changed and it were clear and they had more of an ability to cut off the money and to starve these rogue websites and get at the offshore operators and to block those sites here, the question would still be, would you still be ahead of the problem? Or would you still be limited to kind of the really, really big, grossly infringing sites?

And so the question that I think is down the road is whether there should be some additional right of private actors to get into court on their own without always going through the Department of Justice or ICE, for example. And you will hear that from stakeholders as you talk to them.

Mr. Reed. Thank you. I yield back, Mr. Chairman.

Mr. Goodlatte. I thank the gentleman.

The Chair now recognizes the gentleman from California, Mr. Berman.

Mr. Berman. Thank you very much, Mr. Chairman.

Mr. Sohn, one very quick, hopefully, answer to a quick question.

You write in your testimony CDT recognizes the problem of websites that seek to profit by distributing copyrighted material without authorization and without paying the lawful rights holders.

We are having a debate on what you meant. Is it one or the other? Or even if they are paying the lawful rights holders, if they did it without authorization that is wrong and you oppose it?

Mr. Sohn. I think all we intended by that phrase was to refer to entities that are violating the law because they had not properly licensed the material that they are distributing.

Mr. Berman. So paying rights holders what you think is just compensation if you don't have their permission or the license from them is still wrong.

Mr. Sohn. Correct. I was envisioning by that phrase a voluntary transaction in which the rights holder is paid a licensing fee that the rights holder has agreed to.

Mr. Berman. Mr. Sohn's testimony, as he says there, acknowledges the problem, talks about solutions that involve the forfeiture and blocking of a website as ineffective. His testimony, if you have a chance to read it in detail, it is filled with lots of very interesting things which you can't do justice to in 5 minutes. But challenging the effectiveness of this approach, raising issues about the potential for encompassing websites that may be doing some infringing work but also are exercising non-infringing First Amendment expression raises the philosophical question of the right of U.S. law to try and affect behavior by parties in other countries and then raises consequences of that approach in terms of cybersecurity and inefficiencies in terms of the Internet functioning.

Mr. Castro, I don't know if you have read the testimony, but I would like to get your reaction to some of the points Mr. Sohn raised in his much longer written testimony.

Ms. Castor. Absolutely. And, obviously, in the shortened time, if you look at my written testimony, I believe I have addressed all of those objections that have been raised. They have been raised in a number of forums before.

If you look at the issue of DNS blocking, which is I think where most of the objections have been raised, or blocking even at the IP level, DNS blocking is something that is used already today. There is a service, for example, called open DNS. People actually subscribe to this service, and this service provides users a number of tools like parental controls. It corrects typos and URLs, and it ensures people get to only safe sites.

We can do something very similar with DNS blocking for rogue sites. If you look at the objections that are raised, most of them are speculative. If you look at the data, there is none that supports it.

And if you look at what even the creators of DNS—for example, Paul Vixie, he runs ISC, which is the company that creates BIND which is a software that actually runs DNS on the computers all over the world. He has even come out and said that the idea that any site should be able to just have a domain name, if they are a rogue site, that you should be able to—the purpose of DNS is not to facilitate rogue sites. It is not to facilitate piracy. It is not to facilitate counterfeiting.

We can change the way these standards are written to respond to this. We can create secure DNS protocols that allow for the types of controls and mechanisms that we are talking about today that would allow you to block rogue sites but still have a very secure, even more secure, Internet architecture.

And that is the result we want. We want a result that protects consumers and also gives a secure Internet experience.

Mr. Berman. Mr. Sohn, if I could, well, hopefully, I can get this question in.

The issue of diplomacy and cooperative approaches—if you look at Attachment 8 to Mr. Huntsberry's testimony, which lists reasons why Pirate Bay based in Sweden refuses to comply with DMCA takedown requests from copyright owners, it says it is not a U.S. company and damned if it has to follow U.S. law. It will not comply with requests to take down unlawful material and then proceeds to call the victims of that theft morons and suggest a number of acts which I prefer not to repeat in public. But it is in Attachment 8 for those who want to read it.

What do we ask the Government of Sweden to do? And if they don't do it, do we put them on the USTR's 301 list? Lay out the diplomatic strategy that might work in all the remaining time that you have.

Mr. Sohn. Well, I think absolutely. What you try to do is work with Swedish authorities to identity the people behind the site and actually go after the individuals. That is where you have a real deterrent effect, and that is where you have the ability to seize the computer servers that the bad guys are using.

My understanding is that in a number of ICE actions they have done exactly this. They have cooperated with the Netherlands, for example, in connection with some of the domain name seizures. They have actually taken down some bad guys in cooperation with foreign authorities. And I guess —

Mr. Berman. We have a good example, WikiLeaks. They go after them on sexual misconduct charges.

Mr. Sohn. Ultimately, I think it is very difficult to use the DNS system in a way that is going to effectively make these sites inaccessible. That is why I am saying we have to do so the hard work of actually trying to get the bad guys. Because I think however much we like to use the DNS for that purpose, it is not ultimately going to work.

Mr. Berman. I think my time is more than expired.

Mr. Goodlatte. I thank the gentleman, very pertinent question.

The Chair now recognizes the gentleman from Arizona, Mr. Quayle for 5 minutes.

Mr. Quayle. Thank you, Mr. Chairman. Thanks to all of you for coming.

Mr. Sohn, during your testimony, you were talking about how we shouldn't he overreaching in any law just to go after a few bad actors. And I found that curious that you said "a few bad actors." Because if you are basing it on in comparison to everybody who uses the Internet I think that might be accurate, but when you are actually basing it on people that are legitimately using copyrighted material, do you still believe that it is just a few bad actors, not a large number of people or entities that are doing this?

Mr. Sohn. Well, it is interesting. I think there are certainly a large number of users that engage in infringement.

There was a recent study that looked at a couple of the top BitTorrent sites and found that actually a relatively small number of users, on the order of 100, were responsible for uploading the large majority of the infringing material that was found there. So it does appear that there are some power users who are burning up their Internet connection trying to upload pirated stuff day in and day out. So I do think that going after some of the worst of the worst can make a dent in the problem.

I also think that is where you send a strong deterrence message to everybody else to say, look, you are not as anonymous as you think you are. We will go through the effort to track you down, and we can shut you down. If we do come after you, there is going to be criminal penalties to pay.

Mr. Quayle. Going to the whole shutting-down part, in your testimony you also presented several reasons why domain name seizures would not be 100 percent effective and focused primarily on how such a block might be circumvented. Can you gave other examples of situations where authorities should not take action against criminals because they can find a way around it?

Mr. Sohn. I certainly don't think that a law enforcement action has to be 100 percent effective in order to be worth taking. I do think, though, that at the outset, when we are talking about what new authorities we could create, we would want to at least make sure it meets a certain minimum bar of effectiveness.

And I guess my argument would be not that domain name seizures and blocking are less than 100 percent effective but that it is really going to be hardly effective at all, that if you had a graph you will see a brief dip and then you will see piracy levels go right back up because it is so easy to circumvent for everybody in the system. And at the end of the day what I think would happen is, if domain name seizures and blocking are something that happens on an occasional basis, I don't think that causes any great consequence. I think if that becomes a mainstream tool of law enforcement, it will lose all of its bite. People will just build other ways around the navigation system.

To use an analogy that Mr. Castro bought up, he said it is kind of like taking some of the bad guys' numbers out of the phonebook. It is kind of like that. But, unfortunately, on the Internet there are lots of ways to get information. You don't have to use the phonebook. There are lots of navigation opportunities to find out how to get to these sites. So just purely on a practical level I think it is not a tactic that is effective enough to be worth the risks that it causes.

Mr. Quayle. So you don't have any examples of other laws where we cannot push for it without 100 percent ability to not having a circumvention of that law.

Mr. Sohn. I think when Congress weighs legislation on a daily basis, probably the scrap heap floor is littered with examples where we thought of ideas and decided they won't work.

Mr. Quayle. Thanks.

Now, Ms. Pallante, I was just wondering, to go back to illegal streaming, as technology advances, do you think that illegal streaming of copyrighted material is now the primary chosen method to actually use and deliver those copyrighted material over the Internet?

Ms. Pallante. I think for some works it will be. I am not sure— I am sure Mr. Huntsberry can tell us what the breakdown is between downloading and streaming for movies, for television programming, and for sports streaming. It is very, very big.

Mr. Quayle. And so if that continues to kind of be the wave of the future, do you think that it makes sense to actually have a lesser penalty for those that illegally stream videos or stream copyrighted content over the Internet rather than those that provided them in downloaded form?

Ms. Pallante. Thank you for that question.

If that is a business model that is a primary way for bad actors to pirate material and to make it available without authorization, it doesn't make sense from a policy perspective for that to be a misdemeanor and not a felony, as is the reproduction and distribution right under copyright law.

Mr. Quayle. Thank you very much. I yield back.

Mr. Goodlatte. The gentleman from Florida, Mr. Deutch, is recognized for 5 minutes.

Mr. Deutch. I thank you, Mr. Chairman.

Mr. Sohn, you say in your written testimony that quantifying the problem is exceedingly difficult, and you point out that parties commissioning studies that show the impact of this type of piracy have vested interest in the results, seeming to suggest that perhaps we are taking this more seriously than we ought to.

I guess, Mr. Huntsberry, let me turn to you. Can you speak to the vested interest that might exist here and can you talk for a moment about the overall impacts on our economy?

Mr. Huntsberry. Well, I can tell you that there are a lot of jobs at stake and they occur at different levels. So, for one, you have the films themselves that, as I said, hire between a few hundred up to 5,000 employees to actually produce a movie. And so as volume of films decreases, there is a direct correlation to the number of people who are being hired to make those films.

The second part is that, at a local level, when we produce films in the 50 States, we are not spending money in those States, i.e., not hiring people in those States.

And then, finally, also at the studio level, where you have people that are in the business of helping to produce those movies, market, and distribute them, you have a direct impact there as well, and we have seen decreases in the last few years.

Mr. Deutch. Mr. Sohn, you can agree that there is no reason for us to argue about the relative impact, that this is a vitally important issue we ought to be tackling?

Mr. Sohn. It is an important issue, and my only point was to try to emphasize that I think that some of the specific statistics that get thrown around, when the GAO looked at it, the GAO said, we can't really verify any of these statistics.

Mr. Huntsberry. Congressman, may I add something to that.

In fact, it plays also to a question that was raised earlier. Last year, just Paramount alone, we actually issued 40 million infringement notices. Now infringement notices are specifically targeted at peer-to-peer sites or users of peer-to-peer networks who are downloading content. So we issue the notice to the ISP, who then forwards it to the consumer.

With respect to cyberlockers, which are the online storage sites, we issued 1.5 million takedown notices. That means there were 1.5 million places where anybody in the world would have been able to stream or download the movie.

Mr. Deutch. I want to go back—Mr. Sohn, you point out in your written testimony that in 2007, 2008, which is generations ago in terms of what we are combating, what we are dealing with now, particularly in terms of cyberlockers and video streaming, that CDT compiled a music download warning list.

Now if you agree that the primary focus here ought to be on addressing—focusing the rogue sites so that they can't make a profit, make this a profitable enterprise, which you said earlier, shouldn't we be looking not only at advertising, as you point out, but shouldn't we also be looking at the way that they ultimately do make this a profitable venture, which is making people—driving traffic to their site?

Isn't there an opportunity for the Internet service providers to be involved here? Why shouldn't we be focusing on that component as well? Since without those ISPs and without a discussion about the various ways that we can ensure that these sites don't come up and we can watch pirated content in one or two clicks, without that, these aren't profitable ventures. Shouldn't that be a key piece of this legislation?

Mr. Sohn. Well, the hard question there is, what is the role that ISPs could play that would be effective? Because, again, the kind of DNS blocking that was suggested in the Senate bill last year I think just doesn't have any ultimate effect if you actually track through what would likely happen and if you look at the many ways to avoid it —

Mr. Deutch. Let me interrupt you for a second, because I am running out of time.

Instead of—it seems like you are bending over backwards to acknowledge that there are lots of ways to get around efforts that we might wish to take in order to make this a less profitable venture. Shouldn't we be looking at it the other way, to come up with the technological ways that we can make it more difficult for others to access this, as Mr. Castro points out is eminently doable?

Mr. Sohn. I guess I disagree with Mr. Castro that it is eminently doable to make sites hard to reach. If you look at something like the WikiLeaks controversy, the lesson is it is very hard on the Internet to just make stuff not reachable. That is why I think the more effective approach would be to say, if they can't process payments, for example, if they can't —

Mr. Deutch. I understand that part of your testimony. Can you get back to the ISPs, please?

Mr. Sohn. Right. So on the ISPs specifically, I think it is very difficult to figure out how ISPs could actually block people from getting somewhere in a way that wouldn't be overbroad and have a lot of collateral consequences.

Mr. Deutch. I understand it is difficult. If there is a way that it can be done without the collateral damage that you fear, obviously, that should be something we consider.

Mr. Sohn. I think it is worth considering. I think what Congress will probably find as it looks at that is that those collateral damages, if you are looking at it from the ISP level, are difficult.

Mr. Deutch. Thank you. I yield back, Mr. Chair.

Mr. Goodlatte. I thank the gentleman.

The Chair now recognizes the gentlewoman from California, Ms. Chu, for 5 minutes.

Ms. Chu. Thank you, Mr. Chair.

I wanted to follow up with you, Mr. Huntsberry, about the true economic impact of piracy; and the reason I wanted to get more deeply into it is I represent a district in Los Angeles County. There are many, many jobs that are related to the entertainment industry; and, of course. Paramount Studios are headquartered in Los Angeles County. So what happens to you certainly has a great deal of impact on my constituents.

So in your written testimony you talk about the pre-production investment by the studio. Taking an award-winning move like "True Grit" for an example, can you describe the investment for this economy?

Mr. Huntsberry. Sure. As you said, "True Grit" was shot in Texas and New Mexico but then also produced in Los Angeles, so it had an impact on multiple economies. And in the case of "True Grit," we would have been spending in Texas, New Mexico on hiring local laborers to build sets. That would include carpenters. That would include painters. That would include set designers. It would include caterers and so forth. In other words, these are literally ten, sometimes hundreds of people that we have to have on the set on location to service the production of the movie. And so, again, like in the case of "True Grit," it was an impact of $16 million between those two States alone. That is not accounting for what we spent in Los Angeles, which was even more than that.

Ms. Chu. And I understand residuals from DVD sales are an important part of a compensation package for actors, directors, electricians, painters —

Mr. Huntsberry. Absolutely. The guild members, as well as the union members, are compensated as a percentage of the revenues that we draw from DVD sales or from the sales of the movies in general.

Ms. Chu. I understand "True Grit" was officially released on December 22, 2010. How long did it take before the movie was available on line for free?

Mr. Huntsberry. It turned out that in the case of "True Grit" it took about 5 days, and it was a copy of a screener that we had sent out to Academy members for the voting. And the screener, by the way, was copyright protected.

Ms. Chu. Thank you. I yield back.

Mr. Goodlatte. Thank you.

The gentlewoman from California, Ms. Lofgren, is recognized for 5 minutes.

Ms. Lofgren. Well, thank you, Mr. Chairman. I have so many questions. I hope I can get them out and get answers promptly.

Mr. Huntsberry, I am wondering, the Senate bill last year would have given government the exclusive power to initiate legal actions to block domains. Is this satisfactory to you, or do you believe that there should be a private right of action to obtain DNS blocking orders?

Mr. Huntsberry. Well, first of all —

Ms. Lofgren. If you could just say "yes" or "no," I have only got 5 minutes.

Mr. Huntsberry. We don't know yet.

Ms. Lofgren. Okay, you have here 20 slides, and I am wondering, of those, according to your written testimony, it is about 90 percent of what is of concern was represented in those 20 slides. How many lawsuits have been brought against the actors in those 20 slides?

Mr. Huntsberry. Against the what? I am sorry.

Ms. Lofgren. The actors that you identified in your slides, how many lawsuits?

Mr. Huntsberry. It is not a number that I could quote you here right now. But it is a large number.

Ms. Lofgren. Could you provide it to me later?

Mr. Huntsberry. Absolutely.[88]

Ms. Lofgren. Thank you very much. I appreciate it.

I am wondering about digital locker sites. Do you believe that Congress should give the government the right or power to seize those domains, even if they comply with the DMCA?

Mr. Huntsberry. Well, today they don't comply with the DMCA.

Ms. Lofgren. But the question is, if you give the notice in take down and they comply, do you think they still ought to be subject to —

Mr. Huntsberry. If "complied" is defined as that you can no longer find stolen content on the site, then yes.

Ms. Lofgren. You said in your testimony that, even with DMCA takedowns, there is never a moment that stolen copies of "True Grit" are not accessible. Is your goal really to make sure that there is not available anywhere a stolen copy of "True Grit?" Do you think that is achievable?

Mr. Huntsberry. What we are trying to do, we are trying to level the playing field here between the good guys and the bad guys. Today, even after 40 million infringement notices and 1.5 million takedown notices, the film is still available. So what it has proven so far is that we are not able simply with these notices to bring the problem to a halt.

Ms. Lofgren. You know, I do think that we have a problem here. And the question I am trying to get at is what is an adequate remedy that doesn't cause collateral damage? And I think about we have heard from Hollywood, and that is an extremely important industry for the United States. There is no question about it. I hear from my constituency more about software, because there is certainly a theft problem there. But we have gone round and round with my software constituents and finally agreed that, although it is always wrong to have piracy, not every piracy is a lost sale, because a lot of what is taken would never been sold. It doesn't mean it is right to do it, but it is worth putting a grain of salt, as the GAO has done, in terms of the dollar loss.

Thinking about that, how do we focus on dealing with bad actors without avoiding the collateral damages?

I was listening to some of our freshmen Members about illegal. I was designing this scenario in my mind. You have a Tea Party website, and they are running without authorization clips of the Patriot to inspire those who come to their website, and they are also ad supported. Republican candidates are buying ads on the site, and they are soliciting funds from people who visit the site, and they are also hosting blogs from people who believe in the Tea Party principles.

They have violated the copyright act. They are subject to blockage, if I am reading the Senate bill correctly; and yet there would be significant First Amendment collateral damage.

---

[88] The information referred to was not received by the Subcommittee at the time this hearing was printed.

How would you deal with that, Mr. Sohn, that scenario?

Mr. Sohn. Well, I think, at a minimum, any step that Congress takes here needs a much narrower definition than the Senate bill contained about what constitutes a website dedicated to infringing activity. The Senate bill used that phrase, "website dedicated infringing activity," but I fear the actual definition they used was much broader than that and could apply to any of a range of sites that do a range of things and then happened to get some infringement on them because users post some there.

Ms. Lofgren. For example, I notice this is not just foreign nationals. Most of the companies listed on the site are California companies, Google and Netflix and on and on and on, Facebook. Facebook has tons of infringing material on it that people have uplifted, and yet I wouldn't call Facebook a rogue site. And yet I think it would be subject to—the entire site, if ICE is to be believed, that whole thing would be taken down, wouldn't it?

Mr. Sohn. Well, one certainly hopes that law enforcement would not pursue a case like that, but there is no question that —

Ms. Lofgren. Well, are the facts any different?

Mr. Sohn. And, furthermore, the process for seizures is essentially a one-sided process. So law enforcement decides it wants to target a site. It goes in and tells that to the judge. The site can get seized without having an opportunity for the site operator to come in and say, no, wait a minute, here is why I am actually a lawful enterprise and why you've got this wrong. And I think whenever you have a one-sided process like that, the risk of either mistakes or just overaggressive action is significant.

Ms. Lofgren. I see that the red light is on, Mr. Chairman. I don't want to abuse your courtesy to me.

I yield back.

Mr. Goodlatte. We may have a question or two more here, and so the gentlewoman might hang in.

Mr. Sohn, as you know, ICE has used authority provided by PRO-IP over the past year to seize more than 100 domains that judges found were engaged in online IP theft. In every instance, the domain name owner had the right to petition a Federal judge to require the return of the domain name. Can you tell the Committee how many of these owners have actually filed such a petition and appeared in Federal District Court?

Mr. Sohn. It is my understanding that nobody has done that to date.

Mr. Goodlatte. Is that not an indication that seizing domain name might be somewhat effective?

Mr. Sohn. Well, the fact that they haven't done it could indicate a number of things. Number one, it could indicate that some of them think that challenging the Federal Government in a lawsuit is going to be costly litigation, and some of them may figure it is just easier to —

Mr. Goodlatte. Has anyone come forward and said that of these 100 sites, said, we are right. We have a legitimate complaint that our domain name was seized improperly. We are not engaged in facilitating pirated works, yet we don't want to take on the Federal Government because of the cost or other concerns?

Mr. Sohn. Sir, there are some entities that have publicly said that they believe they were wrongly targeted. There were some music blogs that said they actually had obtained the material they posted from the record labels on a promotional basis.

There was the example—I guess this is not an intellectual property example, but there was an example just last month of a service called moo.com which shares a domain among 84,000 registrants, as I mentioned in my testimony. And the entire domain got seized because, presumably, there were some individual sites there that were engaged in that criminal activity, and a number of innocent individuals were affected there. So there certainty have been cases where innocent individuals have been affected.

I actually think the real reason that you probably don't see entities challenging it is, number one, certainly the bulk of them probably are just illegal enterprises and they have an easy way around it. They can just go register a domain with a foreign registrar that isn't subject to U.S. jurisdiction. So why bother challenging it when you have that easy route around?

Mr. Goodlatte. Amongst these 100, have we seen evidence of that occurring?

Mr. Sohn. Absolutely.

Mr. Goodlatte. Mr. Castro, what do you have to say in response to that?

Ms. Castor. I would say that if the fear is that these sites will go abroad that is why exactly why we need to be blocking these sites. That is specifically the reason that enforcement mechanisms that only target domestic sites and domestic bad actors ultimately will be ineffective. You can think of the problem of having four —

Mr. Goodlatte. But what do you say to Mr. Sohn's contention that that is not effective because they simply go and get another domain name and keep right on going?

Ms. Castor. Well, I would say this Committee could perform an experiment. If you have a domain name that everyone knows, if that disappeared for a day, I bet your traffic would disappear as well. I don't think it is that easy for people to find sites when a domain that they know and use is gone.

Mr. Goodlatte. What do you have to say to that, Mr. Sohn?

Mr. Sohn. Well, I did a little experiment myself after ICE seized I think 10 sports streaming domains back in January. And I was curious. By the way, I did not want to engage in piracy on these sites. I just wanted to find out if they had resurfaced somewhere. So I just did a little bit. It really only took 5 or 10 minutes of sleuthing on the Internet, if that, really just a few searches. And what I discovered was that there were plenty of people out there discussing precisely this issue, people who had various posts and comments, various places saying, hey, where did that site go? And someone answers the question. Well, it has moved, and it is now located at this other foreign top-level domain.

So what I found was, in looking at those sites, it is actually quite easy to figure out where they had gone. And this kind of gets back to my point —

Mr. Goodlatte. But no one knows what happened to the volume at the site. I understand that the more dedicated person would do exactly what you are talking about, and they will find the new domain name and the new address and reach it fairly easily. But the more casual customer can't find the site. Is that having an effect? Is that reducing the volume of piracy or is it not? I think that is a question I would like to have an answer to.

Mr. Huntsberry.

Mr. Huntsberry. Yes, I think that is precisely the point. We know that theft is always part of the business model. It is no different than in the brick-and-mortar business. Brick and mortar every day has to deal with theft, and so this will also occur in the online space.

What we are trying to do here is level the playing field so at least the average consumer is doing the right thing. The bad guys will always find ways to find the content.

Mr. Goodlatte. What do you and Mr. Castro have to say about the collateral damage that Mr. Sohn cited with regard to a domain name that is shared and one violator messed up the other 63 or— how many? More than 63. You had —

Mr. Sohn. There were 84,000 registrations.

Mr. Goodlatte. There were 84,000 registrants.

Mr. Castro. What you have to do in this case is you want to make sure that there are the right kind of processes in place. This is something that this Committee can exactly work on, how can you set up the right processes so mistakes aren't made? Certainly in law enforcement this isn't the first time mistakes were made. This won't be the last time. But the idea that free speech trumps theft is I think absolutely ridiculous, and there is no reason we can't take action.

Mr. Goodlatte. Thank you.

Mr. Watt, does that prompt any further questions?

Mr. Watt. Yes, let me pick up on right there. Because, really, the question I was trying to get to, wanted to get to is how can we set up a due process mechanism that takes these things into account? What would be the ideal due process mechanism, Mr. Sohn? How would you change the current process that ICE is authorized or is undertaking?

Mr. Sohn. The ideal due process mechanism is always to let the defendant have his day in court essentially and come in and explain why it is not —

Mr. Watt. And what is the problem with doing that, Mr. Castro? If I go to a judge and I have got a captive judge and I got all the facts and no opportunity for anybody on the other side to respond, that says, hey, I am legitimate, I got free speech issues, how do those issues ever get raised before the takedown?

Ms. Castor. I think there are a number of things you have to keep in mind. If you are talking about domestic sites, you have to have processes that can respond in Internet time. You have to have, I think —

Mr. Watt. Well, you got to tell me what the processes are. That is what we are here for. We are trying to set up a mechanism now. I don't mean to be impatient like Mr. Conyers has been, but you can't just tell me, you got to do this, you got to do this. I don't understand what it is you are asking me to do.

Ms. Castor. I think the right solution would be —

Mr. Watt. And while I think I agree with you that most of the First Amendment defenses are crap, even though I am probably the biggest First Amendment defender on this Committee—or one of them at least, I would think—but I am not much on allowing somebody's property to be taken without some kind of opportunity to defend themselves. I am kind of on both sides of this issue with you and Mr. Sohn.

But you got to tell me how to get around this. If one side can go to a judge and get an immediate order, it seems to me that the other side could come to that same judge and defend themselves immediately. That is Internet fast time, I would take it.

Are you advocating something different than that?

Mr. Castro. Well, I think there are a number of things you could do. Well, one thing you could do is you could set a limit on how long to have a site taken down without, you know, the right to appear before a judge.

Mr. Watt. But once the site is taken down, the damage is done, if it's done wrong.

Mr. Castro. Well, you could do it, a very short site. You could have administrative and other kinds of reviews before it could be taken down in the first place, and you could also, of course, have liability.

Mr. Watt. Well, that is I am asking you. Are you telling me you can't get an administrative review? What's a judge? That's an administrative review.

Mr. Castro. Well, before it's done internally.

Mr. Watt. Before it's done, internally, that is right. Why can't I, as the site owner, have the opportunity to appear and present my side at that administrative review?

Mr. Castro. You could certainly do that.

Mr. Watt. Okay, all right. So you all are saying the same thing, then. I mean, that satisfies you, Mr. Sohn?

Mr. Sohn. I think, that, yes —

Mr. Watt. Okay. Then we agree we finally got some reconciliation. It satisfies you, Mr. Huntsberry?

Mr. Huntsberry. I think I am not prepared yet to agree with my colleagues here at this point.

Mr. Watt. Well, are you disagreeing with them or you just not prepared to agree with them?

Mr. Huntsberry. No, no. I think that, look. I think due process—

Mr. Watt. You told Ms. Lofgren that too. You didn't have an answer to the question. We need you to answer questions here today, otherwise we won't get anywhere.

Mr. Huntsberry. So, again, the parallel I like to draw here is that if a store is selling —

Mr. Watt. I don't want you to draw parallels. I want you to tell me how I can do this and give due process, and give you what you are looking for at the same time.

Mr. Huntsberry. I think that once a site has been blocked, I think, very quickly, the site owner has the ability to say was it done justly or not done justly.

Mr. Watt. But the blockage of the site for somebody who is legitimate, to give them the opportunity to the next day come back and say you really blew this up, you screwed up, I don't think is fair.

Mr. Huntsberry. But we know today who is stealing our content. It is very obvious to us, because we know exactly who we license to. Therefore any site at which we find our content that we do not license is stealing our content.

Mr. Watt. Even the Facebook Tea Party people that Ms. Lofgren described?

Mr. Huntsberry. Again, if we know our content is on a site that we have not licensed to, we know that it is fraud.

Mr. Watt. Even if it's the Tea Party people on the Facebook site that Ms. Lofgren described that you said you didn't have an opinion about yet.

Mr. Huntsberry. And I still don't have one.

Mr. Watt. Well, but you just made a very broad statement, anybody who puts something up that you haven't licensed is violating your license.

Mr. Huntsberry. Yes. Well, that's true because that is how the licensing agreement is reached. It is reached formally between the studio and the site, and to the extent that the site has not entered into a license —

Mr. Watt. So if law enforcement is going to go out and seize that site, the Facebook site that Ms. Lofgren described, without a hearing, and without that person, without the Tea Party or whoever it is being able to come in and say, this is legitimate First Amendment protected, you would say they are violating it and they shouldn't be given that right?

Mr. Huntsberry. They should absolutely be given the right to speak. I think what we are talking about is before —

Mr. Watt. But 2 days later you want to be given the right.

Mr. Huntsberry. Right. To me it should be the day after.

Mr. Watt. The day after?

Mr. Huntsberry. It should be after the seizure.

Mr. Watt. I don't know about that. Mr. Castro, you wanted to make a point. Go ahead.

Mr. Castro. I just wanted to say that if you look at physical goods, physical goods are seized before there is court review. So if you want to have a similar —

Mr. Watt. I wasn't too hard on that process either. You know, I am at least, you know. I try to be consistent. I am not a big pre-seizure person. I never have thought that it was all left there. Even if you are seizing unlawful stuff, you ought to give people an opportunity to tell people that it's not unlawful.

Anyway, my time has expired and I am far, far over.

But I wanted to ask Mr. Huntsberry one other question, and you can answer for the record.

Mr. Goodlatte. Go ahead.

Mr. Watt. I am trying to find out what authority you are advocating for on the civil side. I heard you say authorized law enforcement to go do stuff in foreign countries. I need to know what authority you need on the non-law enforcement side that you don't currently have? We don't have time to have you answer that not now.

Mr. Huntsberry. I will follow up.

Mr. Watt. You didn't seem to have a lot of opinions about a lot of this stuff anyway, so this will give you a chance to answer some of the questions that you haven't formulated opinions about, and that's one you can spend several days and then get back to us about.

Mr. Goodlatte. We will afford all the Members of the Subcommittee the opportunity to submit questions in writing, and we will afford you an opportunity to respond. Let me see if anyone has a question they would like to ask right now. The gentleman from Florida.

Mr. Deutch. Thank you, Mr. Chairman. It's a fascinating conversation about whether or not the government has the right to shut down Facebook.

But I believe that we have gone slightly astray here. Mr. Sohn, let me ask you a question. When CDT put out that list of 47 sites that were falsely posing as legitimate music stores, which is the way your testimony describes it, you put that list together. When you put that list out, were you worried that these might be legitimate sites that somehow by an organization like yours putting on this list that somehow you might be doing damage to them?

Mr. Sohn. Well, I will say first we did do due diligence there.

Mr. Deutch. Right. I understand that. You did due diligence. Of course you did.

Would we be wrong to suggest or to believe that there is a difference between something that might get posted on Facebook and what SolarMovie does or what a site—a movie site that clearly is illegally streaming movies is doing, number one; or a hook site that is clearly permitting the illegal downloading of copyrighted material; or in the case of music, a site that is clearly permitting the illegal downloading of music without respect for the intellectual property there.

Aren't there instances where, yes, we need to he worried about the broader implications and making sure we get it right. But aren't there instances where we ought to have enough, enough faith in the Federal Government that they, just like CDT, could get it right?

Mr. Sohn. Well, I think there is a big difference between a private actor taking action and a small group like ours, and the Federal Government taking action.

Mr. Deutch. Right, Mr. Sohn, I agree. Just, Mr. Chair, if I may. I agree that there is a difference. And I don't know about CDT's ability to gather, to do their due diligence before putting out a list.

But I believe that probably most of us here would acknowledge that there is no one who has more resources at their disposal than the Federal Government in compiling such a list, number one.

And number 2, with respect to some of these very specific sites where there is nothing except what's illegal being done, clearly, we ought to be in a position to acknowledge that and the Federal Government ought to be in a position to make that determination before moving forward on shutting down that domain there.

Mr. Sohn. I think whenever you have government action involved you do want to have due process, you want to have some procedural guarantees of fairness, and, you know, unfortunately we have already seen an example where the Federal Government made a mistake here, went after moo.com and there were lots of innocent users of that. Why?

Because they didn't quite understand that this was a—I think, because they didn't quite understand because this domain was shared between many users. So I think any time you don't have due process, there are risks.

Mr. Deutch. Mr. Chairman, just before yielding back. I would acknowledge. I would just point out that I think this hearing was incredibly helpful in starting to flesh out some of the tough issues that we need to grapple with.

At the same time, I think, also putting us in a position to realize that if we grapple with those issues, that we can draft legislation that will be respectful of due process, that will build in sufficient due process, but will also permit us to protect the intellectual property rights that are being violated every single day.

I yield back. Thank you.

Mr. Goodlatte. Well, said. The gentlewoman from California.

Ms. Lofgren. Thank you, Mr. Chairman. I realized that I wanted to ask Ms. Pallante if, you mentioned that you had convened a group of stakeholders, a large number, I can't remember the number you said.

Could you provide, later, a list of who have those stakeholders were that you met with?

Ms. Pallante. Yes, I would be happy to.

Ms. Lofgren. Thank you very much.

You know, I was thinking about the DMCA, and I remember very well, Mr. Chairman, I was a freshman, but the years that we spent trying to sort through that, and although I don't think it was perfect, by the time we finished it, it was a lot better than it was when it started. I mean, the original draft outlawed Web browsing, although I don't think it intended to.

Now we are being asked for new remedies. The question isn't whether we shouldn't consider remedies, but whether they are narrowly tailored to deal with a specific problem, and we won't have collateral damage. That's, I think, one of the big issues.

And I was interested in, I think, this is a rough, I didn't write down word for word, but that search engines and ISPs should be required to prevent access to the bad actors, essentially, that that was asserted as something that should happen.

And in thinking about that, since the bad actors are not a static list, I mean, there's constant movement in the Internet, I am wondering how that squares with the Supreme Court's decision in the Betamax case that basically says that technology is capable of substantial non-infringing users, are not inherently guilty of copyright infringement, and really, our position as the government has been that we are not going to either shut down non-infringing technologies if they have substantial non-infringing uses, nor are we going to go in and do the engineering from the government's point of view of technologies that are in that category.

How does that precedence square with the assertion that we should require ISPs and search engines to block an ever-expanding list and technologies that we probably haven't thought of? Can you think of that, Mr. Sohn, how that would work?

Mr. Sohn. Yes. I think you raise a very good point. There's a long tradition in this country of dealing with Internet service providers and information tools like that in a certain way. We have the DMCA that's addressed that.

I do think that one risk is that the current legislative process could take us into really groundbreaking territory where, you know, we toss aside some of our long-standing principles regarding how the Internet operates and how ISPs and intermediaries in the online context work.

One of the fears that I have tried to express here is that I think that some of those proposals just wouldn't work anyway.

So it's asking us to really do a sea change in a legal approach to some of these entities for results that I actually don't think would make much difference in infringement.

Ms. Lofgren. One of the things that I think Mr. Deutsche mentioned it and others, the utility of addressing the payment scheme, and that intrigues me as an opportunity, because if you do have a site where you are getting paid to stream or to download material that you don't have a right to profit from, that is an opportunity, you know, it seems to me, to deal with it.

Visa came in to my office—and I didn't talk to their representatives, but they talked to my staff last week—and said they are watching the Senate bill, that in the last 6 months, they have been asked only 30 times. They have got a voluntary system where they will block payment for infringing uses, but they have only been asked 30 times in the last 6 months to do that.

So I am wondering how, why would that be, and are we using the tools that have already been made available?

I mean, apparently, they are not very agitated about this bill because they don't feel it would—I don't want to speak for them, but my impression was they didn't think it would be a big burden because nobody is asking them to do it now and they are willing to do it.

Maybe you can comment on that, Mr. Huntsberry. Do you know why only 30 times would Visa have been asked to block these sites?

Mr. Huntsberry. No, as a matter of fact, we have been in contact with Visa intensively over the last year, and also I should say with MasterCard. And I will say that MasterCard has done amazing steps forward in correcting this situation.

So we absolutely agree with you that this is a very good area, as is, by the way, working with the ad providers, because advertising revenue is another type of revenue that these sites benefit from.

Ms. Lofgren. I know my time is up. I just would like to make one comment that you are right. I mean, you have got counterfeit goods. We don't have a due process issue when you have got counterfeit goods, but you never have a problem usually that counterfeit goods could be engaging in First Amendment rights activity. It's a whole different type of risk that we have as a country when we move into this.

And some of the, you know, there is a concept, of fair use in the United States. It is possible to use some material and have it be protected by the First Amendment. That's been really not mentioned here today.

And just a final thought, if we move into designing technology by the United States Government, that too will move offshore as we know, Mr. Chairman, not all engineers currently live in the United States. Not all technology is designed in the United States.

That's another collateral issue that we should be discussing and mindful of as we continue to discuss this important issue.

I yield back with that. Thank you.

Mr. Goodlatte. I thank the gentlewoman. I thank all the members of the panel. This has been a very good hearing. I agree with some of the Members who have said that a number of good ideas have been discussed here, a number of good caveats about how to make sure how we don't violate legitimate operators, due process, have been brought forward as well, and I would encourage everybody involved here, the Internet service providers, the content owners, everyone, to find as many business model solutions to this problem as possible as well, because while it is imperative that this Committee act, and I believe that we will act in this area, and the Senate is hard at work on this as well, that just like with the DMCA, we won't find all the solutions here. They are going to have to be found through the use of technology and through the use of better business models to protect intellectual property as well.

So I thank everybody for their contribution today. We will be hard at work at this. This is not our last hearing on this subject. We will be working on legislation.

I would like to thank our witnesses for their testimony today.

Without objection, all Members will have 5 legislative days to submit to the Chair additional written questions which we will forward to the witnesses and ask them to respond to as promptly as possible so that their answers may be made a part of the record.

Without objection, all Members will have 5 legislative days to submit additional materials for inclusion in the record.

With that, I again thank the witnesses and adjourn the hearing.

[Whereupon, at 6:15 p.m., the Subcommittee was adjourned.]

*Chapter 4*

# SUBMISSIONS FOR THE RECORD

CFIF
CENTER FOR INDIVIDUAL FREEDOM

917-B King Street
Alexandria, VA 22314
703-535-5836
Fax: 703-535-5838
www.cfif.org

March 11, 2011

Ms. Olivia Lee
House Judiciary Committee
Subcommittee on Intellectual Property,
Competition and the Internet

VIA ELECTRONIC MAIL

Dear Ms. Lee:

On behalf of the Center for Individual Freedom (CFIF) and its 250,000 supporters and activists across the nation, I write to address the growing menace of rogue websites, and Congress's urgent need to address that threat in order to defend American jobs and innovation.

CFIF was established over a decade ago to advance the fundamental principles that made America the most prosperous and benevolent nation in human history – property rights, the rule of law and free markets. Our Founding Fathers considered intellectual property such a critical manifestation of those principles that they specifically protected it in Article I, Section 8 of the Constitution by empowering Congress, "To promote the Progress of Science and useful Arts, by securing for limited Times to Authors and Inventors the exclusive Right to their respective Writings and Discoveries." Today, in our increasingly knowledge-based global economy, intellectual property is more important than ever and constitutes the primary wellspring for future American growth, jobs, exports and life improvements.

Unfortunately, those same principles are under constant attack from rogue websites that wrongfully profit from pirated and counterfeited American intellectual property. Such violations not only deprive our citizens of the rightful fruits of their labor and investments, but ultimately jeopardize American security, jobs, trillions of dollars of income and even lives.

Accordingly, we at CFIF respectfully encourage Congress to address the rogue website threat, and protect American intellectual property. This effort is particularly critical during this period of protracted economic difficulty, high unemployment and international competition. Thank you very much for your attention to this important matter.

Sincerely,

Timothy Lee
Vice President of Legal and Public Affairs

## Committee on the Judiciary, Subcommittee on Intellectual Property, Competition and the Internet, "Promoting Investment and Protecting Commerce Online: Legitimate Sites v. Parasites, Part I," Statement of Sandra Aistars, Executive Director. Copyright Alliance

The Copyright Alliance is a coalition of more than 40 organizations representing artists, creators, studios, sports leagues, guilds, and labor unions. We are committed to promoting the cultural and economic benefits of copyright, providing information and resources on the contributions of copyright, and upholding the contributions of copyright to the fiscal health of this nation and for the good of creators, owners and consumers around the world.

We applaud the Chairman, and Subcommittee members for holding this series of hearings on the important topic of promoting investment and protecting commerce online. Our organization unites individuals and industries including, photographers and filmmakers, authors and songwriters, videogame developers and musical recording artists, newspaper publishers and graphic artists, magazine publishers and TV producers, business software developers and music publishers, and broadcasters and sports leagues. Our membership spans individual artists and creators, as well as the organizations and corporations that support and invest in them. Besides the 40 organizations allied as our members, we have more than 7,000 individual "One Voi(c)e Artist Advocates" who give of their personal time and creativity to support our work.

All of these individuals and organizations have chosen to work together because the protection and strengthening of copyright is fundamental to our country's creativity, jobs and growth. Whether operating as a small business or individual entrepreneur, or working within a larger business or corporation, each creative individual who captures an image, writes a song, produces an album, films a documentary, writes a software program, publishes or contributes to a novel, magazine, newspaper or scholarly journal, orchestrates, plays in or broadcasts a live sporting event not only adds to the cultural and educational fabric of our country through his or her work, but typically generates employment of dozens, and in many cases hundreds, of additional individuals outside the creative sector.

For instance:

- A media photographer might hire numerous additional crew' members to complete an assignment, employ makeup artists, hairdressers, wardrobe stylists, location scouts, camera operators, helicopter pilots and helicopters, car hauling transporters, and model builders.

- A singer songwriter doesn't toil alone, but instead contributes to the economy through employing individuals all the way from additional songwriters, band members (including by paying them for practice sessions, performances and recording), crew' for set up and strike of shows; and additionally rents rehearsal space, studio space, often pays for venues in which to perform, purchases and maintains instruments and other equipment, and employs sound engineers, graphic artists, IT professionals, cleaners, and caterers.
  All of these inputs to the economy may be exponentially increased and geographically dispersed when artists travel for tours.
- To capture a news story networks, newspapers, and magazines often take writers, photojournalists, cameramen, and other crew into dangerous and remote locations. Only by making investments in the security, transportation, healthcare and logistic support needed to carry out this work are stories such as those surrounding the conflict in Afghanistan or the revolutions across the Middle East brought to our TVs, desktops, laptops, tablets and morning breakfast tables. See http://blog.copyrightalliance.org/2011/02/a-photographer-stands-up-and-a-community-stands-with-him/.
- And much behind the scenes work goes into producing a live event such as the Super Bowl or March Madness. The planning and execution requires thousands of man hours over more than year and includes behind the scenes work by directors, camera operators, graphics artists, audio engineers and the production personnel who put together all the interview segments, ensure games are delivered where and when consumers expect to see them. The investment in personnel likewise includes everyone from hourly per-diem runners to caterers to digital recording operators.

All creative sectors of the economy have long ago moved online, and are at the forefront of delivering news, entertainment, and information to consumers in creative, cutting edge formats. In fact, the success of the Internet and other new media is grounded largely in the availability of professionally created films, programs, and creative works. The Internet has also benefited from technologies developed by and for the creative industries.

- Filmmakers have always been on the front lines of developing new technologies to advance the art and science of filmmaking. Examples include groundbreaking work in 3D technologies, advances in performance capture and development of new camera technology specifically adapted to the needs of visionary directors. Magazine media and newspapers have been swept up in a tide of reinvention and experimentation. While the bond between the reader and print is as strong as ever, publishers are also experimenting with augmented reality (which makes the newspaper or magazine interactive with digital devices), 2D barcodes (enabling readers to buy products they see advertised with their smartphones), and other emerging technologies to make their work more interactive and to drive readers to digital experiences on the web and mobile devices. Publishers are daily creating tablet-friendly content that showcases the enduring qualities of professional journalism: curated stories, long-form journalism, a strong sense of community, and award-winning photography and design. Forward-thinking brands have additionally launched successful books, events, retail products, and so much more. See http://blog.copyrightalliance/org/2011/02/a-big-week-for-magazines/.

- Motion picture companies are daily releasing their works on virtually every and any digital device and format, including in apps and on Facebook, to ensure that consumers around the world can receive their content legally, and with additional features and functionality, even in cases where the content may not be available in their jurisdiction via popular services such as iTunes. See http://blog.copyrightalliance.org/2011/03/stuck-on-rewind/; and http://blog.copyrightalliance.org/2011/03/in-syn%c2%a9-movies-on-the-social-network/
- The recording industry likewise delivers legal content via innovative services, partnering with technology companies. For instance, Sony has recently launched a new subscription-based music service, Music Unlimited powered by Qriocity. The service will give subscribers access to more than 6 million songs through the cloud-based network used by more than 60 million PlayStation gamers. Music Unlimited subscribers can stream millions of songs infinitely on Internet-connected devices like personal computers, as well as Sony's PlayStation 3 game console, Blu-ray Disc player and Bravia televisions. Fans can also import their personal music collections and iTunes libraries into their Qriocity accounts to access all of their music in one place and receive personalized music recommendations.
- And some companies, like Atlantic Records are offering websites so music fans can get an insider's view of what goes on at a record company. Atlantic's site features memorabilia including Ray Charles' first contract and a vintage ad for an Aretha Franklin album, and exclusive videos of artists recording at Atlantic's Studio 1290. Atlantic's acts include Led Zeppelin to John Coltrane, Flo Rida to Death Cab for Cutie and the site is fully customizable via social networking sites to enhance each visitor's experience.

Yet despite the Herculean efforts taken by individual entrepreneurs and corporate stake holders to bring high quality, professional work to audiences on line, legally, and in virtually any format or mode of distribution desired by consumers, individual livelihoods and corporate investments alike are jeopardized by relentless battles with rogue site operators who steal the content, and redistribute it, often profiting handsomely from the work of artists and creators by monetizing it through payment systems, and subsidizing it by advertising.

Numerous studies have been released recently demonstrating the devastating impact of parasitic sites on legitimate commerce.

- According to the Organization for Economic Cooperation and Development, international trade and counterfeit and pirated physical goods was as high as $250 billion in 2007; but if the significant volume of online distribution of pirated goods via the Internet were included, the total could be "several hundred billion dollars more."
- Also recently released is research by Envisional, estimating that nearly 25 percent of internet traffic consists of pirated copyrighted works. According to the study: 23.8 percent of global internet traffic is infringing; more than 17 percent of internet traffic in the U.S. is infringing; bitTorrents account for around half of the global and U.S. infringing traffic; and cyberlockers and infringing video streaming sites also contribute significantly. It is notable that this study confirms earlier research by Princeton Professor Edward Felten, who is often critical of the creative industries, and his student Sauhard Sahi that approximately 99 percent of content shared on a bitTorrent system they surveyed last year was infringing.
- Finally, building on the OECD's research, Frontier Economics issued a report predicting that by 2015, the annual global economic impact of piracy and counterfeiting will reach $1.7 trillion and put 2.5 million jobs at risk each year. According to Frontier's research the total global economic and social impact of counterfeiting and piracy is $775 billion every year.

See http://blog.copyrightalliance.org/2011/02/new-study-provides-further-details-on-the-impact-of-piracy/

At a time when communities and individuals across the country are struggling to recover from a lengthy recession, when not only individual but local, state and Federal budgets are stressed beyond measure, these data points demonstrate that the case for combating piracy, and improving IP protection and enforcement could not be clearer.

We applaud the Subcommittee for its focus on this issue, urge the parties participating in the hearings to work to address these issues, and stand ready to assist in the Subcommittee's consideration of this important topic.

# STATEMENT OF A. ROBERT PISANO PRESIDENT AND CHIEF OPERATING OFFICER MOTION PICTURE ASSOCIATION OF AMERICA, INC. BEFORE THE HOUSE JUDICIARY COMMITTEE'S INTELLECTUAL PROPERTY, COMPETITION, AND THE INTERNET SUBCOMMITTEE HEARING: "PROMOTING INVESTMENT AND PROTECTING COMMERCE ONLINE: LEGITIMATE SITES V. PARASITES, PART 1" RAYBURN HOUSE OFFICE BUILDING, ROOM 2141 WASHINGTON, D.C. MARCH 14, 2011, 4 P.M.

## A. Background and Introduction

We want to thank the Committee for the opportunity to submit this Statement on behalf of the Motion Picture Association of America, Inc.[89] and its member companies regarding the serious and growing threat of Internet sites that profit from the theft and unauthorized dissemination of creative content. As the primary voice and advocate for the American motion picture, home video and television industries in the U.S. and around the world, we have witnessed the proliferation of web-based enterprises dedicated solely to stealing the product of our industry's workforce and are gravely concerned about the detrimental impact that digital theft has on the millions of American men and women who work in our industry.

The U.S. motion picture and television industry plays a unique role in today's American economic infrastructure, providing high-paying jobs to workers in all 50 states; fueling small business growth; injecting capital into local, state, and national revenue pool and consistently generating a positive balance of trade. Of the 2.4 million American workers who depend on the entertainment industry for their jobs, about 12% are directly employed in motion picture and television production and distribution - from behind-the-scenes production technicians to make-up artists and set-builders - across all 50 states. These are high-paying jobs, paying an average salary of nearly $76,000, 72 percent higher than the average salary nationwide. More than 95,000 small businesses—93 percent of whom employ fewer than 10 people—are involved in the production and distribution of movies and television. On-location filmed productions infuse, on average, $223,000 per day into a local economy. Nationwide, our industry generates more than

[89] The Motion Picture Association of America and its international counterpart, the Motion Picture Association (MPA) serve as the voice and advocate of the American motion picture, home video and television industries, domestically through the MPAA and internationally through the MPA. MPAA members are Paramount Pictures Corporation. Sony Pictures Entertainment Inc., Twentieth Century Fox Film Corporation, Universal City Studios LLC. Walt Disney Studios Motion Pictures, and Warner Bros Entertainment Inc.

$15 billion in public revenue. As one of the few industries that return a positive balance of trade, our industry is critical to the U.S. export economy.

## B. Websites Peddling Stolen Digital Content Create Consumer Confusion, Harm the Online Marketplace and Damage the Motion Picture and Television Industry

High-speed broadband networks present tremendous opportunities for exchanging information and ideas; unfortunately, the laws and regulations put in place to protect consumers and innovation in the physical marketplace have not kept pace with the growth of illegal conduct online. The illicit use of online networks can facilitate the anonymous theft and rapid, ubiquitous illegal distribution of copyrighted works. The key foundation of American industry - the expectation that hard work and innovation is rewarded - is imperiled when thieves, whether online or on the street, are allowed to steal America's creative products and enrich themselves along the way.

Rampant theft of American intellectual property puts the livelihoods of the workers who invest time, energy and fortune to create the filmed entertainment enjoyed by millions at risk; to these men and women and their families, digital theft means declining incomes, lost jobs and reduced health and retirement benefits.

Currently, the most pernicious forms of digital theft occur through the use of so-called "rogue" websites. The sites, whose content is hosted and whose operators are located throughout the world take many forms, but have in common the simple fact that all materially contribute to, facilitate and/or induce the distribution of copyrighted works, such as movies and television programming.

These websites present a two-pronged threat: They simultaneously weaken the film and TV industry by undercutting, eliminating or reducing the market for, and thus the financial support for film and television production, which millions rely on for jobs, bringing down the U.S. economy as a whole, and jeopardize the entire online marketplace. Exposing consumers to criminals who routinely pilfer personal and financial information from unsuspecting targets puts consumers at risk, and if not dealt with, will ultimately dissuade consumers from conducting legitimate business online. Furthermore, legitimate companies that want to usher in new business models and provide high-quality content and more consumer choice online have a limited potential for growth when they are forced to compete with free content distributed through illicit means.

Rogue websites typically engage in one or more of the following forms of online theft of copyrighted content:

- Streaming an unauthorized copy of a copyrighted video;
- Downloading an unauthorized copy of a copyrighted video;
- Streaming or downloading of an unauthorized copy of a copyrighted video by linking to a torrent or other metadata file that initiates piracy;
- Linking to a specific offer to sell an unauthorized copy of a copyrighted video;
- Hosting an unauthorized copy of a copyrighted video.

These rogue websites are increasingly sophisticated in appearance and take on many attributes of legitimate content delivery sites, creating additional enforcement challenges and feeding consumer confusion. Among the steps taken by rogue websites to deceive consumers into believing they are legitimate are:

- The use of credit card companies, such as Visa and MasterCard, to facilitate payments to rogue websites.
- The use of "e-wallet" or alternative payment methods such as PayPal, Moneybrokers, AlertPay and Gate2Shop to allow for the receipt of payment from the public for subscriptions, donations, purchases and memberships.
- The use of advertising, often for mainstream, Blue Chip companies, on the websites.
- Reward programs for frequent purchasers.

The impact of this nefarious activity is documented in a recently published report by Envisional, an independent Internet consulting company. Envisional's "Technical Report; An Estimate of Infringing Use of the Internet" estimates that almost a quarter (23.8 percent) of global Internet traffic and over 17 percent of U.S. Internet traffic is copyright infringing. This staggering level of theft cannot be sustained without significant damage to the motion picture industry and the workforce it supports.

Our studios are not alone in grappling with this threat. According to Deluxe Entertainment Services Group, the leading provider of post-production creative services for the film industry, hackers from around the world attempt to penetrate Deluxe's network 20 million times a month on average - seeking financial gain by stealing movies and television content while it is in their possession. Four million -a quarter of the hacker hits - come from Chinese IP addresses. These criminal networks are undermining U.S. competition abroad and harming American workers.

Unfortunately, American companies - knowingly or not - often provide the financial fuel that enriches the criminals profiting from these rogue sites. Online advertisement brokers such as Google's AdSense advertise their clients on these sites, paying the website operators for the right to do so. Online pay processors and credit card companies similarly operate on these websites, turning a blind eye to the willful infringement of copyrights that they are facilitating. Internet service providers (ISPs) allow these websites to operate on their networks. Search engines present a menu of illicit materials with a few strokes of the keyboard, while demonstrating over the past few months that they are, in fact, able and willing to change their search algorithms as they see fit. These American businesses are contributing to the problem.

## C. Legislative Action and Administration Enforcement Is Effective and Necessary to Address the Assault of Online Theft

We are encouraged by the strong commitment this Committee and this Administration have shown to protecting intellectual property and the American workers who create it. The positive effects of government's willingness to intervene have been palpable: Since U.S. Intellectual Property Enforcement Coordinator (IPEC) Victoria Espinel was confirmed by the Senate, we have seen increasing cooperation from our partners in the private sector intermediaries— whether pay processors, ad brokers, or ISPs. The combined efforts of the Department of Justice, Immigrations and Customs Enforcement (ICE) and the Intellectual Property Rights (IPR) Center have not only put numerous rogue sites out of business but have raised awareness with the public, deterred bad actors, and resulted in many websites voluntarily ceasing criminal activity or becoming legal platforms for online content.

ICE's "Operation in Our Sites, v.1.0" demonstrates the positive effects of the Administration's involvement. Of the top 304 infringing websites that were monitored during the 2010 calendar year, including both sites that compile links to stolen content and sites that allow unauthorized streaming, nine were seized during both phases of "Operation in Our Sites." An additional 81 websites, over one quarter of the landscape (26%) voluntarily stopped offering illegal content or completely shut down, and of the 81 sites, 12 transitioned to legal movies or TV, or became promotional websites that do not offer illegal content. This is a significant development and demonstrates the effectiveness and positive impact of government intervention to curb illicit behavior.

Recently, the Office of the IPEC released its first annual report to Congress pursuant to the PRO-IP Act and the report reiterated not only the detrimental impact of copyright infringement on the economy but also the need to work with the Congress to update intellectual property laws to improve law enforcement effectiveness. To quote:

> "The digital environment is at its core an economy of intellectual property. Digitalization of goods, services, data, ideas and conversations creates intrinsically new assets, often built on or derived from assets for which there are existing protections. The application of intellectual property rules to the digital environment are therefore essential to enabling creators to be rewarded for their work. Lack of intellectual property

enforcement in the digital environment, by contrast, threatens to destabilize rule-of-law norms, with severe effects on jobs and economic growth. Undermining respect for rule-of law values impacts a range of other policy goals affected by the Internet (e.g., privacy). In short, criminal laws and intellectual property laws that apply in the physical world are based on a tradition of rules, checks and balances that must be applied to and tailored to the digital world. "

We believe that rogue sites legislation, combined with the Administration's work with intermediaries and enforcement by the IPR Center, will go a long way towards shutting down the unauthorized distribution of copyrighted works and close a gap in the intellectual property law.

Again, we thank the Committee on behalf of our member companies for the opportunity to provide this Statement to underscore the severity of the pernicious threat posed by digital theft to our workers, whose jobs, pensions and benefits are most vulnerable to its impact. We look forward to working with you, Chairman Goodlatte, Ranking Member Watt, and other members of the Subcommittee on crafting legislation to deal with this criminal activity.

National Association of Theatre Owners
750 First St. NE Suite 1130; Washington, DC 20002 (202) 962-0054
March 14, 2011
The Honorable Bob Goodlatte Chairman
House Judiciary Subcommittee on Intellectual Property,
Competition and the Internet B-352 Rayburn House Office Building
Washington, DC 20515

**Re: "Promoting Investment and Protecting Commerce Online: Legitimate Sites v. Parasites, Part I"**

Dear Chairman Goodlatte;

The National Association of Theatre Owners (NATO) respectfully submits this letter in support of meaningful legislation that will provide law enforcement with tools to combat the growth of counterfeiting and digital theft by illicit websites. We ask that it be included in the hearing record.

NATO is the world's leading trade association for motion picture theaters, representing more than 30,000 movie screens in all 50 states, and additional cinemas in 50 countries worldwide. Our membership includes the largest cinema chains in the world and hundreds of main street theater owners.

Going to the cinema is one of the most popular forms of entertainment throughout the country. Without swift legislative action on Capitol Hill, however, rampant online intellectual property (IP) theft threatens to undermine the motion picture business—and virtually all sectors of industry. Each year, rogue websites that profit off IP stolen from our country's innovative and creative industries undermine the U.S. economy, endanger millions of American jobs, and pose significant health and financial safety risks to consumers.

Movie theater operators are acutely aware of the increasingly harmful effects that rogue websites have on our economy. The illegal online distribution of movies delivered through the Internet across unlimited geographic markets is a devastating problem that costs the exhibition industry hundreds of millions of dollars every year in lost ticket sales domestically and billions of dollars globally. Furthermore, the rampant growth of movie theft threatens to impact the incentive of movie studios to invest in new film productions, thereby threatening the quality and number of films available for movie theaters to show, with the ancillary effect that would have on jobs in the industry.

In every slate, movie theater operators are important partners in small and large communities— urban and rural. Faced with decreased revenues caused by the negative effects film theft has on box office and concessions sales, the movie theater industry —a vital sector of the nation's economy—may be forced to lay off workers and eliminate employee benefits. Furthermore, a devastating ripple effect in local economies is spurred by a decline in retail and restaurant traffic when neighboring movie theaters are forced to shutter or lose patronage as a result of movie theft. Movie theaters are not the only businesses harmed by the infringing activities of rogue websites that also profit from a range of counterfeit products, including electronics, luxury items, sports merchandise and pharmaceuticals.

If rogue websites masquerading as legitimate retailers sold their illegal goods in brick-and-mortar buildings, there is no question that they would be subject to criminal penalties and civil lawsuits. Since these sites can remain anonymous and operate across multiple national boundaries, however, federal officials are hamstrung in their enforcement efforts. That is why it is important to enact legislation like the Combating Online infringement and Counterfeits Act (COICA), which would enable law enforcement authorities to disrupt websites that profit off the innovation and creativity of American companies and workers. To protect the rights of Internet users, this bipartisan measure includes strict protections that ensure only the most egregious websites dedicated to the sale or distribution of infringing goods are targeted.

We encourage lawmakers to work with their colleagues on both sides of the aisle to enact balanced IP enforcement legislation that combats rogue websites that threaten American ingenuity and undermine the nation's economic growth.

Sincerely, John Fithian
President & CEO
National Association of Theatre Owners

## Letter for Entry into Official Record House Judiciary Subcommittee on Intellectual Property, Competition, and the Internet

On behalf of Arts + Labs, an alliance of the technology, content and creative communities, we wish to commend the subcommittee's efforts to address the growing challenge of protecting intellectual property in the digital age. The ability to protect one's intellectual property and enjoy a fair opportunity to earn an economic reward for one's creativity has long been key to the innovation that drives the U.S. economy. Conversely, threats to intellectual property rights, especially in the form of digital theft, drains valuable resources, billions of dollars in revenue and precious jobs from our economy.

Among those most at risk are independent artists, filmmakers, writers, musicians, who simply lack the resources to track down pirates and seek corrective action under the procedures mapped out by current law. The theft of creative works by digital means also jeopardizes tens of thousands of production crews and other specialists who work behind the scenes to bring creative arts to the public. When a film is pirated or a song is illegally copied, the economic loss lands squarely on these individuals in the form of lost royalties, lost wages and lost jobs. Add up these individual costs, and the cumulative effect deprives the economy of billions of dollars every year. At a time when this country is trying to revive the economy, restore our employment picture and increase our competitiveness, we cannot afford to ignore the growing wave of online piracy.

Arts+Labs recognizes the difficulty Congress faces in identifying the best way to enhance enforcement of copyright and other IP laws, and we are well aware that finalizing the details of any enforcement regime will require a careful balance among the rights of individual consumers, the interests of individual creators, and the responsibilities assigned to private enterprises. But every member of Arts+Labs strongly supports your efforts to find an effective and balanced path to stronger enforcement.

We look forward to working with the subcommittee and individual members in this vital effort.

Sincerely,

Michael McCurry
Mark McKinnon

Chairman, Arts+Labs

# MiMTiD

## The World's Leading Content Protection Company, Promoting Investment and Protecting Commerce Online: Legitimate Sites v. Parasites, Part I

Search Engine inclusion into this new legislation and search engine immediate cooperation[90] with existing law can be the most efficient tool to combat "Parasites."

Most search engines do not cooperate with existing Law.

MiMTiD is the world's largest issuer of DMCA take down notices to Search Engines and we have the data.

### Problem

- Content is being illegally streamed, downloaded and systematically monetized, creating lost sales, job loss and future uncertainty.

### Assertion

- Search Engines are systematically promoting and monetizing stolen Intellectual Property.
  - Providing potential customers with immediate access - globally.
  - Enabling revenue generation through ad networks.
  - Exploiting DMCA construct to avoid removing infringing links.
  - Increasing global governmental spheres of influence.
  - Enabling billions of dollars to flow into these businesses.

### Solution (What We Do Now.)

- Notice Search Engines
  - Notice all search engine infringing links.
  - Notice all ad networks monetizing infringing content.

---

[90] We use the term "cooperate" because the DMCA term "expeditiously" to a Search Engine means whenever a Search Engine gets around to responding to takedown notices for repeat infringing sites, which can be 45 days or more, if they respond at all. As the largest issuer of these notices to repeat infringing websites dedicated to copyright infringement, we have the data.

- Provide law enforcement and lawmakers with access to repeat infringing data.

## Our Concerns

- Search Engine Compliance with existing law would reduce the Bill's burden on ISPs and others negatively affected.
  - The Google assertion that the Bill should only affect foreign domiciled websites is injudicious. Google; "The Bill should not rewrite or undermine *existing law that works*."
  - MiMTiD sends thousands of DMCA notices to Google targeting primarily U.S. and many foreign domiciled repeat infringing sites. Many of these notices are not actioned for more than forty five days and many notices are completely ignored.
- Immediate compliance with the Law, removing the infringing links from search when noticed and permanently removing repeat infringers, would eliminate the earnings power of these websites dedicated to repeat infringement.
- Immediate compliance with the Law would eliminate venture capital flows into business models that exploit the loophole in the current Law (DMCA). Approximately $23[91] billion in 2010.

Make no mistake, it's all about advertising dollars. They themselves are the principal Advertising Network or are participating with the Advertising Networks monetizing the infringed content appearing on these repeat infringing sites that are being repeatedly noticed.

- Google, et al. must comply with the Law.

  Most agree that the first line of defense against rogue web sites is to have the sites completely removed from search results. While Congress struggles to strike a balance between creating legislation that will be effective whilst preserving existing protections to the vast economy of the internet, the Digital Millennium Copyright Act (DMCA) is being tactically abused by Google and others whose observance of the law would lead to the most effective deterrent to the very issues that new legislation seeks to rectify.
- The new legislation (COICA) must address this critical issue to prevent the complete destruction of U.S. intellectual property rights and related jobs loss.

---

91 'Source: CB Insights and MiMTiD Corp.

The new law needs to compel Search Engines to remove links to websites dedicated to copyright infringement immediately, upon receipt of notice. Google, "takes numerous steps above and beyond our legal obligations." Based on the data contained in the MiMTiD Chilling Report, this is a purely fantastical statement.

## Why Is This Happening?

- How do you find infringing sites where content is being stolen?
- How do most potential consumers locate infringed content - globally?
- Where does traffic to websites dedicated to infringement come from?
- How do websites dedicated to infringement monetize content?
- Why are the websites dedicated to infringement in the top Alexa rankings?
- Who benefits the most from infringement activity?
- Who has the most to gain by finding infringing links?
- Who has the most to lose by removing infringing links?
- Who continues to index the most notorious infringing sites in the world?
- Who continues to monetize content on the most notorious infringing sites in the world? Who continues to index replacement sites that have been seized?
- Who continues to monetize content on replacement sites that have been seized?
- Who regularly exploits Interpretation of chapter 5 of the DMCA?
    - Search Engines
- Why are billions of dollars flowing into businesses that will continue to exploit this opportunity?
    - Because It is a billion dollar opportunity with very little risk and enormous upside.

"The fact is, it's a revenue issue versus protecting intellectual property in this country," Senator Tom Coburn, an Oklahoma Republican.

"I contend that America is on the losing end of the largest transfer of wealth through theft and piracy in the history of mankind," Senator Sheldon Whitehouse, a Rhode Island Democrat. "We're doing virtually nothing about it."

## What Tools Do We Have to Help You Assess and Address the Problems?

- MiMTiD, on behalf of our customers, sends Search Engines, most notably Google hundreds of thousands of notices targeting repeat infringing sites.

- Search Engine Compliance rates are precisely tracked along with the Advertising Networks to demonstrate clear financial benefit Search Engines gain from websites dedicated to copyright Infringement.
- Advertisers can be messaged through the IAB or directly with data.
- Law enforcement can be given tools that enable accuracy and sustainability.
- The vagueness of historical messaging to Lawmakers is being replaced with real-time data representing criminal, monetary benefits to enable meaningful additions to COICA (The Chilling Report - chillingreport.com).
- We do not charge for access to this information.

## MIMTID THE WORLD'S LEADING CONTENT PROTECTION COMPANY

In closing, "existing law that works," as indicated by Google's letter to the Senate Judiciary Committee, certainly works for Google in that the DMCA term/phrase "remove expeditiously" has no legal definition and/or cannot be precisely defined therefore limiting if not eliminating legal recourse that as a result is only symbolically afforded to the private sector under the DMCA.

For a New Law to be effective, it must compel Search Engines to; remove search links to Websites Dedicated to Copyright Infringement and terminate direct and indirect advertising relationships with Websites Dedicated to Copyright Infringement immediately, upon receipt of notice or court orders.

- We hope we have inspired some new thinking today.
- We appreciate you allowing us to present here today.
- We look forward to working with you and providing you ongoing information, (Precise Data) about this critical issue.

## THE WORLD'S FIRST COMPREHENSIVE DATABASE OF WEBSITES DEDICATED TO COPYRIGHT INFRINGEMENT

### The Chilling Report

Complete forensic record of all activity.

- Tracks Search Engine Monetary Flows from Repeat Infringing sites.

- Tracks Search Engine and Other Ad Networks
- Tracks Repeat Infringing Sites
- Tracks DMCA Compliance

www.chillingreport.com

## Before the U.S. House of Representatives Committee on Judiciary Subcommittee on Intellectual Property', Competition and the Internet, Regarding "Promoting Investment and Protecting Commerce Online: Legitimate Sites v. Parasites, Part I," March 14, 2011 Statement of the Consumer Electronics Association

On behalf of the Consumer Electronics Association (CEA), I would like to raise several key policy questions and concerns for your consideration as the Subcommittee begins to address the issue of online commerce and IP infringement in the 112$^{th}$ Congress. We appreciate and thank the Committee for their thoughtful deliberation on this important topic.

CEA is the preeminent trade association promoting growth in the consumer electronics industry. CEA members include product and component manufacturers, internet providers and both small and large retailers. Our industry^ accounts for more than S165 billion in annual domestic sales and directly employs approximately 1.9 million United States workers. We support strong intellectual property enforcement. Indeed, our members' businesses rely on robust and balanced intellectual property^ law that protects the rights of authors and inventors while preserving and encouraging innovation, free expression and competition.

When considering any legislation relating to online commerce and IP infringement it is critically important for the scope of the language to be specific and finely tailored to the targeted issue. If it is not, legitimate commerce may unintentionally be limited and restricted.

For example, the scope of S.3804 - Combating Online Infringement and Counterfeits Act ("COICA") - as introduced only in the U.S. Senate in the 111$^{th}$ Congress, was significantly broader than its intended purpose of shuttering "rogue" websites engaging solely in the exchange of infringing content or goods. Instead, the legislation as written could have inadvertently subjected lawful domestic retailers, consumer electronics manufacturers, communications storage and data-sharing companies, to unwarranted burdens, expense, litigation, and loss of property. If this Committee were to contemplate similar legislation on this topic, then it is the hope of CEA that the definitions and scope be limited only to sites primarily dedicated to infringing activities and that are used only as a means for copyright infringement under 17 U.S.C. Section 506 or trademark infringement under 18 U.S.C. Section 2320.

Further, Congress must be careful not to borrow' broad definitions relating to civil causes of action in other statutes and inject them into a different and inappropriate context. For example, definitions used in S.3804 would have put at risk any site that could be broadly characterized as "enabling and facilitating" any violation of Section 17 of the United States Code (COICA § 2(a)(l)(B)(i)(I-II)).

This exceedingly broad definition, combined with a lack of civil due process, would have severely undercut the Supreme Court's landmark *Betamax* decision. That decision, commonly referred to as the "Magna Carta of the Innovation Industry," protects technology products with substantial non-infringing uses. The *Betamax* holding is crucial to our members' ability to sell new and innovative products without fear of crippling lawsuits.

Under such a broad definition, if the Internet had existed when suit was filed against the Betamax VCR in 1976, and adjudicated in 1979 (lawful), 1981 (unlawful), and 1984 (lawful), the websites of retailers selling VCRs on-line could have been subject to seizure from 1976 through 1979, and again from October, 1981 until January, 1984, when the Supreme Court finally ruled that offering a VCR for sale was not copyright infringement.

Today, if COICA had passed as introduced, a consumer electronics retailer's web site today could have been subject to seizure by the Department of Justice because printers and computers for sale on it (which are central to the site's activities) could be used to "enable" "violation[s]" of title 17. While the targeting of legitimate commerce was undoubtedly not intended by the bill's drafters, S.3804 authorized such overreaching and harmful actions. Any legislation considered in the 112$^{th}$ Congress should by all means possible protect concepts upheld in the *Betamax* decision.

In addition, while CEA strongly believes that intellectual property rights should be enforced, we take issue with legislative language that grants vigilante powers to the private sector. As originally drafted, 8.3804 provided complete immunity- for domain name registrars and registries, financial transaction providers, and advertising services, allowing them to take voluntary action against an Internet site if the entity "reasonably believes the Internet site is dedicated to infringing activities." As written, under this "vigilante provision" a site could be removed from the Internet or otherwise disabled by private actors without any Department of Justice or court determination that the targeted site met any standard of infringement.

Consider this example: a U.S. District Court recently awarded summary judgment to YouTube in a lawsuit brought by Viacom in which damages potentially amounting to $1 billion were claimed. Again, had COICA passed without change, Viacom arguably would have been empowered to approach a domain name registrar with evidence that YouTube was "dedicated to infringing activities" without filing suit and the registrar, now hyper-sensitive to such accusations, could have removed YouTubc.com from the Internet. Under this regime, the registrar would have had full immunity and YouTube no legal recourse. Any legislation considered in the 112$^{th}$ Congress should uphold due process, and monetary- remedies should be allowed if a site was targeted by' mistake or for competitive reasons.

Lastly, new legislation should tread carefully to avoid the establishment of a new-secondary-liability concept for Internet companies. S.3804 relied upon the undefined terms "enable or facilitate," which could have rendered these companies liable for inadvertently "enabling" or "facilitating" the conduct of third parties. This runs contrary to 13 years of w ell-settled federal policy under the Digital Millennium Copyright Act. Such claims could ensnare legitimate U.S. social media platforms, video sharing sites, auction sites, third-party retail sites, grey-market sales sites, and countless sites that are overwhelmingly lawful and integral to the U.S. economy.

As the Committee is doubtlessly aware, domain name seizures are a blunt and powerful instrument ripe tor misuse in the absence of adequate protections. Late last year, the Department of Homeland Security (DHS) seized the domains of alleged "pirate" music sites that included a number of legitimate music blogs promoting music with the express permission of the copy right owners. Last month, while targeting a small number of child pornographers, DHS mistakenly took down 84,000 legitimate sites, many of which were used by small businesses. Such unwarranted government confiscation of private property- can be best avoided with narrow definitions and the assurance of due process and adversarial court proceedings before websites are seized.

As an industry' that relies on intellectual property protection, we suffer the damaging effects of counterfeit products in international trade. We are committed to working closely with copy right owners to shut down web sites that are truly dedicated to infringement, and we are confident that legislation introduced and considered by this Committee in the 112$^{th}$ Congress can do so without inadvertently punishing legitimate U.S. retailers, internet companies, and manufacturers.

Respectfully submitted.
Michael Petricone
Senior Vice President, Government Affairs

March 10. 2011
Representative Bob Goodlatte
Chairman, Committee on the Judiciary, Subcommittee on Intellectual Property, Competition, and the Internet
U S. House of Representatives
Washington, D.C.

Representative Howard Coble
Ranking Member, Committee on the Judiciary, Subcommittee on Intellectual Property, Competition, and the Internet
U S. House of Representatives
Washington. D.C.

Dear Chairman Goodlatte, Ranking Member Coble and Members of the Committee,

I am writing on behalf of Canada Goose, an internationally recognized Canadian apparel company based in Toronto and deeply concerned about the problem of counterfeiting. We have joined forces with the Outdoor Industry Association and its members to address this significant problem, as it impacts our brand in the United States and around the world. This statement is submitted in anticipation of the hearing this coming Monday being hosted by the House Judiciary Committee Subcommittee on Intellectual Property, Competition and the Internet on the problem of rogue websites

Canada Goose manufactures a wide range of jackets, vests, hats, gloves and other cold weather apparel, designed and manufactured to protect Canada Goose customers against the most extreme cold weather conditions All Canada Goose jackets are manufactured in Canada The company has built its reputation on core values of product quality, authenticity and technical innovation.

We have been aggressively fighting this battle on a global basis and have taken the following steps:

- Listing sites on the Canada Goose homepage that have been identified as counterfeiting sites
- Hired a professional resource to police online counterfeiting
- Utilizing a hologram label to authenticate our product (very expensive and difficult to replicate)

In addition, I have spoken at numerous conferences on this topic. We are also working hard with law enforcement agencies around the world, federal policymakers in the United States and Canada and global brands to address this important issue. We believe that consumer education is essential and a critical part of the solution. We are grateful to see the U.S. Congress taking action, as counterfeiting is a global issue that hurts consumers and businesses, large and small.

We look forward to continuing these important discussions in this respected forum.

Sincerely,
Kevin Spreekmeester
Vice President of Global Marketing
Canada Goose

# PART II: OPENING STATEMENTS

## PROMOTING INVESTMENT AND PROTECTING COMMERCE ONLINE: LEGITIMATE SITES V. PARASITES (PART II)

WEDNESDAY, APRIL 6, 2011
House of Representatives,
Subcommittee on Intellectual Property,
Competition, and the Internet,
Committee on the Judiciary,
Washington, DC.

The Subcommittee met, pursuant to call, at 10:49 a.m., in room 2141, Rayburn Office Building, the Honorable Bob Goodlatte (Chairman of the Subcommittee) presiding.

Present: Representatives Goodlatte, Smith, Quayle, Coble, Chabot, Issa, Jordan, Poe, Marino, Adams, Watt, Conyers, Berman, Chu, Deutch, Sanchez, Wasserman Schultz, Lofgren, Jackson Lee, and Waters.

Staff present: (Majority) David Whitney, Counsel; Olivia Lee, Clerk; and (Minority) Stephanie Moore, Subcommittee Chief Counsel.

Mr. Goodlatte. Good morning. The Subcommittee on Intellectual Property, Competition, and the Internet will come to order.

And I will recognize myself for an opening statement.

Today's hearing is the second of two oversight hearings the Subcommittee will conduct to examine issues that surround digital theft and online counterfeiting.

At our first hearing on March 14, we received testimony from the Acting Register of Copyrights, a representative from the Center for Democracy and Technology, a representative from the Information Technology and Innovation Foundation, and the Chief Operating Officer of Paramount Pictures. While there was disagreement as to solutions, each witness affirmed the importance of protecting intellectual property online.

They also acknowledged the need to ensure that whatever legislation Congress considers is appropriately balanced and takes into account the views of a variety of stakeholders.

In discussing the first hearing, I want to take a moment to clarify a point that arose and that we may revisit today. The seizure process for IP crimes committed within the jurisdiction of the United States is current law. It was enacted as part of the PRO-IP Act that this Committee originated and passed on a bipartisan basis several years ago. That process utilized by the Government is the remedy for infringing sites over which the U.S. can bring a seizure action. This includes, for instance, domestic and foreign sites that are registered on the dot com and dot net top level domains.

The purpose of these hearings is in a broad sense to examine current and anticipated threats to IP online. As part of that inquiry, we are looking into the adequacy of existing laws that were enacted to protect investment and promote creativity online. Foreign-based and foreign-registered infringing sites are not reachable by U.S. authorities. Yet, the Internet enables criminals anywhere in the world to defraud and jeopardize U.S. consumers while generating revenue from U.S.-based businesses.

Any legislation that grants new authority to protect Americans and deny access to our market to wholly foreign parasites will not be based on our seizure laws and processes. That is because there is no property such as a server or a domain name in the U.S. to be seized.

However, it has become increasingly clear that new tools are, indeed, necessary to meet the growing levels of theft online. Online theft significantly impacts the music, movie, software, digital book, and other industries that are increasingly moving to digital delivery of goods and services.

However, it is not limited to these industries. Indeed, it also impacts traditional manufacturers. I hold in my hands a real and a knock-off Vibram shoe. I challenge anyone to tell me which one is real. They both have the toes that you all are familiar with. And these fake goods, along with even more dangerous goods, like fake medicine, car parts, and others, are being sold illegally online and shipped directly to consumers in the U.S.

These foreign sites go to great lengths to make their illegitimate goods appear legitimate, including promoting the logos of financial services companies, hosting advertising on their sites from legitimate companies, and even charging close to the same prices for fake goods that the lawful owner charges. We must aggressively combat this theft.

Today we will receive testimony from an outstanding panel of witnesses. First, ICE Director John Morton is here to describe the critical role his agency plays in combating IP theft in the physical world and on the Internet. Director Morton will discuss the important role of the IPR Center which brings together 17 key domestic and foreign investigative agencies to leverage resources, skills, and authorities in order to provide a comprehensive response to IP theft.

He will also describe the Operation in Our Sites initiative, a law enforcement operation that uses the authority contained in PRO-IP to target websites used to sell counterfeit goods or distribute pirated merchandise and copyrighted digital materials. Since June 2010, this high visibility and labor-intensive operation has executed judicially authorized search warrants and resulted in the seizure of 119 domain names as part of ongoing criminal investigations. According to the Motion Picture Association of America, the seizure of nine sites that trafficked in infringing movies and TV programs in the first operation had a huge deterrent effect and resulted in the voluntary suspension of 81 of the 300 most active pirate websites.

Our second witness, Floyd Abrams, is one of our Nation's leading authorities on the First Amendment. Appearing on his behalf, Mr. Abrams refutes the suggestion that the Internet, while free, should also be lawless.

Our third witness is Kent Walker, the Senior Vice President and General Counsel of Google. Best known for its interactive search function, Google is the dominant player in web-based advertising and applications and it is increasing its market share in Internet-enabled mobile devices. Mr. Walker states Google leads the industry in helping to combat copyright infringement and the sale of counterfeit goods online. To their credit, Google has taken positive steps such as developing the content ID technology it uses on its YouTube platform. Google has also announced the intention of taking additional steps to improve copyright enforcement online.

That said, the question is isn't so much what Google has done as much as it is what Google ought to do. Many rightsholders have serious questions about Google's willingness to cooperate in a meaningful way. Among their concerns, they note the revenue that flows from Google's ad networks to unlicensed sites that are clearly infringing, the prominent posting of infringing files on Google's blogspot which is hosted on Google-owned servers, and the time it takes for Google to comply or even respond to DMCA notice and takedown requests.

Time will not permit a complete discussion of all of these concerns with Mr. Walker today, but I will appreciate his public and personal commitment to myself and the other Members of this Subcommittee to work closely with us to respond fully and promptly to any further questions we have that we might forward after today's hearing.

Our final witness is Christine Jones who serves as the Executive Vice President and General Counsel of the Go Daddy Group. As the world's largest registrar of domain names and a hosting provider. Go Daddy maintains a large, 24/7 abuse department whose mission it is to preserve the integrity and safety of Go Daddy's network by investigating and shutting down websites and domain names engaged in illegal activities. Go Daddy's policy is to immediately investigate complaints that a customer is engaged in unlawful online activity and to permanently suspend services to any domain name, website, or registrant they conclude is engaged in illegal activity. Go Daddy voluntarily and permanently suspends support for all the parasites associated with such a customer's account.

Ms. Jones has several specific recommendations on steps we can take to make the Internet a safer and more trustworthy place for consumers and owners of valuable IP.

In my own estimation, the need to fashion new tools to more effectively and meaningfully combat digital theft and online counterfeiting is beyond reasoned discussion. The most serious questions relate to the scope of appropriate relief and the balance of interests among stakeholders and the public.

In addition, I want to note that this is the furthest thing from censorship. A civilized society respects property and promotes lawful individual expression whether it occurs online or in the public square. This hearing is another important step in advancing the public debate and enhancing the ability of our members to assess the true character and impact of criminal infringement on the Internet and to design new tools that will be adapted to current and emerging technologies.

I look forward to working with Members on both sides of the aisle and with our colleagues on the other side of the Capitol as we advance this effort.

It is now my pleasure to recognize the Ranking Member of the Subcommittee, the gentleman from North Carolina, Mr. Watt.

Mr. Watt. Thank you, Mr. Chairman. And let me thank Chairman Goodlatte for providing the Subcommittee with two hearings on this important issue. I think it is critical that we look more broadly at how we promote investment and protect legitimate commerce online, and a primary means of doing that is deterring the electronic theft of legitimate commerce and products just as aggressively as we try to deter theft of products on the ground. These hearings are affording us the opportunity to do that.

I look forward to working with you, Mr. Chairman, to fashion an appropriate remedy for what might romantically be called piracy but what we still refer to in my neighborhood as theft or simple stealing.

As I noted in our first hearing, online theft of intellectual property is increasing and negatively affecting both the rightsholders and the Nation's economy. Theft of digital work such as music and movies carries with it substantial downstream damage, hitting the pockets and livelihoods of businesses, large and small, and their workers and artists. Who wants to make something or use their intellectual innovation or creative talents if the fruit of their labor is just going to be stolen?

Businesses are hemorrhaging profits, shrinking staff, and in some instances facing extinction. Counterfeit products of all kinds sold online not only create a drain on the economy, but they can also pose serious health and safety risks for an unknowing public and jeopardize the financial security of individuals. Luxury goods, automobile parts, foodstuffs, and pharmaceuticals have all been hijacked by criminals with the tacit assistance of credible payment processors and, yes, reputable players in the Internet ecosystem and spurred by the demand of consumers. The criminals would rather use their ingenuity to deceive and exploit than to conduct legitimate business. The magnitude of digital theft and online counterfeiting together is simply staggering, and they have to be stopped.

While the anti-circumvention provisions of the Digital Millennium Copyright Act, the DMCA, have provided rightsholders with some protections against theft, the scope of these protections is narrow and their reach provides no protection against threats from foreign websites.

Similarly, the notice and takedown provisions of the DMCA established an enforcement model that, while engaging many actors in the Internet ecosystem, relies in the final analysis upon ISP's and other online service providers to implement enforcement.

The gaps in the DMCA suggest that the time to supplement its provisions to address the broader range of theft is upon us. The scope of the problem has become so immense that every participant within the Internet ecosystem must assume some responsibility for taking the profit out of piracy.

As a member also of the Financial Services Committee, I am familiar with the laws and regulations imposing obligations on banks to curb the tide of money laundering. While we require banks, not because they are bad actors, to report deposits in excess of $10,000, we do so because we want to deter criminals from using reputable financial institutions to further their criminal enterprises.

Similarly, I believe it is incumbent on us to ensure that legitimate Internet intermediaries are protected from criminal elements which the evidence overwhelmingly suggests are exploiting U.S.-based businesses to infiltrate the U.S. market, reaping profits while undermining our economy.

This applies also to criminals who operate beyond our borders and register domain names with foreign registrars. Despite current efforts of IP rightsholders and law enforcement officials, it seems clear that new authorities and enforcement strategies and enhanced cooperative partnerships are critically needed to combat the use of foreign websites by criminals to reach American consumers.

Additionally, any law we craft must, to the greatest extent possible, account for new technologies and anticipate the creativity of criminals to circumvent the law. This is even more important in a global economy.

I look forward to the recommendations of our witnesses and thank them for being here.

And, Mr. Chairman, I yield back.

Mr. Goodlatte. I thank the gentleman for his very cogent remarks.

And I am now pleased to recognize the Chairman of the Judiciary Committee and a leading advocate for efforts in this area, the gentleman from Texas, Mr. Smith.

Mr. Smith. Thank you, Mr. Chairman.

This important hearing is the second of two of the IP Subcommittee devoted to the destructive effects of online parasites, web-based entities that steal intellectual property.

Practically anything capable of being reproduced digitally or available for sale in stores is only a click or two away today. That is a good thing when consumers purchase from legitimate businesses, but increasingly consumers are being steered to web stores that traffic in counterfeit products.

According to the Alliance for Safe Online Pharmaceuticals, 95 percent of online pharmacies are unlicensed or traffic in counterfeit drugs. When patients go online and end up buying fake medicines, more than a trademark is in jeopardy. The lives of those or their loved ones are placed at risk. So this is about both protecting lives and intellectual property.

It is also about jobs, jobs lost as a result of digital theft and online counterfeiting. The jobs lost in legitimate industries tend to be high-paying jobs that provide income and security to tens of thousands of Americans. For instance, jobs in the U.S. entertainment industry have an average salary of $76,000. This is 72 percent higher than the national average. When jobs like these are lost, entire families become victims.

With digital theft, what is distributed was created by those who have had their property stolen. Perfect reproductions of movies, sound recordings, books, software, and musical compositions compete directly with licensed goods.

The Constitution provides for the progress of science and useful arts by giving Congress the specific responsibility and duty to spur creativity and innovation by securing those IP rights. Our job on the House Judiciary Committee is to protect the right of free expression and to provide due process of law.

A recent study of online activity revealed that nearly one-quarter of global Internet traffic involves stolen IP. This digital theft is now so pervasive, profitable, and pernicious that it discourages creative companies from investing in the production of new licensed content. IP theft not only adversely affects creators but also undermines investments in new technology by innovative companies such as Netflix.

Securing property rights and protecting IP is a matter that unites Members on both sides of the aisle and on both sides of the Hill. While we will never achieve unanimity, there is a great deal of consensus that new legislation is needed to deal with threats that have emerged as technology has progressed.

Thank you, Mr. Chairman.

I yield back.

Mr. Goodlatte. I thank the Chairman.

And it is now my pleasure to recognize the Ranking Member of the full Committee, the gentleman from Michigan, Mr. Conyers?

Mr. Conyers. Thank you, Mr. Chairman.

We were yesterday over on the other side meeting with the Chairman of the Senate Judiciary, the Chairman of this Committee, the Subcommittee Chairman of this

Committee, the distinguished gentleman from California, Mr. Berman, and myself pledging publicly to be as cooperative as we can in this ongoing examination of how to get a bill out of here that will satisfy at least a few, maybe even most of you that are present in the room today.

Now, there are a number of companies—and Google is not the only one—and other search engines that act as intermediaries that facilitate what all this lecturing is about on piracy and stealing and so forth. We are beginning to examine what responsibility do they have? Are we all the innocents, and all the bad guys are overseas doing all this?

Under title 17 and sections 501 and 506, this Government and copyright holders cannot adequately stop, so far, online infringement at the speed that is necessary to stop the crimes. On the Internet, once a file of an illegal movie has been uploaded, for example, days and even minutes can result in copies of the file traveling to every corner of the Web. The Department of Justice and our civil suit system move at a very slow pace. The DMCA has been insufficient to stop what is going on. There has been a proliferation of sites operating off our shores. As fast as we close a few down, others spring up.

And so I am glad that Floyd Abrams is here, the number one man in First Amendment concerns, because we have got a big challenge in front of us.

Now, we are going to move toward closing down some of this international illegal activity, and the challenge is how to do it without violating due process and the First Amendment.

So I join everybody here in all the rhetoric.

But why don't we just cut off some of the money? These streams of pirate sites—instead of cutting off each one every time it pops up to pop up somewhere else, why don't we eliminate some of the financial incentives by cutting off funding from the customer through the payment processing system or cut off the funding from the advertising networks?

What about the Department of Justice with the authority to go after the worst, we could permit them to order court-supervised takedowns and allow them to block access to rogue sites from within the United States? And it may be we need to talk to the Attorney General again on this subject.

Finally—and this is almost unthinkable—we could begin to grant a right of private action to allow people to challenge some of these providers, search engines and payment processors.

I will be the first to be critical if we step over the line, but I think that there is more that can be done and I think that we need to use this hearing as another opportunity to come up with some legislation that we will all be proud of

Thank you, Mr. Chairman.

Mr. Goodlatte. I thank the gentleman.

And without objection, other Members' opening statements will be made a part of the record.

We have a very distinguished panel of witnesses today. Their written statements will be entered into the record in their entirety, and I ask the witnesses to summarize their testimony in 5 minutes or less. To help you stay within that time, there is a timing light on your table. When the light switches from green to yellow, you will have 1 minute to conclude your testimony. When the light turns to red, it signals your 5 minutes have expired.

Before I introduce our witnesses, I would ask them to stand and be sworn.

[Witnesses sworn.]

Mr. Goodlatte. Thank you and please be seated.

Our first witness is John Morton, the Director of Immigration and Customs Enforcement. ICE is the principal investigative arm of the U.S. Department of Homeland Security and the second largest investigative agency in the Federal Government. The primary mission of ICE is to promote homeland security and public safety through the criminal and civil enforcement of Federal laws that govern border security, customs, trade, and immigration.

Before his confirmation in 2009, Mr. Morton spent 15 years at the Department of Justice. While there, he served as an Assistant United States Attorney, Counsel to the Deputy Attorney General, and Acting Deputy Assistant Attorney General of the Criminal Division. During his tenure, Mr. Morton has sought to strengthen ice's investigative and enforcement efforts with a particular emphasis on border crimes, export controls, intellectual property, and child protection.

Our second witness is Floyd Abrams. Mr. Abrams is a partner at the New York law firm of Cahill, Gordon & Reindel. His practice is diverse and includes intellectual property, media, and communications law. An internationally noted trial and appellate attorney, Mr. Abrams is best known for his experience and expertise in First Amendment issues. He is the recipient of countless awards and honors, which I will not attempt to enumerate, but perhaps none is more noteworthy than the description of Mr. Abrams by Senator Daniel Patrick Moynihan as, quote, the most significant First Amendment lawyer of our age. End quote.

Mr. Abrams earned his bachelor's from Cornell University and his J.D. from Yale Law School. I understand he is testifying in his personal capacity today.

Our third witness is Kent Walker. Mr. Walker is a Senior Vice President and General Counsel of Google. In the latter role, he is responsible for managing Google's global legal team and advising the company's board and management on legal issues and corporate governance matters.

Before joining Google, Mr. Walker served in a variety of senior legal positions at other technology companies. These include eBay, Liberate Technologies, Netscape, America Online, and AirTouch Communications. Prior to serving in these positions, he served as an Assistant United States Attorney where he focused on the prosecution of technology crimes.

Mr. Walker graduated magna cum laude from Harvard and earned his J.D. with distinction from Stanford Law School.

Our final witness is Christine Jones. Ms. Jones is the Executive Vice President and General Counsel and Corporate Secretary to the Go Daddy Group, Incorporated. With more than 47 million domains under management, godaddy.com is the world's largest domain name registrar. In addition to being responsible for all legal affairs, Ms. Jones oversees the domain services, network abuse, government relations, compliance, and legal departments of the corporation. She has been active in her support of Internet-related legislation to, among other things, protect children from predators, protect patients from counterfeit and unlicensed drugs, and enhance transparency and accountability among those who operate online.

Before affiliating with Go Daddy, Ms. Jones practiced privately and worked for the Los Angeles District Attorney's office.

She earned her bachelor's from Auburn University and her J.D. from Whittier Law School. In addition to being an attorney, she is also a certified public accountant.

We welcome all of our witnesses to the Subcommittee on Intellectual Property, Competition and the Internet today, and we will begin with Mr. Morton's opening statement.

*Chapter 5*

# WITNESSES

## TESTIMONY OF THE HONORABLE JOHN MORTON, DIRECTOR, U.S. IMMIGRATION AND CUSTOMS ENFORCEMENT

Mr. Morton. Good morning, Mr. Chairman, Ranking Member Watt, Members of the Subcommittee. Good morning as well to Chairman Smith and to Ranking Member Conyers from the full Committee.

As you know, ICE is an aggressive investigator of intellectual property offenses, and we run the National Enforcement Center for IP Crime just across the river in northern Virginia.

Now, why is ICE so heavily engaged in intellectual property enforcement? The answer is simple. American businesses and consumers are under assault from organized counterfeiters and copyright thieves. American jobs, American innovation, the safety of our people are all at risk, not minor risk, serious risk, risk calculated in the billions, risk that threatens the foundation of certain U.S. industries, risks that put people in hospitals.

Remember, counterfeiters and copyright thieves aren't trying to make America great. They don't pay taxes. They don't create jobs. They don't provide health care or pensions. They don't invest in the next Oscar-winning movie, the next lifesaving drug, or the next technological advance. They don't care about safety or health standards. Instead, they wait for others to do the research, for others to work hard, for others to play by the rules, and then they take what they can't make on their own and profit at our country's expense.

In short, we have a significant problem on our hands, and resolute action by Government, by industry, and the consumer is necessary to turn the tide.

Why are we pursuing enforcement online? Again, the answer is simple. That is where crime is taking us. The days of counterfeiting and copyright theft occurring solely through the mails, on the streets, or through our ports are over. Today these crimes are just as likely to occur over the Internet as they are on the corner of 4th and Main.

Let me be clear here. We are investigating crimes online because copyright thieves and counterfeiters have led us there. We are not seeking to regulate the Internet. We are not out to stifle free speech. We are not out to trample anyone's constitutional rights. Any suggestion to the contrary is simply false. Full stop. We are a law enforcement agency out to deter and prevent crime. Nothing more, nothing less. Crime is crime wherever it occurs and we do not accept the view that the Internet should somehow be off limits to enforcement if it is knowingly being used to commit crime.

So what is ICE doing to combat the problem? Well, we are making IP enforcement a priority for the agency and pursuing a record number of IP cases. Last fiscal year, for example, we opened over 1,000 new IP investigations, the largest number in our agency's history.

Wherever we can, we pursue the traditional investigative model; that is, we investigate the alleged crime, we seize the contraband, we arrest and prosecute the perpetrators. That approach doesn't always work well, however, on online cases as online crime is frequently centered overseas and outside of our legal jurisdiction. Take an online counterfeiting site, for example. More often than not, the server, the criminals, and the counterfeiting operation are all outside the U.S. The same is true for infringing sites. Nothing need be based in the U.S.

As a result, we have also seized 119 domain names of sites used to sell counterfeit goods and to illegally distribute copyrighted materials. 119 sites, mind you, out of well over 200 million on the Internet. The majority of the sites were linked to counterfeiting of hard goods; the rest were involved in illegal streaming or downloads of entertainment or software.

Please note that we are not targeting lawful businesses, blogs, or discussion boards. The sites we go after are commercial and have engaged in repeated and significant violation of the law. They are increasingly sophisticated and often seek to dupe consumers.

I don't know if we can throw up—so here is just two quick examples. Here is a website purporting to be an authorized Louis Vuitton outlet and it offers Louis Vuitton products—and I quote— 100 percent handmade from France. The website has the Louis Vuitton logo, name, and designs. What is missing, of course, are any genuine Louis Vuitton products. Instead, none of the products are handmade in France, but they are all counterfeit in China and shipped to the United States.

The next slide, if you would. This is allegedly an authorized retailer of Nike shoes, another site that we seized. In fact, none of these shoes are authorized or made by Nike. They are all counterfeit. Here you have Nike, one of the major U.S. manufacturers based in Oregon, and it is if not the most targeted, one of the most targeted companies in terms of counterfeiting.

Let me close very quickly by saying we spend a lot of time and attention on process. We can talk about that more in detail.

I also recognize that good people can have different views on how to solve counterfeiting and copyright infringement. That is okay. I don't pretend to have all of the answers. Addressing online crime is not an easy task and criminal investigation is but one part of the solution.

I do know this, however, Mr. Chairman. If we do nothing to keep pace with online criminals or give up this fight, little good will come of it.

Thank you. [The prepared statement of Mr. Morton follows:]

## U.S. Immigration and Customs Enforcement Statement of John Morton Director, U.S. Immigration and Customs Enforcement Department of Homeland Security, Regarding a Hearing on "Promoting Investment and Protecting Commerce Online: Legitimate Sites v. Parasites, Part II," before the U.S. House of Representatives Committee on the Judiciary, Subcommittee on Intellectual Property, Competition and The Internet

Wednesday, April 6, 2011- 10:45 AM;
2141 Rayburn House Office Building

### Introduction

Chairman Goodlatte, Ranking Member Watt, and distinguished Members of the Subcommittee:

Thank you for the opportunity to highlight the important role U.S. Immigration and Customs Enforcement (ICE) plays in combating intellectual property (IP) theft in today's global economy.

Simply put, American business is threatened by those who pirate copyrighted material and produce counterfeit trademarked goods. Criminals are attempting to steal American ideas and products and sell them over the Internet, in flea markets, in legitimate retail outlets and elsewhere. From counterfeit pharmaceuticals and electronics to pirated movies, music, and software, IP thieves undermine the U.S. economy and jeopardize public safety. American jobs are being lost, American innovation is being diluted and the public health and safety of Americans is at risk - and organized criminal enterprises are profiting from their increasing involvement in IP theft.

The Administration is responding to this organized criminal activity through a first-of-its-kind, coordinated, and strategic offensive that targets counterfeiters and those who pirate copyrighted material. This offensive involves multiple departments and agencies within government coming together in an ICE-led task force, the National Intellectual Property Rights Coordination Center (IPR Center). IP enforcement policy across many different federal agencies is being coordinated by the first presidentially appointed, Senate-confirmed Intellectual Property Enforcement Coordinator (IPEC), Victoria Espinel, with whom I have had the great privilege to work. ICE and the IPR Center contributed and consulted frequently with the IPEC on the creation of the first-ever Joint Strategic Plan on Intellectual Property Enforcement released in June 2010. Additionally, we contributed to the IPEC's 2010 Annual Report to Congress, released in February 2011, and a variety of other reports to Congress and the Vice President.

## Background

America's entrepreneurial spirit and integrity are embodied by the creativity and resourcefulness of our workforce. New inventions, innovations, works of art, and discoveries create new jobs and new industries and add to our country's heritage. Innovation drives commerce and enables the United States to compete in the global marketplace. Intellectual property rights and the ability to enforce those rights encourage American companies to continue the tradition of American innovation and develop products, ideas and merchandise.

Intellectual property rights are intended to discourage thieves from selling cheap imitations of products that are often far less safe or reliable than the original products. More importantly, intellectual property rights protect public safety by preventing the proliferation of counterfeit pharmaceuticals and other materials that are potentially harmful. They also protect our military members by preventing the spread of untested and ineffective knockoff components. Intellectual property rights violators unfairly devalue America's contributions, hinder our ability to grow our economy, compromise American jobs, and put consumers, families, and communities at risk. They also protect the actor, director, writer, musician, artist, and countless others who labor in and around America's entertainment industry from having a movie, manuscript, song or design illegally sold by someone who had no part in the artistry of creating it.

As the members of this Subcommittee well know, globalization provides boundless opportunities for commerce. But it also brings a growing set of challenges, especially in combating the theft of intellectual property. In a global economy, enforcement of intellectual property rights is crucial to ensuring that legitimate manufacturers and companies can expend capital developing overseas markets, exporting goods and creating jobs.

## ICE's Role

ICE has a legacy of engagement in IP theft enforcement - stretching from our past years as U.S. Customs Service investigators to our present role as homeland security investigators. ICE is a leading agency in the investigation of criminal intellectual property violations involving the illegal production, smuggling, and distribution of counterfeit and pirated products, as well as associated money laundering violations. We target and investigate counterfeit goods entering the U.S. through our ports from various countries overseas and we seize counterfeit goods associated with these investigations, such as those that infringe on trademarks, trade names and copyrights. ICE has become increasingly innovative in how we combat counterfeiting and piracy. Our goal is not mere marginal increases in enforcement, but to disrupt the manufacturing, distribution, and financing segments of these criminal organizations.

ICE recognizes that no single U.S. law enforcement agency alone can succeed in the fight against IP theft. Rather, it is essential that all relevant federal agencies work together and with industry to confront this challenge. ICE initiated the IPR Center to leverage government resources to combat IP theft.

## The IPR Center

The mission of the IPR Center is to address the theft of innovation and manufacturing that threatens U.S. economic stability and national security, restrict the competitiveness of U.S. industry in world markets, and place the public's health and safety at risk. The IPR Center promotes coordination and communication across the many U.S. government agencies with roles in enforcing IP laws. The IPR Center brings together key domestic and foreign investigative agencies to efficiently and effectively leverage resources, skills and authorities to provide a comprehensive response to IP theft.

The IPR Center, located in Arlington, Virginia, is an ICE-led task force of 17 relevant federal and international partners. The Department of Justice (DOJ) is a participant, prosecuting federally for all partners. The IPR Center includes embedded team members from, among others, U.S. Customs and Border Protection (CBP), the Food and Drug Administration Office of Criminal Investigations (FDA OCI), the Federal Bureau of Investigation (FBI), the U.S. Postal Inspection Service (USPIS), the Department of Commerce International Trade Administration, the U.S. Patent and Trademark Office, the Defense Criminal Investigative Service, the Naval Criminal Investigative Service, the Army Criminal Investigative Command Major Procurement Fraud Unit and the Inspector General's Office from the General Services Administration. Last year, the Government of Mexico and INTERPOL joined the IPR Center as our first international partners.

Since February 2011, the IPR Center has welcomed the following new partners: the U.S. Consumer Product Safety Commission; the Defense Logistics Agency; the U.S. Department of State Office of International Intellectual Property Enforcement; and our third international partner, the Royal Canadian Mounted Police. Together, the partners at the IPR Center have created a one-stop shop for industry and victims of IP theft, reducing duplication and allowing us to leverage and benefit from our different areas of expertise. ICE and the IPR Center have repeatedly teamed with the World Customs Organization (WCO) and its member countries in several multilateral enforcement operations targeting counterfeit goods.

## ICE's International Efforts

ICE'S Homeland Security Investigations International Affairs (HSI-IA) represents the largest investigative law enforcement presence abroad for the Department of Homeland Security (DHS) with an international footprint of 69 offices in 47 countries, including representatives at seven combatant commands, staffed by more than 380 personnel. The mission of HSI-IA is to protect the United States by enhancing its security through international investigations involving transnational criminal organizations responsible for the illegal movement of people, goods, and technology, and through strong and integral intelligence and removal programs. There are 11 countries on the U.S. Trade Representative's Priority Watch List as part of its annual review of the global state of intellectual property rights protection and enforcement. ICE maintains a presence in nine of these countries, with a total of 14 offices. The FBI, an IPR Center partner agency, maintains a presence in the other two countries.

ICE Attachés work with international organizations and foreign law enforcement counterparts to build capacity, strengthen relationships, and conduct joint enforcement activities. ICE is recognized as a worldwide subject matter expert on criminal customs matters, and holds positions as Vice Chair for the Enforcement Committee and Chair of the Commercial Fraud Working Group with the WCO.

### *ICE's Work in China*

The primary source country for the manufacture and distribution of counterfeit merchandise is China. In FY 2010, ICE and CBP seized at U.S. ports of entry IPR violative goods from China with a domestic value (as opposed to manufacturer's suggested retail value) of more than $124.6 million. These seizures accounted for approximately 66 percent of the total domestic value of counterfeit merchandise seized by DHS.

ICE has a presence in central and southern coastal China with offices in Beijing and Guangzhou, with our Assistant Attaché in Guangzhou designated as ICE's first "IP Attaché" and ICE's point of contact for all IP matters involving China. These two offices deal largely with commercial fraud and IP. Moreover, the ICE office in Guangzhou is working with the U.S. Consulate on a project to make Shenzhen a model IP enforcement city. ICE has made a commitment to work with the Consulate on this project and provide training to the Chinese Public Security Bureau on IP investigation and enforcement.

Last September, I traveled to China for meetings with my Chinese law enforcement counterparts, including the Ministry of Public Security (MPS), and signed an agreement to cooperate on joint investigations of IP theft. The IPR Center also regularly liaises with MPS representatives from the Chinese Embassy in Washington.

This new agreement builds on our previous work with China. In September 2003, ICE collaborated with Chinese authorities on Operation Spring, a joint IPR investigation that resulted in the extradition and conviction of DVD pirate Randolph Guthrie, who was sentenced to 48 months incarceration and ordered to repay $878,793 in restitution to the Motion Picture Association of America. Another joint ICE-Chinese investigation resulted in four arrests in the United States and the seizure of more than $100 million in counterfeit computer software and approximately $4 million in counterfeit cigarettes.

### *ICE's Work in Other Countries*

More recently, ICE worked with our Korean partners in Seoul to combat IP violations occurring in that country. In September, I signed a Memorandum of Understanding between ICE and the Korean Supreme Prosecutor's Office to work collaboratively on IP investigations. Since FY 2008, seizures in Korea involving our Attaché in Seoul have increased dramatically: in FY 2010, 22 subjects were arrested, and merchandise valued at approximately $18.7 million was seized. So far in FY 2011, 42 subjects have been arrested and ICE has assisted in seizures valued at approximately $13 million.

In July 2009, ICE opened an office in Brussels to work directly with the WCO on multilateral operations addressing bulk cash smuggling and explosives precursor chemicals. ICE also works with INTERPOL, the Asia-Pacific Economic Cooperation Forum, and the Departments of State, Commerce, and Justice on a variety of initiatives, including providing training on IPR enforcement to our international law enforcement partners.

## ICE's Contributions to Foreign Training and Capacity Building

In May 2009, the IPR Center initiated the U.S. interagency "IPR in Africa" Working Group, with participation by the Departments of State, Justice, and Commerce, to improve coordination of the U.S. government's IP training and resource commitments in Africa. In coordination with these U.S. entities, the WCO and INTERPOL, the IPR Center serves as a subject matter expert in IPR training specifically focused on strengthening enforcement and investigations.

ICE provides training on IP theft enforcement and interacts with foreign officials worldwide through our participation in the Department of State International Law Enforcement Academy (ILEA) program. The mission of the ILEAs — located in Budapest, Gaborone, San Salvador, Bangkok, and Lima — is to help protect U.S. interests through international cooperation and the promotion of stability by combating crime.

ICE is an active member of the U.S. delegation negotiating the Anti-Counterfeiting Trade Agreement (ACTA). The goal of ACTA is to work with other countries interested in promoting strong enforcement of IPR. ACTA aims to strengthen legal frameworks to bridge existing gaps between laws and dedicated enforcement, and to foster ongoing cooperation among ACTA participants.

## State, Local, and Tribal Training and Outreach

ICE and the IPR Center assert that an effective enforcement strategy must include the participation of our state, local, and tribal law enforcement partners. On April 26, 2010, designated as World IP Day, I announced the creation of local IP Theft Enforcement Teams (IPTETs), The IPTETs are partnerships with state, local and tribal law enforcement built on the best practices identified by the IPR Center. They use an informal task force approach to enhance coordination of intellectual property investigations at the state, local and tribal level. There are currently 26 IPTETs across the country, which include federal, state, local and tribal law enforcement partners, including sworn personnel from police and sheriff departments and local prosecutors. The IPR Center has been conducting training for the IPTETs around the country and since their creation.

## Recent Enforcement Successes

### *Operation in Our Sites*

Last year, the IPR Center launched Operation In Our Sites, a new initiative targeting websites being used to sell counterfeit goods and distribute pirated merchandise and copyrighted digital materials. During the first enforcement action as part of this initiative, ICE agents, working with the U.S. Attorney's Office for the Southern District of New York, obtained judicially authorized seizure warrants for seized seven illegal domain names providing more than 500 movies and television programs. After ICE shut down the websites, 20 million visitors attempted to access the sites.

On November 29, 2010, I joined the Attorney General to announce the results of Operation In Our Sites v. 2.0. Timed to coincide with "Cyber Monday," reportedly the largest online shopping day of the year, the operation targeted online retailers of counterfeit goods, including sports equipment, shoes, handbags, athletic apparel and sunglasses, as well as illegal copies of copyrighted DVD boxed sets, music and software. ICE and DOJ obtained federal court orders to seize the domain names of 77 internet sites selling counterfeit goods, five websites selling pirated movies, music and software, and one server. The operation was spearheaded by the IPR Center, in coordination with DOJ Computer Crime and Intellectual Property Section, nine ICE field offices, and ten U.S. Attorneys' Offices.

In 2011, ICE added to the In Our Sites initiative on February 4 with In Our Sites V. 3.0, and on February 14 with In Our Sites v. 4.0. In Our Sites v. 3.0 coincided with the Super Bowl, and resulted in the seizure of 10 domain names of websites that provided access to pirated telecasts of the National Football League, the National Basketball Association, the National Hockey League, World Wrestling Entertainment, and the Ultimate Fighting Championship. Last month, ICE and DOJ announced the arrest of the operator of one of these websites on charges of federal copyright violation. These are lucrative criminal endeavors, and ICE and DOJ froze one bank account with over $500,000 in cash that resulted from the illegal operation of the website. Operation In Our Sites V. 4.0 coincided with Valentine's Day and resulted in the seizure of 18 domain names of commercial websites engaged in the illegal sale and distribution of counterfeit goods.

The domains seized pursuant to court order now display a banner announcing the seizure of the site by the government and an explanation of the federal crime and punishment for copyright theft and distribution or trademark violations. Since the initial seizures in June 2010, there have been over 38 million hits to the seizure banner that notifies viewers a federal court order has been issued for the domain name and educates them that willful copyright infringement is a federal crime. The resulting public education about pirating is a significant benefit of this enforcement operation in deterring future crimes and in raising awareness.

The Operation In Our Sites initiative will continue through 2011 and beyond. ICE'S efforts through this operation successfully disrupt the ability of criminals to purvey copyrighted materials illegally over the internet. In addition to the domain names that are seized through this operation, evidence suggests that the operation has a deterrent effect. In fact, following Operation In Our Sites v. 1.0, ICE was notified that 81 of the most active websites that had been offering pirated material voluntarily shut down.

### *Due Process in Operation in Our Sites*

Operation In Our Sites was developed with the Department of Justice to respect free speech, to provide due process, and to work within the statutory framework provided to us by Congress. Domain names seized under Operation in Our Sites are seized only in furtherance of ongoing criminal investigations into violations of U.S. federal laws. As with all criminal investigations, the initial leads are obtained through a variety of sources including, but not limited to, leads from the general public, tips from industry representatives and information uncovered by special agents. For each domain name seized, ICE investigators independently obtained counterfeit trademarked goods or pirated copyrighted material that was in turn verified by the rights holders as counterfeit. After such verification, ICE applied for federal seizure warrants based on probable cause.

Federal magistrate judges approve criminal seizure warrants based on probable cause for the domain names that are targeted. The standard is exactly the same as in any other criminal investigation. As with all judicially authorized seizure warrants, the owners of the seized property have the opportunity to challenge the judge's determination through a petition. If a petition is filed, a hearing is held in a federal court to determine the validity of the affidavit supporting the seizure, at which point the government would have the burden of proof. Of course, all rights of appeal, ultimately even to the Supreme Court of the United States, would adhere to the website owner, should the judge determine the issue in favor of the government.

Under existing federal law, the website owner may also choose to demand return of the property through the law enforcement agency itself, by writing a letter to ICE. If ICE does not return the website within 15 days, the owner can petition the U.S. District Court in which the seizure warrant was issued or executed.

Further, if the website owner determines he or she does not wish to pursue either of these avenues of due process, a challenge may be filed directly with the law enforcement agency conducting a forfeiture action under administrative processes.

So, there are four avenues of due process along the path, including the initial determination by a neutral and detached magistrate that the website was engaged in violations of federal criminal copyright or trademark law.

***Other Notable Investigative Successes against IP Theft***

ICE'S IP theft enforcement efforts have continued to increase under this Administration. In FY 2010, ICE initiated 1,033 intellectual property infringement cases—a 42 percent increase over FY 2009—and achieved 365 arrests, 216 indictments and 170 convictions. In FY 2010, criminal charges flowing from ICE-initiated intellectual property investigations increased by 86 percent over the previous year. These figures include both federal and state prosecutions. The below cases illustrate some of our notable IP enforcement successes.

In the past year, ICE agents continued to seize millions of dollars in counterfeit items as a result of significant criminal investigations including an investigation into a criminal organization smuggling counterfeit shoes and luxury goods through the Port of Baltimore, with an estimated manufacturer's suggested retail price of more than $219 million had the products been legitimate goods. This investigation resulted in nine federal arrests. ICE was able to develop evidence on a parallel operation in the United Kingdom, and our ICE Attaché in London passed the information on to relevant UK law enforcement. This resulted in six arrests, seizures of 50,000 counterfeit luxury items and approximately $617,000 in U.S. equivalent currency, making it one of the largest IP theft enforcement cases in UK history.

We have broadened our reach by partnering with foreign counterparts, such as the Mexican Tax Administration Service, which seized 306 tons of counterfeit merchandise at mail facilities and land, air and sea ports of entry during just one joint operation.

Earlier this year, the IPR Center partnered with the NFL, NBA, NHL, the National Collegiate Athletic Association (NCAA), industry and local law enforcement to conduct operations targeting counterfeit sports merchandise sold during the Super Bowl, the NBA All-Star Game, the Stanley Cup championship, and the NCAA Final Four and Frozen Four tournaments. These operations resulted in seizures of more than 14,000 counterfeit items valued at more than $760,000.

In June 2010, ICE and CBP completed the U.S. portion of Operation Global Hoax, a three-month multilateral enforcement action proposed by the IPR Center and coordinated with the WCO. Global Hoax is the first-ever worldwide enforcement action targeting counterfeit DVDs and CDs as they are shipped around the world. The five-day surge operation at mail and express courier facilities resulted in the seizure of more than 140,000 pirated DVDs, 28,000 CDs, and more than 270,000 other counterfeit items worldwide. Domestically, ICE HSI and CBP seized 22,371 pirated DVDs, 2,658 pirated DVD box sets, 133 pirated CDs and 8,556 other counterfeit items worth a total MSRP of approximately $5.3 million.

In October 2010, the IPR Center coordinated U.S. efforts in Operation Pangea III, a global operation targeting illegal pharmaceutical sales over the Internet that involved the participation of ICE, CBP, FDA OCI, USPIS, DEA, 45 countries, the WCO, INTERPOL, international organizations, and industry. The U.S. operation was conducted at mail facilities in several U.S. cities. Internet monitoring revealed more than 820 websites engaged in illegal activity, including those offering controlled or prescription-only drugs. Nearly 300 of these websites have been taken down and investigations continue. Participants inspected over 278,000 packages, seizing nearly 11,000 packages which contained more than 2.3 million illicit and counterfeit pills worth more than $56.7 million. Globally, 130 search warrants were executed and 87 individuals were arrested or are under investigation for a range of offenses.

ICE remains steadfast in ensuring that IP theft is not used to support those who would harm the United States or our interests abroad. Last November, ICE and the FBI worked with the New Jersey State Police and the Philadelphia FBI Joint Terrorism Task Force on a case that identified a three-cell criminal organization; a U.S.-based stolen property and counterfeit goods group; an overseas procurement group; and an international group tied to Hezbollah procuring weapons, counterfeit money, stolen property, and counterfeit goods. Ultimately, the investigation resulted in 25 indictments, 15 criminal arrests, 15 administrative arrests, and 10 red notices in INTERPOL.

However, we recognize that we are not going to be able to prosecute our way of this problem. There are simply too many criminals operating online today. This Administration believes strongly that we need to have the private sector and the companies that make the internet function take action if we are going to address this problem effectively. We are working with the White House Intellectual Property Enforcement Coordinator and other agencies to support the efforts to establish voluntary agreements with payment processors, ad networks, and other intermediaries to do the right thing. Combined with our law enforcement efforts, having the private sector step up to take voluntary action against infringers can have a tremendous effect.

## ICE's Partnership with the Private Sector

The IPR Center recognizes that law enforcement cannot fight IP theft alone and we look to partner with private industry in our efforts. In a market economy, no one has a greater incentive for protecting intellectual property rights than private industry.

Companies want to protect their investments in research, development, manufacturing, sales, marketing and product distribution.

To help enhance and facilitate productive partnerships within both the public and private sectors, the IPR Center provides industry with valuable information about ICE's efforts to combat the importation of hazardous and counterfeit products, and it provides points of contact in ICE field offices that industry can use to provide ICE with leads and tips. Since July 2008, the IPR Center and ICE agents have conducted approximately 638 outreach efforts, to include formal presentations and meetings, speaking with more than 34,000 industry representatives.

## Building Public Awareness about IP Theft

ICE believes the only way for us to be truly successful in our efforts against IP theft is to change public perception of IP crimes. Too many individuals believe buying knock-off goods or downloading films or songs from piratical sites is a victimless crime. The public must recognize that counterfeiting, piracy, and diversion is theft: theft of innovation, jobs, and revenue that sustains jobs, advances American business, funds health insurance, and supports industrial growth and economic stability.

The IPR Center is leading an effort to educate the public and other audiences about IP theft and international organized crime connections. In June 2010, the IPR Center hosted a Symposium titled "IP Theft and International Organized Crime and Terrorism: The Emerging Threat." Panels of academics, industry leaders and domestic and international government officials discussed links between international organized crime, terrorism and IP theft. Attendees included congressional staff, domestic law enforcement, media and others. A similar symposium is being planned for later this year.

## Challenges Ahead

I am regularly asked what challenges lie ahead in IP theft enforcement. First, I note that there are more criminals engaged in IP theft than ever before, and counterfeiting materials and items that clearly can affect public health and safety. As international criminal organizations have yielded huge profits through trafficking in counterfeit goods, they have opened their existing criminal infrastructures and smuggling routes to the flow of counterfeit merchandise. Because criminal penalties for commercial fraud violations as imposed are less severe than traditional drug or weapons trafficking offenses, many IP thieves and organized criminal organizations view IP theft as a relatively "low risk" endeavor. As I noted, ICE is working closely with international law enforcement partners to facilitate global investigations and crack down on transnational criminal organizations.

Moreover, over the last 10 years, the Internet's growth as a global commerce medium has caused it to develop into a key means for facilitating IP theft. The 2010 Cisco Visual Networking Index forecasts that global IP traffic will quadruple by 2014. Moreover, Cisco notes that download speeds of DVD quality movies have been reduced from three days 10 years ago, to just around two hours this year; an MP3 audio download time has been reduced from three minutes to approximately five seconds. This increase in access to the Internet, while of great benefit for global communication and commerce, presents a challenge with regard to IP enforcement.

In addition, while ocean-crossing shipping containers are necessary to move bulk quantities of counterfeit items such as handbags, shoes, batteries or holiday lights, other high value items including counterfeit pharmaceuticals, mobile phones, computer network components, microchips, MP3/4 Players, pirated DVDs/CDs and others are being smuggled in smaller and smaller quantities through mail and/or express courier parcels. ICE and CBP, using our customs authorities, will need to increase surge operations at foreign mail and courier facilities to generate seizures, controlled deliveries, intelligence and investigative leads.

IP theft cases have grown in both magnitude and complexity. A crime previously viewed as limited to luxury goods (such as high-priced handbags, apparel, and watches) has quickly grown to include all types of products and consumer goods at every price point, presenting more challenging and involved investigations.

Another challenge we face is that criminals are willing to counterfeit and market any product if it will sell, regardless of whether such sale could result in serious and significant injury to consumers or the public. ICE has investigated cases involving counterfeit toothpaste that contained a component found in antifreeze. Likewise, in 2007, ICE and the FDA arrested Kevin Xu, one of the world's most prolific counterfeiters of pharmaceuticals. Xu has been linked to distribution of counterfeit medications such as Plavix, Zyprexa, and Casodex that are used to treat blood clots, schizophrenia, and prostate cancer, respectively.

ICE and the FBI, along with DOJ, investigated the potential sale of counterfeit Cisco Gigabit Interface Converters to the U.S. Department of Defense for use by U.S. Marine Corps personnel operating in Iraq. Failure of these counterfeit devices on the battlefield would have endangered the lives of American service members. The defendant's profit would have been only approximately $120,000, showing the callousness with which many counterfeiters treat human life. I am pleased to report one defendant in this case investigated by ICE was recently sentenced to more than four years in prison.

These cases are troubling and demand attention from criminal investigators and regulatory agencies. At ICE, we are prioritizing our investigative resources to focus on IP theft enforcement that protects health and safety including the safety of our soldiers serving abroad and protects the American economy.

## Conclusion

Thank you for the opportunity to appear before you today to discuss the work of ICE in protecting U.S. intellectual property rights. I would be pleased to answer any questions that you may have at this time.

## Attachment

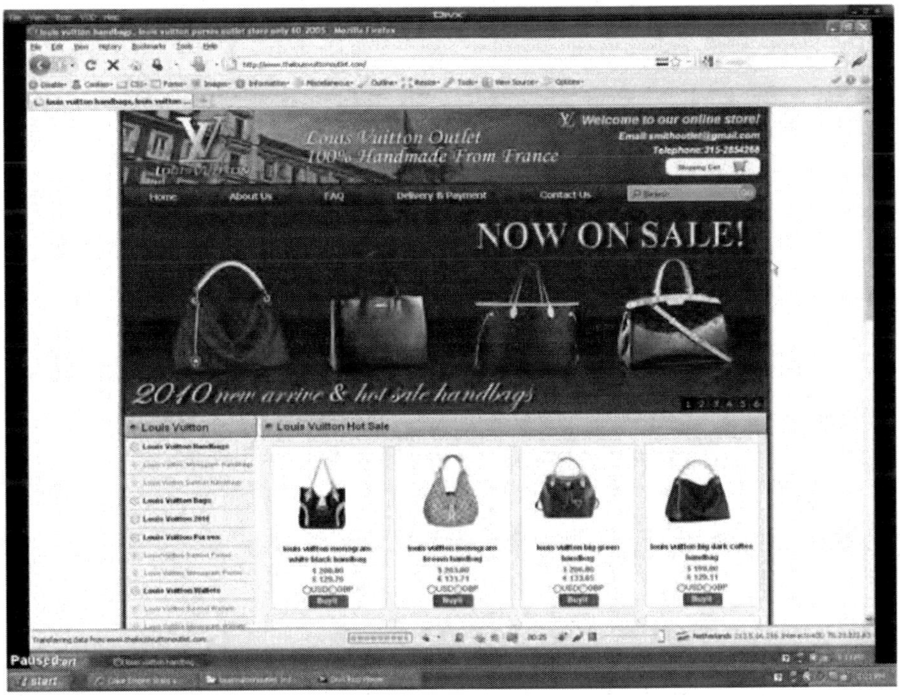

Mr. Goodlatte. Thank you, Mr. Morton.

Mr. Abrams, welcome.

## TESTIMONY OF FLOYD ABRAMS, SENIOR PARTNER, CAHILL GORDON AND REINDEL LLP

Mr. Abrams. Thank you. Mr. Chairman, Mr. Ranking Member, Mr. Chairman, Mr. Ranking Member, Members of the Committee, I appreciate the opportunity to be here today and to offer a few First Amendment views on the topic you have.

You have got three competing, sometimes overlapping themes here today. We deal with the Internet, which is probably the greatest enabler of free speech by everyone in the history of the world.

We deal with the copyright law which is a great enabler of free speech by providing a basis for people to engage in it, to create, and to profit from it. And we deal with the First Amendment which limits the ability of government in many areas to control free speech.

That we deal with the Internet does not mean that we are dealing with an entity that is so unique that we must act as if we are in a law-free zone. The law is the same with respect to libel on the Internet as it is with respect to libel in a newspaper. The law is the same with respect to invasion of privacy on the Internet as it is with respect to television broadcasts, and the law is the same with respect to copyright on the Internet and off the Internet.

It is simply then not so for some people to suggest that the Internet is the Wild West and that we should leave it that way. Even the Wild West had sheriffs and even those who use the Internet have to abide by our laws.

Now, how should you address the question which every Member of this Committee has agreed is a significant one and, indeed, a dangerous one as it currently exists in a way that complies with the First Amendment?

First, any legislation has to be narrowly drafted, really narrowly drafted so it only impacts websites, domains that are all but totally infringing. We don't want a situation, either as a matter of public policy and certainly not as a matter of the First Amendment, where we are wiping out in some sense or blocking in any sense protected speech. But if an entity, as so many of the ones at issue here are, is nothing but a transmitter of infringing products, which is to say acting criminally under our laws, you are permitted to deal with it so long as you do so without getting into an overbreadth situation.

I suggest to you that so far as you can, you ought to base any legislation on the law that currently exists. You don't have to start from scratch as if there is nothing that can guide you. We have a copyright law. We have means of enforcement. Injunctions have been issued by courts since 1790 when the copyright law was first enacted by Congress before we even had a Bill of Rights.

I would recommend to you that any legislation should include some reference to and, I would urge, inclusion of Federal Rule 65 which is the Rule of Civil Procedure which deals with the modalities of assuring that people have notice to appear, that judges don't have to issue injunctions, but that they may do so, and which provides great procedural protections for all that may be affected by legislation.

And I would simply sum up what I have to say in greater length in my prepared statement by saying that by enacting legislation in this area, we are not abdicating America's leadership of the world with respect to freedom on the Internet. We are simply enforcing well established, deeply rooted, frequently abided by, until rather recently, copyright law which exists for the purpose of furthering free expression in the first place. There is no constitutional right to steal someone else's intellectual property. And I urge the Committee to act with that in mind.

Thank you, Mr. Chairman.

[The prepared statement of Mr. Abrams follows:]

## TESTIMONY BEFORE THE SUBCOMMITTEE ON INTELLECTUAL PROPERTY, COMPETITION, AND THE INTERNET, COMMITTEE ON THE JUDICIARY, UNITED STATES HOUSE OF REPRESENTATIVES 112TH CONGRESS, 1ST SESSION, FLOYD ABRAMS, SENIOR PARTNER, CAHILL GORDON AND REINDEL LLP

Chairman Goodlatte, Ranking Member Watt and Members of the Committee:

Thank you for the opportunity to testify before your Committee today regarding online commerce and the challenges of legislating and enforcing copyright and piracy laws in an Internet age. I am a senior partner at the law firm of Cahill, Gordon and Reindel in New York and the author of "Speaking Freely: Trials of the First Amendment." T appear today at your request, speaking on my own behalf For your information, I have previously advised, in writing, the Directors Guild of America, the American Federation of Television and Radio Artists, the Screen Actors Guild, the International Alliance of Theatrical and Stage Employees, and the Motion Picture Association; of my view that legislation introduced in the Senate relating to online privacy of copyrighted works was consistent with the First Amendment.

While I will discuss potential legislative approaches to online infringement in some detail today, I think it is useful to start with a few broader observations regarding the application of copyright law and the First Amendment online. 1 begin with what should not be controversial.

The Internet is one of the greatest tools of freedom in the history of the world. That is why there is an "urgent need" to protect freedom of expression on the Internet throughout the world, as Secretary of State Hillary Clinton observed last month. At the same time, however. Secretary Clinton pointed out that "all societies recognize that freedom of expression has its limits," and that those who use the Internet to "distribute stolen intellectual property cannot divorce their online actions from their real world identities" - indeed, our ability to "safeguard billions of dollars in intellectual property [is] at stake if we cannot rely on the security of our information networks."

It is no answer to this challenge to treat loose metaphors—the Internet as "the Wild West," for example—as substitutes for serious legal or policy analysis. It is one thing to say that the Internet must be free; it is something else to say that it must be lawless. Even the Wild West had sheriffs, and even those who use the Internet must obey duly adopted laws.

Thus, it is no surprise that libel law routinely applies to material that appears on the Internet just as it does to other material. And that libel precedents regarding printing information on paper are just as applicable to information posted online. (A recent holding to that effect was the Fifth Circuit's ruling in *Nationwide Bi-Weekly Administration, Inc. v. Belo Corp.*) And, as well, that principles of privacy law are applied to personal information posted online, just as they are to personal information when recorded in more traditional media. (That approach was affirmed in *Benz v. Washington Newspaper Publishing Co.*)

Copyright law is no different. One current treatise succinctly notes, "[a]ll existing copyright protections are applicable to the Internet." The seizure provisions of copyright laws have been applied to authorize the seizure of online property that facilitates infringement, such as domain names, just as physical property has often been seized to stop its use to facilitate infringement. Under current law, for example, recent enforcement actions against infringing sites involved seizing and locking domain names, and compelling registries to route visitors to a government address notifying the public of the seizures.

Copyright law has existed throughout American history. The Constitution itself authorizes Congress to adopt copyright legislation. The first such legislation was enacted in 1790, a year before the First Amendment was approved by Congress. And from the start, injunctions were one form of relief accorded to victims of copyright infringement. Courts applied the first copyright act to grant injunctions under traditional principles of equity. Since injunctions in cases outside of the specific copyright context have been held to be unconstitutional prior restraints on speech, including the landmark Supreme Court cases of *Near v. Minnesota* and *New York Times Co. v. United States*, there has been an ongoing debate about the application, if any, of the First Amendment to copyright principles. Indeed, the question of whether and, if so, how certain elements of the Copyright Act should be read to accommodate various First Amendment interests remains open.

The law could not be clearer, however, that injunctions are a longstanding, constitutionally sanctioned way to remedy and prevent copyright violations. That premise was explicit in the critical concurring opinion in the Supreme Court's most famous prior restraint case, assessing publication of the Pentagon Papers in New York Times Co. v. United States. As Justice Byron White's concurring opinion observed in that case, "no one denies that a newspaper can properly be enjoined from publishing the copyrighted works of another"

Current treatises reflect this judicial consensus. To quote from the 2010 Practicing Law Institute discussion of prior restraints, which I authored with my colleague Gail Johnston: "[C]ourts have found no constitutional obstacle to enjoining, pursuant to federal legislative mandate, the unlawful use of a registered trademark or copyright." Similarly, in an article focused squarely on the issue of injunctions in the copyright arena. Judge James L. Oakes observed that a "pirated or copied edition, record, movie, song or other work . . . cries out for an injunction."

The Supreme Court's most detailed treatment of the interrelationship between the First Amendment and copyright, the seminal case of *Harper & How' Publishers, Inc. v. Nation Enterprises*, stressed that the Copyright Act actually advances the very interests which the First Amendment protects.

"First Amendment protections," the Court noted, are "already embodied in the Copyright Act's distinctions between copyrightable expression and uncopyrightable facts and ideas" The Constitution supports the explicit protection of such expression and creativity, the Court stated, within a framework that defends both the right to speak and the ability to profit from speech. "[T]he Framers intended copyright itself to be the engine of free expression," explained the Court, and "[b]y establishing a marketable right to the use of one's expression, copyright supplies the economic incentive to create and disseminate ideas." Copyright law thus fortifies protections for speakers and creators, in a First Amendment context, while stimulating future creativity.

These mutually reinforcing linkages between protections for speech and protections for copyright are especially important in today's digital age. The Center for Democracy and Technology's David Sohn, who testified before this Committee to raise concerns about targeting rogue sites — and who does not share all of my views in this area - recently stated a proposition with which I think there can be no serious disagreement: "Large-scale copyright infringement undermines First Amendment values in promoting expression and threatens the growth of new media."

Of course, the evident constitutionality of injunctive relief for copyright violations does not mean that injunctions must automatically or always be issued in response to a copyright violation. As this Committee is well aware, the Supreme Court has recently held to the contrary, warning against the error of a "categorical grant" of injunctive relief for patent infringement in *eBay Inc. v. MercExchange*. The Second Circuit applied that conclusion in a recent, celebrated copyright case, *Salinger v. Colling*. What no court has ever denied is that injunctions are a valuable and constitutional response to copyright violations.

With these foundations in mind—the Internet is not a law-free zone, and copyright law with injunctive relief has always been part of the constitutional framework protecting free speech—I turn to a few priorities worth considering when legislating in this area.

Your hearings are entitled "Promoting Investment and Protecting Commerce Online: Legitimate Sites v. Parasites," drawing an important distinction between two types of sites on the Internet. In the copyright context, legitimate sites distribute work that they own or may legally use through fair use principles, or otherwise, while parasites distribute work that they have stolen. A sound policy to combat infringement must target these infringing websites, without overly burdening legitimate ones. In fact, I think it is fair to say that the primary constitutional questions that must be addressed in shaping legislation in this area revolve around this very distinction: How do we separate infringing sites from legitimate sites? Or, in First Amendment lingo: What is the potential overbreadth of a regulation's impact on speech, and what procedural protections must a regulation provide to satisfy First Amendment norms?

## Potential Overbreadth

It is axiomatic in First Amendment jurisprudence that government restrictions on speech should be narrowly tailored to avoid unnecessarily burdening protected speech.

Courts apply strict scrutiny to statutes that potentially interfere with protected speech, with special scrutiny of rules that may sweep too broadly. This Committee must thus consider the potential overbreadth of any legislation impacting speech, including legislation designed to combat online infringement and piracy. I offer a few questions to consider in doing so, in the context of legislating against online infringement.

First, how does a bill define the requisite level of infringement that the government must prove in order to seek remedies against particular content, or a given site or domain?

In other words, how high is the bar set? A "zero tolerance" policy towards any instances of infringement enforced at the level of a website or domain — where an entire website could be blocked or seized for a single, or just a few, offenses — would plainly raise the most troublesome First Amendment concerns. By contrast, setting a high bar, by statute, can help avoid the risk of unnecessarily burdening protected speech.

The Combating Online Infringements and Counterfeits Act, or "COICA," which was sent to the floor by the Senate Judiciary Committee in the last Congress, provides one potential approach to establishing such a bar. The bill would establish a statutory category of sites that are "dedicated to infringing activities," defined as sites that are "marketed" or "primarily designed" for infringement, or have no other "commercially significant purpose or use" besides infringement. Such infringement is defined under current copyright and trademark law, and which would otherwise be "subject to civil forfeiture." Thus for copyright violations, a site must be "dedicated to infringing activities" and offering goods or services in violation of title 17 U.S.C, or facilitating such violations by means such as downloading, streaming, transmitting or linking. For trademark violations, a site must be "dedicated to infringing activities" and offering, selling or distributing goods, services or counterfeit materials in violation of section 34(d) of the Lanham Act (15 U.S.C. 1116(d)). There are obviously other words that might be used to describe a site subject to regulation in this area, but however phrased, the speech at issue must be overwhelmingly violative of the Copyright Act for any such regulation to be constitutional.

Beyond setting the bar high, another issue is how authorities carry out enforcement actions in a manner that respects First Amendment norms. In an action that drew significant attention, on February 15, 2011, the Homeland Security Department seized several domain names on child pornography charges and accidentally blocked other websites that had not been deliberately targeted. Media reports estimated that up to 84,000 sites were temporarily shut down. Three days after the seizure, the Homeland Security Department acknowledged that it had "inadvertently seized" a "higher level domain name," which impacted other sites, and the department sought to restore those sites "as soon as possible." Such an error, even for a short period of time, is obviously of great concern and it is important to explore how safeguards and technical standards might be effectively incorporated into legislation to prevent or minimize such abuse.

Third, how does a bill compliment or interact with existing remedies against infringement and piracy? Under current copyright law, for example, copyright violations can be remedied by injunctive relief, forfeiture or impoundment. Statutory schemes that follow these approaches, and include their protections and processes under federal precedent, are likely to operate on a clearer, more sound constitutional foundation than remedies that are developed from scratch. Indeed, while the Internet does pose some novel and unique regulatory challenges, Congress should generally aim to apply already existing standards wherever possible, rather than treat cyberspace as a land with laws unto itself.

Fourth, does a bill's remedy focus on combating infringement where it occurs, or does it act as a bar to future, protected speech? Any bill providing injunctive relief should be limited to halting infringement and prohibiting future infringement online, not acting as a prior restraint on protected speech in the future. For example, if a site or domain is seized or blocked for infringement, operators must be free to post all their non-infringing content elsewhere, as well as on their original site, once the infringing content is removed. Indeed, I do not think a court would find constitutional any regulation or order barring individuals from finding ways to use the Internet to post or relocate protected speech.

## Procedural Protections

The Constitution requires due process for all, and the procedural protections afforded to expression, for speakers and listeners alike, carry special weight in First Amendment law. Individuals accused of infringement, by the government or civil litigants, must be afforded notice and an opportunity to be heard. Thus the most straightforward approach in this area, both constitutionally and practically, is to ensure that any new legislation provides the same process and protections that federal litigants currently have when facing the possibility of injunctive remedies.

One way to achieve this aim is to incorporate Rule 65 of the Federal Rules of Civil Procedure into legislative proposals in this area. That would ensure that any injunctive relief against infringing sites is governed by the rules protecting all litigants in civil actions in the United States today. That is the approach of COICA, and while this Committee will make its own, independent judgments about how best to craft a legislative approach to combat infringement, the inclusion of Rule 65 is a worthwhile element in any regulatory framework.

Under Rule 65, courts "may issue a preliminary injunction only on notice to the adverse party." For temporary restraining orders to be issued without notice. Rule 65 requires that two conditions must be met. "[S]pecific facts in an affidavit or verified complaint [must] clearly show that immediate and irreparable injury, loss, or damage will result. . . before the adverse party can be heard in opposition." And "the movant's attorney certifies in writing any efforts made to give notice and the reasons why it should not be required." The rule then requires that hearings for orders without notice are to be held "at the earliest possible time, taking precedence over all other matters," and the adverse party may move to dissolve or modify an order on two days' notice to the moving party. Therefore, a website operator that prefers to respond later, or learned of an action later because the operator did not provide accurate contact information to the registry, would still retain the right to seek later relief from the order.

In the cases of delay caused by the submission of false contact information to a domain registrar, a relevant complication for many infringing and foreign websites, it is worth noting that federal copyright law already treats the knowing submissions of "materially false contact information to a domain name registrar" as a rebuttable presumption of willful infringement. In a similar vein, some operators of infringing websites, including operators abroad, may knowingly decline to participate in U.S. court proceedings. Such a choice, after legitimate notice and procedural safeguards are provided, can lead to ex parte proceedings and default judgments. Courts routinely enter default judgments in civil lawsuits, including comparable online copyright cases. Indeed, under current law, after initial notice has been served, courts have granted permanent injunctive relief for copyright violations in default judgments without additional attempts at notice.

Nonetheless, the ultimate test for any legislation providing injunctive relief is not the words in the statute, but the words of a judge interpreting or passing judgment upon its validity. While a court is empowered to grant injunctions, it need not. While a court is empowered to grant temporary restraining orders, it may not. That does not excuse Congress, of course, from its duties to craft constitutional legislation and carefully weigh the tradeoffs in a given public policy. The irreplaceable role of an independent judicial officer should anchor, however, our reasonable expectation that legislation which provides proper process will ensure website operators accused of infringement and piracy shall be entitled to their day in court. Whether they accept or evade that obligation will be up to them.

## Conclusion

Addressing infringement and piracy in a manner consistent with our constitutional protections for speech is an important and complex challenge. The Senate has already chosen one route, which I believe would be held constitutional, and whether this House chooses to legislate similarly or not, it should plainly take the greatest care to abide by First Amendment norms.

I offer a final thought about the broader debate. I would like to directly acknowledge that potential action by Congress in this area has drawn objections from groups and individuals advocating their deeply held beliefs about civil liberties, human rights and a free Internet, including many groups that I have worked alongside, and for which I have the highest regard. Among a range of objections, however, two core critiques stand out.

First, there is a recurring argument that the United States would be less credible in its criticism of nations that egregiously violate the civil liberties of their citizens if Congress cracks down on rouge websites.

Second, there is the vaguer notion, which I discussed earlier, that stealing is somehow less offensive when carried out online.

Neither of these propositions is correct.

Copyright violations are simply not protected by the First Amendment. Rogue websites, which live off theft and are plainly dedicated to infringement and piracy, are not engaging in speech that any civilized, let alone freedom-oriented, nation protects. That these infringing activities occur on the Internet makes them not less, but more harmful. The fear that by combating these specific acts through legislation, the United States would compromise its role as the world leader in advancing a free and universal Internet seems to me insupportable. As a matter of both constitutional law and public policy, the United States must remain committed to defending both the right to speak and the ability to protect one's intellectual creations. Legislation designed to enforce old laws in a new, wired era does not thwart the constitutional right to engage in speech. Quite the opposite. It protects creators of speech, as Congress has since this Nation was founded, by combating its theft.

Mr. Goodlatte. Thank you, Mr. Abrams.

Mr. Walker, welcome.

## TESTIMONY OF KENT WALKER, SENIOR VICE PRESIDENT AND GENERAL COUNSEL, GOOGLE

Mr. Walker. Thank you, Mr. Chairman, Ranking Member Watt, Mr. Chairman, Mr. Ranking Member, Members of the Committee.

As you have mentioned, Mr. Chairman, before I joined Google, I was a Federal prosecutor. As an Assistant United States Attorney, I prosecuted cybercrime. I brought some of the first cases against criminal copyright enforcement in the country. I recognize the challenges and the difficulties of protecting intellectual property online.

The legal issues that we will discuss today are complex and challenging. They require thoughtful approaches to preserve and enhance the benefits of the Internet for consumers and businesses in America and the world. And Google is dedicated to addressing issues of online copyright infringement and counterfeiting. We know that the future growth and the success of our industry relies on fighting the bad guys who break the law. And we stand ready to support further enforcement measures against rogue foreign websites, focusing on financial transactions and advertising where those measures are appropriate and narrowly targeted against the worst of the worst foreign websites, in line with Mr. Abrams' comments this morning.

We do have concerns, however, about extending new law to dictate natural search results. We would like to work together to ensure that these efforts are effective, while not harming legitimate services and technologies that drive U.S. economic growth and our country's leadership in the global information economy.

Let me share several ways that Google combats copyright infringement and counterfeiting and then discuss principles for how to address rogue foreign websites.

At YouTube as, Mr. Chairman, you recognized, we designed a powerful tool that rights holders use to block or monetize infringing content. Our content ID system, developed using 50,000 engineering hours at a cost of over $30 million, scans every video uploaded to YouTube and typically within seconds compares it against more than 4 million reference files provided by rightsholders. Today over 1,000 media companies, including every major U.S. studio and record label, use content ID, and most of them choose to monetize rather than to block the content. This shows the win-win possibilities that Internet technologies can bring, getting money to rightsholders and innovative services to users.

When it comes to online services like our search engine, a major part of the explosive growth of the Internet in the United States and around the world is due to the strong legal foundation created by Congress in the Digital Millennium Copyright Act. Last year, Google processed over 3 million DMCA takedowns across our products, including search. These came from copyright owners of all sorts from big movie studios to small publishers of needlepoint patterns. And currently Google engineers are building new tools so we can act on reliable copyright takedown requests on our search engine within 24 hours. We are already testing the new tool with a content industry partner and we hope to invite other partners into that test in the weeks ahead.

When copyright owners tell us about infringement, we disable access to the infringing content whether that content comes from foreign or domestic sources. The shared responsibility of the DMCA works. It assures that online platforms like Google or Facebook or Twitter will not face crippling liability when users post comments or files to online sites. And as we committed last year, we are already excluding several piracy-related terms from appearing in "autocomplete," a feature on Google that predicts queries as users type. And we have asked content industry representatives to provide other terms for consideration.

Turning to our advertising programs, in AdSense we prohibit ads on infringing web pages and we use automated and manual review to weed out abuse. Last year alone, we took action on our own initiative against over 12,000 sites for violating that policy.

To address counterfeiting our policies ban selling ads to advertisers who market counterfeit goods, and they always have. We use automated tools to prevent violations of our policies, and last year alone, we invested over $60 million in these efforts. After all, a Google user who is duped by a fake good is less likely to click on another Google ad. So the integrity of the sponsored links on our sites is of paramount importance to us. In the last 6 months of 2010 alone, we shut down 50,000 accounts for attempting to advertise counterfeit goods, and 95 percent of those shutdowns came not as a result of a complaint but as a result of our own efforts. While it sounds like a lot—and it is—the legitimate complaints we received concerned less than one-quarter of 1 percent of advertisers.

We have also committed to an average response time of 24 hours to handle counterfeit complaints involving sponsored links, and that too is in process and should be rolling out fairly soon.

So finally, as you address the challenge of rogue foreign sites, I would ask that you keep in mind the following three points.

First, aim squarely at the worst of the worst foreign websites without hurting legitimate technologies and businesses. We agree with the goal of going after websites that are outside the reach of U.S. law and whose main purpose is commercial infringement. Procedural safeguards are critical, though, to ensure due process and to avoid mistakes costing legitimate businesses the use of their domain names.

Second, don't rewrite the DMCA and existing law that works. Businesses benefit from stable and predictable rules with clear standards. Targeted legislation to address rogue foreign websites must not inadvertently dismantle the legal framework that America's technology companies and innovators rely upon. The DMCA strikes the right balance between thwarting infringement and preserving free speech and we should build upon it, not undermine it.

Third and last, tailor intermediary obligations appropriately. Let me repeat Google is open to working with the Subcommittee on additional enforcement tools. Search engines already remove infringement by domestic and foreign sources, so we think it is right for additional measures to focus on financial transaction providers and advertising services, both of which Google provides. But any legislation should avoid a private right of action that would invite shakedowns against companies making good faith efforts to comply with the law.

To sum up, these are complex issues. We need to address the enforcement problems, while protecting the overwhelmingly positive benefits of the Internet for our country and the world. And we look forward to working with each of you to do just that.

Thank you very much.

[The prepared statement of Mr. Walker follows:]

## TESTIMONY OF KENT WALKER, SENIOR VICE PRESIDENT AND GENERAL COUNSEL GOOGLE INC., BEFORE THE HOUSE JUDICIARY SUBCOMMITTEE ON INTELLECTUAL PROPERTY, COMPETITION, AND THE INTERNET HEARING ON "PROMOTING INVESTMENT AND PROTECTING COMMERCE ONLINE: LEGITIMATE SITES V. PARASITES, PART II," APRIL 6, 2011

Thank you Chairman Goodlatte, Ranking Member Watt, and members of the Subcommittee for this opportunity to testify.

I am Google's Senior Vice President and General Counsel. As a former federal prosecutor, I am well aware of the need to enforce laws against the infringement of intellectual property rights, the complexities of such cases, and the fact that the internet can be used for unlawful purposes, often by sophisticated criminals. As an assistant U.S. Attorney in San Francisco, I specialized in cybercrime and brought one of the first criminal copyright infringement cases in the country. I was also involved in the successful prosecution of a prominent computer hacker.

Google supports developing effective policy and technology tools to combat large-scale commercial infringement. As I'll describe below, Google has dedicated tens of millions of dollars in engineering and other resources to help weed out notorious bad actors. But such activity- accounts for only a very small percentage overall of the creative, political, social, and commercial opportunities created and empowered by the web. As this Subcommittee considers new enforcement tools against rogue foreign websites, it should not jeopardize the legitimate Internet services and technologies that underlie the United States' lead in the global information economy.

My testimony will focus on three main points. First, I will underscore how the internet is a critical driver of American economic growth and job creation, and offers enormous benefits to creators. Second, 1 will highlight the many ways in which Google leads the industry in helping to combat copyright infringement and the sale of counterfeit goods online. Finally, I offer recommendations for addressing the exceedingly complex challenge of rogue foreign websites.

## The Internet Drives U.S. Economic Growth and Delivers Enormous Benefits to Creators

Internet technologies are used every- day in amazing and perfectly legal ways. Without question, the information technology industry is the fastest growing business sector in the world, regularly experiencing double-digit growth and accounting for nearly one-fourth of our nation's real GDP growth. The Internet adds an estimated $2 trillion to annual GDP. Interactive advertising alone is responsible for $300 billion of economic activity in the U.S., employing 3.1 million Americans.

For just over a decade, Google has invested in the power of the Internet to bring groundbreaking new services and technologies to millions of users around the world. Today we have more than 24,000 employees worldwide, and we recently announced that 2011 will be the biggest hiring year in our company's history. We offer search, advertising, and other products that help other businesses thrive. In 2009, for example, Google estimated that our search and advertising tools generated $54 billion in economic activity in the U.S. alone.

But the Internet is about much more than just Google or other leading U.S. Internet companies like Facebook, Twitter, Amazon, and eBay. The Internet has been a boon to businesses of every kind and size across the country. The efficiencies of the web reduce transaction costs for suppliers and consumers in every sector, while creating entirely new markets. Thanks to the Internet, it's never been easier to start a business and reach a wide audience. More than a million small and large advertisers use Google as a platform to find customers in an increasingly global marketplace—from Twiddy, a vacation rental business in North Carolina that attributes recent growth and job creation to Google's advertising tools, to two brothers in Austin Texas who use Google to grow loyalty and demand for premium YETI Coolers, certified to withstand smashing by hungry grizzly bears.

The innovations brought about by the Internet economy have also delivered enormous benefits to content creators. Google empowers traditional artists and an emerging generation of new creators to promote their work to a global audience. Google drives traffic to creators' websites, sending, for example, four billion clicks a month to news sites. Every minute, users upload 35 hours of video content to our YouTube site. YouTube has allowed performers to rocket from oblivion to fame; has given politicians, pundits, and protesters a powerful new way to communicate; has facilitated citizen journalism; and has inspired laughter at the antics of dancing babies.

From its startup phase in 2005, YouTube is now monetizing for content owners over 3 billion video views per week. We create revenue for more than 20,000 partners, including mainstream media companies like ABC and Univision and individual members of the YouTube partner program, hundreds of whom are making more than six figures a year. Record labels are now making millions of dollars a month on YouTube. Today over 1,000 media companies—including every major U.S. network broadcaster, movie studio, and record label—use the copyright protection tools that YouTube offers, and a majority of them choose to monetize rather than block their content online.

With the explosive growth of the Internet and skyrocketing demand for Internet-enabled devices, companies that rely on important limitations built into U.S. copyright law have risen quickly to become a central foundation of the American economy. Innovation-friendly limitations and exceptions, principally fair use and the safe harbors of the Digital Millennium Copyright Act (DMCA), work alongside copyright's exclusive rights to foster an unprecedented level of creativity and expression that fuels the economy. It is no exaggeration to note that the DMCA set the legal foundation for e-commerce, The Computer and Communications Industry Association has found that industries that rely on fair use and other limitations generate $4.7 trillion in revenue, represent one sixth of total U.S. GDP, and support 17 million jobs. While online piracy remains a serious enforcement problem, we should not lose sight of the overall balance of our nation's copyright law, which continues to spur a broad array of American-bred creativity and innovation.

## How Google Protects Copyright

Google believes strongly in protecting copyright and other intellectual property rights. We understand that despite the overwhelmingly positive and legitimate uses of

Internet services and technologies there will be some who misuse these for infringing purposes. Google invests millions of dollars in engineering and other resources to help rightholders fight this misuse. Across our search engine and hosted products, we remove or disable access to millions of infringing materials each year at the request of copyright owners. We also voluntarily take several steps well beyond our legal obligations.

Google has been an Industry-leader in developing innovative measures to protect copyright and help rightsholders control their content offline. To date, Google has expended more than 50,000 engineering hours and more than $30 million to develop Content ID, our cutting-edge copyright protection tool that is helping rightsholders make money on YouTube. This powerful technology scans every video uploaded to YouTube and, within seconds, compares it against more than 4 million reference files provided by participating rightsholders. Copyright holders and their advocates—from the MPAA to NBC to Warner -Music—have praised YouTube as a bright light in copyright protection.

We are also working on other major voluntary initiatives to help protect copyright. We committed last year to prevent terms that are closely associated with piracy from appearing in Autocomplete. Without altering search results, Autocomplete is a. feature that algorithmically predicts and displays queries as users type based on what other users have typed. We have begun working to prevent several piracy-related terms from appearing in Autocomplete, and have asked content industry representatives to suggest other terms for consideration that, won't, overly restrict legitimate speech. We are also hard at work on a new initiative to make authorized preview music content appear more readily in search results.

With the flexibility to innovate on top of baseline legal regimes like the DMCA's notice and takedown process, Google is able to design these extra efforts in ways that help both rightsholders and users, encouraging more people to search, find, and enjoy the legitimate offerings available on the web.

Like all Internet companies, the critical foundation tor our anti-piracy efforts remains the DMCA, the seminal law Congress passed in 1998 to address copyright protection online and promote the worldwide expansion of e-commerce. Congress rightly understood that some material posted by the millions of people who use online services infringes copyright, and that online service providers in the ordinary course of their operations engage in copying and other acts that expose them to potential copyright liability. Congress also recognized that requiring online providers to engage in pre-screening of every user-posted text, picture, and video would inhibit free expression and stifle the growth of the Internet.

Through the DMCA, Congress established a notice-and-takedown process that provides copyright owners expeditious recourse when they discover infringement online while also giving online service providers the certainty necessary to invest in Internet services and technologies. The careful balance struck by the DMCA created the legal infrastructure for the Internet we know today. The DMCA safe harbors make possible online platforms like eBay, Amazon, YouTube, Facebook, and Twitter, which in turn have unleashed new sources of creativity, economic development, and jobs.

The DMCA's shared responsibility approach works. Copyright holders identify infringement and, if they choose, request its removal. Upon notification, online service providers like Google remove or disable access to the infringing material. This approach makes sense, as only copyright holders know what material they own, what they have licensed, and where they want their works to appear online. Service providers cannot by themselves determine whether a given use is infringing. A text, song, image, or video can infringe copyright in the context of one site but be legal on another, through license or in the context of criticism, political speech, or other legally protected use. Even copyright owners themselves sometimes have trouble determining whether a use of their content is infringing.

Copyright owners in 2010 called on Google to disable access to approximately 3 million allegedly infringing materials across all our products, which accounts for far less than 1% of all the materials hosted and indexed by Google. We received takedown notices by letter, fax, email, and web forms from all sorts of copyright owners including movie studios, record labels, adult entertainment vendors, and needlepoint pattern publishers, from 70 countries and in a wide variety of languages. We maintain a growing team of employees dedicated to receiving, reviewing, and responding to DMCA notices. We check to make sure that the notices are complete and are not attempts by competitors or others to use invalid copyright claims to censor speech with which they disagree.

Last December, I announced that we will invest even more resources to streamline the DMCA submission process. We are designing new tools that will enable us to act on reliable copyright takedown requests within 24 hours. That initiative is well underway, and we have already invested significant engineering resources. The new tool for Web Search is already being tested with a content industry partner, and the Blogger tool will begin resting next month. We are also in the process of improving our transparency efforts to notify site owners and our users when content has been removed as a result of allegations of infringement.

We also employ a wide array of procedures and expend considerable financial resources to prevent our advertising products from being used to monetize material that infringes copyright. For example, our AdSense program enables website publishers to display ads (identified by the "ads by Google" footer) alongside their content. Our policies prohibit the use of this program tor infringing sites, and we use automated and manual review to weed out abuse. Last year, we took action on our own initiative against nearly 12,000 sites for violating this policy. We also respond swiftly when notified by rightsholders. We recently agreed to improve our, AdSense anti-piracy review procedures and are working together with rightsholders on better ways to identify websites that violate our policies.

We are also helping to lead industry-wide solutions through our work with the Interactive Advertising Bureau (IAB), comprised of more than 460 leading media and technology companies. The IAB has established quality assurance guidelines through which participating advertising companies will take standardized steps to enhance buyer control over the placement and context of advertising and build brand safety. Last week, Google certified its compliance with these guidelines.

Despite the best efforts of the online advertising industry, proactive measures will never be a complete solution. Some publishers deliberately take steps to evade detection systems, meaning bad sites will invariably slip through. Technologically sophisticated players use tactics like "cloaking" (showing one version of their site to the public and a different version to Google) to evade the protections that Google and other companies put in place. Because of these tactics, coupled with the sheer volume of ads served per day, finding a particular ad on the web that has circumvented our systems may not always be possible. While the industry is aggressively going after this abuse, it is clearly a cat-and-mouse game to stay technologically ahead of the bad actors, and Google is committed to being an industry leader in eradicating this behavior.

## How Google Helps Combat Counterfeiting

Just as in the offline world, people misuse legitimate online services to try to market counterfeit goods. This abuse hurts our users and our business; combating it is central to Google's operations. The integrity and quality of the sponsored links displayed alongside Google search results are of paramount importance to our overall success. A Google user duped by a fake good is less likely to click on another Google ad in the future. For this reason, Google undertakes enormous efforts to root out ads for sites that sell counterfeit goods.

Google has clear policies against advertising counterfeit goods, and we expend considerable resources to enforce those policies. In the last six months of 2010, we shut down approximately 50,000 accounts for attempting to use sponsored links to advertise counterfeit goods, and more than 95% of these accounts were discovered through our own detection efforts. Even more ads themselves were blocked on suspicion of policy violations. Our automated tools analyze thousands of signals to help prevent bad ads from being shown in sponsored links. Last year alone we invested $60 million in efforts to prevent violations of our ad policies.

But there is no silver bullet. It's a whack-a-mole problem, as we constantly work to improve our practices against sophisticated entities trying to game our protections. While Google's tools are quite effective, it is incredibly difficult for Google to identify a counterfeit product being advertised, this is a challenging task, even for brand owners. Online advertising companies, which do not take possession of the good, cannot know for sure whether any particular item out of millions advertised is indeed a counterfeit. As has always been the case with newspapers and offline advertising platforms, it is essentially impossible for Google to block all attempted abuse.

But we are nevertheless doing our part. We have a fast and easy complaint form for brand owners to notify us of ads for potentially counterfeit goods. Last month, Google announced that for brand owners who use this form responsibly, we will commit to an average response time of 24 hours or less. Brand owner feedback is an important way in which we improve our systems—as we get more data about bad ads, we get better at counteracting the new ways that bad actors try to game the system.

Similarly, we have clear policies against placing Google ads on third-party sites that sell or promote counterfeit goods. As a practical matter we receive very few complaints from brand owners about this problem. Still, to ensure that our practices continue to scale as the Web grows, we have recently committed to working more closely with brand owners to identify violators.

Google also regularly cooperates with a wide array of law enforcement authorities, including working with officials to combat counterfeiting, for instance, an enforcement manager at Rosetta Stone has thanked Google employees for providing him and the Secret Service with tremendous assistance that led to solving a $100,000 fraud case. Google's Trust & Safety team also has trained thousands of law enforcement officials on evolving investigative techniques on the web and emerging trends that Google is seeing, all of which aid in law enforcement efforts.

## The Complexities of Rogue Foreign Sites

Google understands the Subcommittee's desire to consider additional ways to combat rogue foreign websites that traffic in infringing goods yet are outside the reach of U.S. legal process. We urge the Subcommittee to seek input from a broad base of stakeholders and avoid approaches that threaten the growth of new technologies that benefit rightsholders and consumers in an increasingly social, mobile, and inter-connected world. We support increased international cooperation among governments to enforce the law, recognizing that unilateral domestic enforcement tactics are limited in their effectiveness and may risk retaliation against legitimate American businesses by other countries.

Policymakers should aim squarely at the 'worst-of-the-worst" foreign websites without ensnaring legitimate technologies and businesses. Additional enforcement tools should target only those websites that are outside the reach of U.S. legal process and whose main purpose is commercial infringement, where U.S. legal process is capable of reaching a particular website or a site consents to such jurisdiction, new causes of action are unnecessary and will lead to actions that overlap or are potentially inconsistent with existing law.

Defining what is a rogue site is not a simple task. Technology advances often lead to evolving areas of copyright law, as courts sort out the application of common law doctrines to new technologies. An overbroad definition of a rogue site could easily ensnare millions of popular U.S, websites that allow users to sell goods or upload content. Websites that responsibly respond to takedown notices and comply with the DMCA should not be deemed rogue. Procedural safeguards should ensure sufficient due process to avoid mistakes costing legitimate businesses the use of their domain name, which, for e-commerce companies, could very well mean their livelihood.

New legislation should not alter common law secondary liability principles or undermine the DMCA. Targeted legislation addressing rogue foreign websites must not inadvertently dismantle the legal framework upon which America's technology innovators rely. New legislation should not change common law principles of secondary liability or rewrite existing laws like the DMCA. For example, if *in rem* court orders are allowed against rogue foreign websites, the existence of such orders should not be used in civil cases to undermine DMCA safe harbors or increase the risk of secondary liability. Without expressly addressing this overlap, new approaches threaten to reach a much broader array of intermediaries than those directly served with a court order. The DMCA has a practical and real effect in thwarting infringement, and legislation that targets "the worst of the worst" should not increase liability for online services that are playing by the rules.

The DMCA strikes the right balance for search engines. By removing infringing material from domestic and foreign sources, the DMCA's notice-and-takedown process strikes the right balance among the interests of rightsholders, internet users, and intermediaries like search engines, social networks and the vast other ways in which people find and link to information online. The DMCA has a proven 12-year track record as a fast, efficient tool for notifying online services that contain links that lead to infringing material, and it works. Through a process much simpler than obtaining an *in rem* court order, rightsholders send notices and search engines disable links to that infringing material. The DMCA already allows copyright owners to target every link to any infringing material online, and numerous entities assist them with that task.

Google users (including rightsholders searching for infringement) count on Google's Web Search to be as comprehensive as possible, serving as an index that accurately reflects the full range of what is lawfully available on the World Wide Web. No search engine or other high-volume web platform is in a position to determine which uses are authorized, which are unobjectionable, or what qualifies as a fair use. Even copyright owners themselves find the task difficult. The good news is that a vibrant industry in online enforcement has sprung up, with companies making the process of locating infringing material taster and cheaper for rightsholders.

When it comes to offshore rogue sites, no one should think that imposing additional obligations on search engines, social networks, directories, or bloggers beyond the

DMCA will be a panacea. If the site remains on the web, neither search engines nor social networks nor the numerous other intermediaries through which users post links can prevent Internet users from talking about, linking to, or referencing the existence of the site. These links or references will themselves appear in search results, and will enable users to reach the site. Simply put, search engines are not in a position to censor the entire Internet, deleting every mention of the existence of a site. If a rogue site remains accessible on the Internet, relying on search engines to try to make it "unfindable" is an impossible endeavor. Even if such a thing were possible for American search engines and other web servers, it would simply spur the growth of offshore search engines like Baidu that do not comply with American law. We have always tried to provide users with a comprehensive picture of what is available on the Internet, which is a core principle that has led people around the world to trust the integrity of America's search engines.

Legislation must not interfere with the health and stability of the Internet. Recent focus on using the domain name system (DNS) to police against undesired activity must be carefully weighed against its limited effectiveness and the significant implications for core American values such as innovation and freedom of expression. Even if service providers block domain names through DNS interference, the site will remain reachable through its IP address, browser plug-in software, alternative DNS providers, or other means. But the DNS blocking itself could affect the Internet's reliability, security, and performance.

Policymakers should foreclose private rights of action and tailor intermediary requirements appropriately. Any obligations put upon payment providers or advertising services to address rogue foreign websites must be reasonable, technically feasible, and appropriately tailored. Given the evasive tactics bad actors employ to avoid detection, no intermediary will be able to prevent all abuse of its systems, and efforts to legislate must be careful not to hold intermediaries responsible for abuses of their systems that could not reasonably be prevented. Legislation should not include a private right of action that would invite suits by "trolls" to extort settlements from intermediaries or sites who are making good faith efforts to comply with the law.

Policymakers should dismantle barriers to licensing to encourage greater proliferation of compelling legal offerings for copyrighted works online. We encourage the Subcommittee to promote the creation of more innovative legitimate offerings in the marketplace that will harness the power of the Internet to compensate rightsholders. Numerous thorny issues still impede the efficient licensing of digital music—a thicket of licensing obstacles prevents consumers from buying lawful goods online and stops services from offering innovations that would benefit rightsholders and users alike. Yet, it is without question that attractive legal options for satisfying consumer demand in a timely, easy, and convenient way will reduce incentives to rely on illegal sources. Internet services are rapidly moving to cloud computing models, and policymakers should encourage content creators to embrace this technological trend at an early stage.

In the past several years, Congress has passed significant enforcement-related legislative measures while other bills aimed at fostering the growth of licensed services did not become law. Too often copyright initiatives impart ever-increasing penalties without clear evidence that such penalties put real money in artists' pockets. We urge the Subcommittee to turn its attention to market-creating measures that will encourage compelling legal offerings for users, make a proven difference in artist revenues, and incentivize the kind of innovation that is needed for our country's future. Licensing reform has the potential to do that.

## Conclusion

Google agrees with the need to fight online infringement. There is of course no silver bullet, no one-size-fits-all umbrella solution. Rather, we urge the Subcommittee to carefully review and tailor measures to address rogue foreign websites without impairing legitimate technologies, innovative businesses, and lawful speech. At a time when the. United States leads the global information economy, with Internet freedom a cornerstone of U.S. foreign policy, we must carefully consider how policies against foreign websites could set international precedents and undermine innovation, e-commerce, and freedom of expression the world over. Issues of jurisdiction and enforcement remedies for Internet-based activities affect matters well beyond intellectual property rights. We must work together to target the "worst-of-the-worst" rogue foreign websites without unintentionally impeding legitimate interests of those innovating and using online services to drive economic growth and global freedom.

Mr. Goodlatte. Thank you, Mr. Walker.

Ms. Jones, we are pleased to have your testimony.

## TESTIMONY OF CHRISTINE N. JONES, EXECUTIVE VICE PRESIDENT AND GENERAL COUNSEL, GO DADDY GROUP

Ms. Jones. Good morning. Chairman Goodlatte. Thanks so much for the opportunity to be heard today.

You know, we put a lot of time and energy into getting rid of bad actors from other Internet at Go Daddy. So we sincerely appreciate that you guys have made parasites a priority for the Subcommittee this Congress.

And I also want to extend my personal thanks to Ranking Member Watt and Chairman Smith and Ranking Member Conyers of the full Committee as well and, frankly, all the Members of the Subcommittee because I spend a lot of my personal time on these issues not because I have to but because I think it is the right thing to do. Let me tell you it is nice to know that I have an ally in this fight because sometimes we feel like we are out there all by ourselves.

Having worked closely with law enforcement, the intellectual property community, and others on a wide variety of issues related to parasites, it is clear to me that we still have a long way to go. I will be the first to admit there is no silver bullet—no silver bullet. It doesn't exist. Just like in offline crimes, it appears there will always be bad guys on the Internet. That is a stark reality we all must face. And although some of us have done a lot, there is still a lot more that some can do. So let's talk about what that looks like.

We have had great success in the past with a hybrid approach to illegal content. That means voluntary industry cooperation on the one hand among all of the industry players accompanied by targeted, specific Federal legislation designed to protect the companies that are doing the right thing, but provide a consequence for those who do not.

We have used this approach in addressing child pornography, for example, to great effect, and Go Daddy and Google recently worked together with the White House Intellectual Property Enforcement Coordinator to gather representatives from all of the major industry players to address rogue online pharmacies. We feel like we are making progress there as well. That effort resulted in the formation of a group known as the Center for Safe Internet Pharmacies. That group's mission is to share information among all of the players, work together to terminate services for illegal online drug sellers. Whatever your service is, if you are a payment card provider, if you are a paid advertising provider, if you are a domain name registrar, whatever it is, turn off your services. We feel like that hybrid approach there is going to make it possible for us to address a significant number of illegal drug sellers who operate online today.

So we support that type of hybrid approach to address a variety of types of criminal activity such as child abuse, rogue pharmacies, spam, phishing, identity theft, intellectual property infringement, terrorism, hate speech, on and on and on. We think it works in all of those situations.

Of course, it is always just as important to focus on enforcement as it is to enact new legislation. To do that, we would suggest a few simple things. I think Ranking Member Conyers mentioned this in his statement, that is, follow the money, and shut down all of the choke points in the system because we have to disincentivize the bad actors. So in the IP context, for example, we would take away the ability to search for, pay for, ship, and make money from selling stolen or counterfeit goods, but we have to do that while encouraging new innovation and research and development. One thing we know is that the better we get, the better we get. That means we have to think of things we can hardly even imagine right now.

So what happens, for instance, in the case of cyberlockers or infringing mobile applications or whatever infringement is going to come up that is invented in the future? If we establish a set of rules and procedures such as the DMCA which can be applied to a wide array of situations, we can possibly address those things that aren't, as if they were.

None of us can predict the next big thing. I mean, who knows what is the next eBay or AOL or Netscape or Go Daddy or Google or Twitter? Who knows? Not so long ago, there was a monopoly for selling domain names. Nobody had ever heard of an Internet browser or even a search engine. The term "social media" didn't exist. It is common understanding now. And not too long from now, there is going to be another idea like that that nobody has ever heard of We have to think in terms of concepts rather than URL's or domain names or IP addresses or whatever to make legislation that is designed to outlast the current ideas.

And because these issues reach outside our borders, we should all take steps to bind our foreign affiliates to the actions that we take here in the United States.

A huge number of our customers make a living operating online businesses. That is how they make their money. And their ability to continue to do so is very important to us. We would challenge our counterparts in the Internet ecosystem to do what we do at Go Daddy, that is, to voluntarily take action against the people that we know to be using our system for illicit purposes, and that includes registrars, registries, hosting providers, payment processors, shippers, ISP's, search engines, online advertising providers and, oh, by the way, whoever joins the community next, whoever that is. We challenge them all to make the same commitment.

And I would submit that unless and until we provide a consequence for the businesses that facilitate criminals in their system, there will always be a safe harbor, a place where crooks can go to engage in crimes online, and we must fix that hole in the fence.

Thank you very much for the time.

[The prepared statement of Ms. Jones follows:]

Go Daddy®.com

## BEFORE THE UNITED STATES HOUSE OF REPRESENTATIVES COMMITTEE ON THE JUDICIARY, SUBCOMMITTEE ON INTELLECTUAL PROPERTY, COMPETITION AND THE INTERNET, HEARING ON "PROMOTING INVESTMENT AND PROTECTING COMMERCE ONLINE: LEGITIMATE SITES V. PARASITES, PART II," STATEMENT OF CHRISTINE N. JONES, EXECUTIVE VICE-PRESIDENT, GENERAL COUNSEL, AND CORPORATE SECRETARY THE GO DADDY GROUP, INC., APRIL 6, 2011

### Introduction

Good morning, Chairman Goodlatte, and thank you for the honor of speaking before you today on the critical issue of combating illegal and nefarious activity on the Internet. I would also like to extend my thanks and appreciation to Ranking Member Watt, Chairman Smith, and Ranking Member Conyers, as well as the other Members of the Committee, for all your efforts in addressing this important issue.

The Go Daddy Group devotes considerable time and resources to working with law enforcement to preserve the integrity and safety of the Internet by quickly closing down websites and domain names engaged in illegal activities. A vast number of our customers earn their livelihood from the successful businesses they have been able to establish and grow online, and their ability to continue to do so is of paramount importance to us. Go Daddy is committed to doing everything it can to ensure that the Internet is a safe and trustworthy way to communicate and conduct business. We challenge our counterparts on the Internet to make the same commitment.

### Background

The Go Daddy Group, Inc. consists of eight ICANN-accredited domain name registrars, including GoDaddy.com. Go Daddy currently has over 47 million domain names under management, and is the number one domain name registrar in the world. In fact, we register domain names at a rate of more than one per second. We are also the world's largest website hosting provider - we currently provide hosting services for more than 5 million websites. Our 50+ additional products and services, including SSL certificates, website builders, and online business tools, are all focused toward helping our customers establish a trusted presence on the Internet.

A domain name registrar serves as the point of entry to the Internet. For example, if you wanted to register the domain name www.ChairmanGoodlatte.com. you could go to www.GoDaddy.com to register that domain name. A domain name registrar is different from a traditional ISP, such as AOL, MSN, or EarthLink. The ISP provides access to the Internet whereas the registrar provides the registration service for com names and the like. In short, in exchange for a fee, the ISP provides the means by which an Internet user connects to the Internet via a dial-up connection, cable modem, DSL, or other connection method. A registrar, on the other hand, enables Internet users to establish a web presence by registering a unique name such as www.ChairmanGoodlatte.com.

A domain name registrar also differs from a domain name registry, in that the registry acts as the database of all domain names that are registered for a particular top-level domain, or "TLD." TLDs are the suffix that appears to the right of the "dot" in a particular domain name - in www.ChairmanGoodlatte.com the TLD is ".com." There are dozens of registries that have received authorization from ICANN to offer particular TLDs, such as .com, .net, .biz, .info, etc. Registrars such as Go Daddy enter into agreements with the various registries to offer the TLDs that are managed by those registries.

Once www.ChairmanGoodlatte.com is registered, you might decide that you want to direct your domain name to a website that contains content, such as items for sale, a blog, news articles, or the like. In order to create and maintain a website on which to store your content, you would need to find a place to store, or "host," that website. Again, you could go to www.GoDaddy.com for content storage, or hosting, services. A hosting provider differs from a traditional ISP in that the hosting provider supplies space on a computer server that is accessible from the Internet, rather than access to the server, which is provided by the ISP.

***How Go Daddy Works to Combat Illegal Activity on the Internet***

Go Daddy has made it a high priority to use its position as the world's largest registrar and hosting provider to make the Internet a better and safer place. As such, we have a large 24/7 Abuse Department whose mission is to preserve the integrity and safety of Go Daddy's network by investigating and shutting down websites and domain names engaged in illegal activities. We work with law enforcement agencies at all levels and routinely assist in a wide variety of criminal and civil investigations. We are also quick to respond to public complaints of spam, phishing, pharming, and online fraud, and work closely with anti-fraud and security groups such as the Anti-Phishing Working Group, Digital Phish Net, the National Center for Missing and Exploited Children, and CyberTipLine. We take each instance of illegal activity very seriously and devote high priority to ensuring that websites containing any kind of illegal content - so-called "Parasites" — are removed from our network

As recent examples of our enforcement and takedown activities, we worked with the United Kingdom's Metropolitan Police Service to shut down or redirect nearly 200 domain names and websites used to sell counterfeit merchandise, including clothing, shoes and jewelry. We also recently worked with the Federal Bureau of Investigation to disable the domain names of more than two dozen overseas websites that were selling counterfeit Tiffany & Co. jewelry. We are currently involved in an investigation by the Computer Crime Division of Scotland Yard to shut down websites that sell counterfeit tickets to sporting events. To date, we have successfully disabled access to approximately 60 such websites by redirecting their domain names. There are, of course, many more past and ongoing examples which would not be appropriate to disclose in this context.

We also continue to lead the charge to stop the proliferation of rogue online pharmacies and websites selling counterfeit medications. In 2010 alone we worked with the Federal Drug Administration and the U.S. Drug Enforcement Agency to investigate and take down over 36,000 such websites.

**The Domain Name Registration Process**

The domain name registration system is entirely automated. There is no human intervention into the process. Because many words have multiple meanings and combinations of words can be used for both legitimate and illegitimate purposes, no domain names are automatically prohibited from registration. As mentioned above. Go Daddy registers a domain name at a rate of more than one per second. This makes it virtually impossible for a human being to verify the legitimate use of every domain name registration, particularly on an ongoing basis. To compensate for this, we have developed a notification system for reporting instances of all types of network abuse to our internal Abuse Department.

**The Notification Process**

With over 47 million domain names under management, most of our data come from third-party complaints or notices. The Go Daddy Abuse Department can receive information that ParaSites may be residing on our network in several ways: 1) direct complaint from a third-party via email, 2) direct complaint via telephone; 3) tip from Go Daddy employees who have either become aware of, or suspect the existence of, illegal content on a customer site; and, 4) notifications from CyberTipLine and other "watchdog" groups.

**The Investigation Process**

Once Go Daddy is made aware that a potential ParaSite is registered through one of our companies, we immediately investigate to determine whether there is in fact illegal content associated with the domain name, such as Scheduled drugs for sale without a prescription or child pornography (hereafter, "CP"), on the site. If so, we determine whether that customer has other domain names resolving to the ParaSite, and whether there are other ParaSites in the customer's account. In some cases, Internet users can only access ParaSites (such as sites containing CP) by supplying a paid-for membership user name and password. While we cannot investigate content that requires payment to access, we do investigate all web pages found to be freely accessible to Internet users without a user name and password for any site that we suspect is a ParaSite.

After we determine that there is content meeting the criteria for classification as a ParaSite, we archive a screenshot (in the case of a registered domain) and all or partial content (in the case of a hosted site) sufficient to demonstrate evidence of illegal activity for future use in law enforcement investigations.

**The Suspension Process**

After domain names, websites, and registrant information have been investigated and determined to be associated with illegal activity, we permanently suspend our services. It is important to note that domain names are not suspended prior to investigation, especially where domain names are not associated with an active website. It is very difficult for us to suspend a domain name before it is associated with an active website because many words have multiple uses. In addition, if there is no ParaSite associated with a particular domain name, there is no reason to suspend the domain name itself because there is nothing unlawful about a domain name, in and of itself.

**Our Results**

Go Daddy has documented proof that our efforts to preserve the safety and integrity of the Internet work. We investigate hundreds of thousands of domain names and websites each year for illegal activity. In 2010, we conducted approximately 672,000 investigations, involving approximately 40,000 unique customers.

The number of domain names and websites investigated each year is much higher than the number of unique customers investigated. This is because one unique customer may have many domain names. Many times, one customer will have literally hundreds of domain names in its account. In those cases, we suspend all the ParaSites associated with the customer's account, not just the ones about which we receive a complaint or notification. In 2010 alone, Go Daddy suspended approximately 150,000 websites found to be engaged in illegal or malicious activity.

Importantly, these numbers are skewed slightly lower because many times when Go Daddy is the registrar, but not the hosting provider, ParaSites have already been removed by the hosting provider by the time we conduct our investigation. This is a result of third-party complaints being sent to both the domain name registrar and the hosting provider at the same time, and illustrates the efficient results that can be obtained by providing concurrent notifications to all the Internet ecosystem players. We are, of course, very grateful when our fellow Internet companies take complaints of ParaSites as seriously as we do and when they fully cooperate with us to terminates their services to Parasites to help rid the Internet of illegal content.

***Our Recommendations for Combating ParaSites***

Go Daddy has a long history of supporting federal legislation directed toward combating illegal conduct on the Internet. For example, our company strongly supported the Ryan Haight Online Pharmacy Consumer Protection Act of 2008, which amended the Controlled Substances Act to significantly increase the criminal penalties associated with illegal online pharmacies. We also vigorously advocated for the passage of the Protect Our Children Act of 2008, which, among many other protections, prohibited the sending of live images of child abuse via the Internet, and authorized an additional $320 million in funding for the fight against CP. Go Daddy always has and always will support both government and private industry efforts to identify and disable all types of ParaSites on the Internet. And, as set forth below, we have several specific recommendations that we believe will make the fight against illegal activity online more efficient and effective.

Direct Complaints Regarding Domain Names To Registrars Rather Than Registries We believe that complaints against domain names should be directed to the appropriate domain name registrar, rather than to the registry. Because it is the registrar that typically has the most contact with the registrant of a domain name, registrars are very often involved in a variety of criminal investigations relating to websites associated with the domain name (for example, CP investigations involving registrants). The registry in many instances has no knowledge of these highly confidential and sensitive matters, and we have experienced several occasions in which the sudden disabling of a domain name by a registry disrupted weeks or months of work investigating serious criminal activity by the registrant. We would like to see future government and private industry efforts focused on naming the registrar as the primary contact for courts and law enforcement regarding all criminal and civil matters relating to domain names. We can then facilitate and coordinate concurrent actions by international, federal and local governments with respect to particular names.

**Direct Complaints Regarding Illegal Content to All Relevant Members of the Internet Ecosystem**

We further ask the Committee to consider establishing notice and takedown procedures, such as those provided for by the Digital Millennium Copyright Act (the "DMCA"), that could be applied to additional types of illegal content and to additional online service providers, including all members of the Internet ecosystem. While it is practically a mathematical certainty that the players and types of illegal content will change in the future, today the relevant members of the ecosystem would include registrars, hosting providers, payment processors, shippers, Internet service providers, search engines, and online advertising providers (hereinafter, the "Ecosystem Members").

The DMCA provides a process for copyright owners to directly contact online service providers regarding websites that contain infringing material, and demand the removal of that content. The law establishes a safe harbor for providers that promptly remove the infringing material following notification, so long as the provider follows the processes outlined in the statute. Go Daddy has found the DMCA to be an extremely useful tool in combating online infringements and counterfeits, and has adhered to its provisions with much success. We have removed tens of thousands of websites that contain counterfeit or infringing material after receiving notification of the existence of the sites from third-parties pursuant to the DMCA. We anticipate that we would make even greater strides in this area if the DMCA were expanded (or new legislation were put into effect) to include notice and takedown provisions for illegal conduct other than copyright infringement -trademark infringement, for example, as well as spam, phishing, fraud, etc. The expanded legislation could and should apply to all of Ecosystem Members.

It is obviously critical that the Ecosystem Members all work together to combat Parasites. To the extent that any Ecosystem Member receives notice that a member of its network is engaged in illegal conduct, that organization should be required (or, better yet, take it upon itself as the responsible thing to do) to disable access to the resources that are allowing the criminal to engage in the nefarious activity. With the help of clearly defined and widely disseminated notification and takedown procedures, the Ecosystem Members should be able to cut off a large portion of the technical and financial resources that have, to date, allowed the proliferation of online bad actors. And, consistent with current law, future legislation should include an immunity provision for the "good actor" members of private industry that act in accordance with or exceed the law's provisions.

Utilize DNS Blocking Instead of DNS Filtering to Combat ParaSites Finally, Go Daddy has some concerns about recent proposals to impose domain name system ("DNS") filtering as a means of combating ParaSites. We strongly prefer "DNS blocking" to "DNS filtering" as an effective strategy for disabling access to illegal and malicious content on the Internet.

The DNS is the standard technology for managing domain names on the Internet. DNS technology allows you to type a domain name into your web browser and locate the address, or URL, for that domain name. A "DNS server" is any computer registered to join the DNS. DNS servers run special-purpose networking software, feature a public IP address, and contain a database of network names and addresses for other Internet hosts. DNS servers communicate with each other using private network protocols.

All DNS servers are organized in a hierarchy. At the top level of the hierarchy, so-called "Root servers" store the complete database of Internet domain names and their corresponding TP addresses. The Internet currently employs 13 Root servers, located in various countries around the world. All other DNS servers are installed at lower levels in the hierarchy, and maintain only certain pieces of the overall database. Most non-Root DNS servers are owned by businesses or ISPs, such as Go Daddy and Google, and are maintained in various locations around the world.

The term "DNS filtering" describes a mechanism through which ISPs prevent outbound DNS inquiries regarding particular domain names from reaching the Root servers for those names. The net effect is to prevent the ISP's customer base (i.e., only those customers that are using the ISP's DNS servers) from being able to access the domain name or website in question. "Filtering," rather than "blocking," is the best name for this mechanism, because the process does not and will not provide 100% protection. At best, it prevents a significant portion of a single ISP's customer base from being able to access a "DNS-filtered" ParaSite.

In our view, DNS filtering is an ineffective mechanism for fighting illegal activity online. The widespread implementation of DNS filtering would result in a large number of Internet users attempting to circumvent such filtering. While the easiest and most common way to do this is to use a proxy site, undoubtedly some users will change their primary DNS resolver to an overseas provider. If more users begin using DNS servers that are not secured, they will be in a position of exposed risk to DNS poisoning and similar security concerns. Ironically, this increases the likelihood of their exposure to Parasites.

In addition, the imposition of DNS filters would diminish the ability of DNS providers in the United States to implement DNS security extensions, and of domestic ISPs and DNS providers to monitor DNS servers. Overseas DNS providers have not yet widely implemented DNSSEC authentication keys. Without such keys, providers have no way of verifying the validity of DNS record responses. As a result, if a significant portion of a provider's customer base uses other DNS servers as a rule, the provider will be unable to effectively protect those customers.

We believe that DNS blocking, as opposed to DNS filtering, is a much more effective vehicle for removing illegal content from the Internet. DNS blocking is different from DNS filtering in that DNS blocking is action taken at the "authoritative" or "response" level of the DNS cycle. As such, it needs to be done by the registrar (which provides the authoritative DNS response), or, in cases where the registrar is unable or unwilling to comply, by the registry (which provides the Root zone file records - the database — for the entire TLD). Though a very similar technical process to DNS filtering, DNS blocking provides a much more thorough solution because it applies to all Internet users, regardless of which ISP they are a customer of or whether proxy services are used.

Where DNS blocking is imposed, Internet users will not be able to access a ParaSite by any common means.

## Conclusion

Thank you again, Chairman Goodlatte, for the opportunity to testify on these important issues. Your commitment and the commitment of the Members of this Committee to bringing attention to the problem of ParaSites on the Internet is sincerely appreciated. Go Daddy is committed to working with you, with law enforcement, and with our fellow Internet Ecosystem Members to remove illegal content from the Internet.

I would be happy to answer any questions you may have.

*Chapter 6*

# LETTERS, STATEMENTS, ETC., SUBMITTED FOR THE HEARING

Mr. Goodlatte. Thank you, Ms. Jones.

I will recognize myself to begin the questioning. Let me warn my Committee Members I may take a little extra time here because I want to go into some detail with this issue with some specific examples.

Let me say at the outset that I want to restate my belief that tech and content, two areas in which this Committee has great interest, are not enemies and that they both bring innovation to the table to solve various problems, and they need each other, and we need both of them contributing to solve this problem.

Mr. Walker, let me just say I am an avid user of Google's search engine, and I welcome your comments here today that you want to work with the Committee on some legislative solutions that might involve your company and other players in the tech community in this. And we hear your concerns as well.

And I want to commend you for a news release, which I will put in the record, that says, "Google boots Grooveshark from Android Market," and it noted that this was done yesterday. Grooveshark is a music app that has been found by many of the top music labels to be violating copyright law, and a Google spokesman said, "We remove apps from the android market that violate our terms of service." And it was also noted that we were having a hearing on the subject here today. But we commend you for that.

[The information referred to follows:]

CNET News

# Google boots Grooveshark from Android Market

Just before a scheduled appearance on Capitol Hill to testify about its antipiracy efforts, Google removes an app provided by a music service long accused of copyright violations.

by **Greg Sandoval** | April 6, 2011 3:41 AM PDT

(Credit: Screen shot by Greg Sandoval/CNET)

WASHINGTON--Google has removed Grooveshark's music app from the **Android Market [http://www.cnet.com/android-atlas/]**, a move that comes after some of the top music labels have accused the service of violating copyright law, sources said.

"We remove apps from Android Market that violate our policies," a Google spokesman said in response to questions from CNET. He did not specify what violations Grooveshark may have committed or whether Google had been pressured by the music industry to remove the app.

A Grooveshark representative was not immediately available for comment.

**Related links**

- **Google to testify on piracy before House subcommittee**

Google boots Grooveshark from Android Market | Media Maverick - CN... http://news.cnet.com/8301-31001_3-20051156-261.html

**[http://www.cnet.com/8301-31001_3-20048939-261.html]**

- **Has Google jumped sides in copyright war? [http://www.cnet.com/8301-31001_3-20024510-261.html]**
- **Grooveshark pulled from App Store [http://www.cnet.com/8301-13526_3-20013850-27.html]**

The recent removal of the app happened as Google prepared to testify at a hearing today before members of the House Judiciary committee in which Kent Walker, Google's general counsel, is scheduled to testify. A subcommittee is **investigating sites [http://www.cnet.com/8301-31001_3-20048939-261.html]** that allegedly traffic in pirated or counterfeit goods. Google has been dogged by accusations that the company profits from piracy by allowing alleged pirate sites to post Google ads. The company denies this and is expected to outline the company's **antipiracy efforts [http://www.cnet.com/8301-31001_3-20024510-261.html]** at today's hearing.

Grooveshark, based in Gainesville, Fla., is a service that offers free music by enabling users to post their own tracks to the site and then share them with other users. The service, which boasts more than 6 million songs, was accused by EMI in a lawsuit of copyright violations, a case that was settled in 2009 when Grooveshark agreed to license the label's catalog.

Months later, however, Universal Music Group, the largest of the top four labels, filed another copyright suit against the company. That case is still pending. Music industry sources say Universal as well as Warner Music Group and Sony Music Entertainment continue to view Grooveshark as a pirate site.

After receiving complaints from the top record companies last year, **Apple removed Grooveshark [http://www.cnet.com/8301-13526_3-20013850-27.html]** from its App Store in August.

**Correction 8:45 a.m. PT:** *This story initially gave an incorrect time frame for when Google removed Grooveshark from the Android Market. The removal occurred recently.*

**[http://www.cnet.com/profile/sandonet/]**

## About Greg Sandoval [http://www.cnet.com/profile/sandonet/]

Greg Sandoval covers media and digital entertainment for CNET News. Based in New York, Sandoval is a former reporter for The Washington Post and the Los Angeles Times.

**[http://plus.google.com/107414072672616197316/]**

Mr. Goodlatte. I want to go into some details about some of the things we found in recent searches, however. In preparation for today's hearing, we conducted searches in Google for free mp3 Taylor Swift, quote/unquote. Over the past several days, the first page of each search return appeared to show all unlicensed sites. We checked with the distributor of Taylor Swift's recordings, and they provided us three screen shots from yesterday that show only two authorized sites out of nearly 30. To access the first of those, a consumer would have to scroll past the first 14 suggested by Google.

You wrote recently that Google was, quote, a big fan of making authorized content more accessible, end quote, 4 months ago, and yet this is the result.

I intend to check in a week, in a month, in 3 months, in 6 months. When I do that, will I find this same problem in existence? What is Google doing about this?

Mr. Walker. Thank you, Mr. Chairman.

Let me go to the Grooveshark example first. I want to flag that this is not the first time we have removed items from the App Store. We have removed almost 2,000 different applications from the App Store over time, something like 200 or 300 in February alone. So we continue to look not just for copyright infringement but malware and many other things. There are I believe about 200,000 different applications. So it is a major challenge for us to go through all them.

Mr. Goodlatte. And we commend you for that.

Mr. Walker. With regard to the additional items in the search results, we do try and remove—when we get notice of these individual infringing items, obviously, we try and take them down. And at the same time, we have said we are eager to work with the content industry on ways of making their sites more accessible. In some cases, when they offer preview content or other kinds of things where you can listen to 30 seconds or a minute or a trial copy of the song, for example, that is very attractive to users. And we talk with them about ways of partnering that would actually make that more visible within the snippets, within the search results that are returned, and so as you get users clicking on that, that is sort of a natural signal. The cream rises to the top even as we try and pull the bad guys out.

Now, that said, the Internet is a big place, and as I think all of the witnesses have said, we are never going to get rid of all the bad guys. We play the Whac-A-Mole problem as much as the content industry does, and it frustrates us. When you hear me talk about taking down 50,000 sites for this or 12,000 accounts for that, that costs us a lot of time and effort. It drives us crazy trying to get rid of these guys because, of course, we take them down one place, they come back up in another place using a different credit card, using a different IP address. So it is a constant battle.

We think the best way to fight that battle is collaboratively, to your point about the content industry and the technology industry working together. We are in the best position to rapidly remove content and build tools and filters to help do that. The content industry is in the best position, maybe a unique position to let us know what is authorized and what is not because, of course, there are multiple authorized sites for different kinds of songs. The music industry is a very complicated place with label rights and publisher rights that expire over time in different geographies and the like. They know what is authorized and what is not, and we rely on them to let us know and then we take action.

Mr. Goodlatte. Let me follow up on that. As I indicated, I use Google frequently. I am frequently amazed at the sophistication of the algorithms that you use in your search process. When I type in things, I like to see how many letters I have to type in before Google knows what I am looking for. And I am frequently very impressed.

3 days ago, we conducted a search for "watch movies online." We typed in those words. Without prompting, the first suggestion that appeared in the dropdown box that comes—which is exactly what I am talking about, anticipating what I want. In the dropdown box, the first suggestion was "watch free bootleg movies online." And I am sure as a former Federal prosecutor, you know the meaning of the term "bootleg." If you click, you go to a results page full of infringing links. Clicking on one of the sites at the top of the page takes you to a website that is a notorious infringing site. It even advertises pre-release movies. We have a movie coming out on Friday that they are advertising now will be available online illegally. "Hanna" is the movie and it is going to appear in the theaters on Friday, and you will be able to see it online on Friday too apparently. It even advertises pre-release movies.

Why exactly does Google suggest to users that they click on "watch free bootleg movies online"?

Mr. Walker. So the functionality you are speaking to is referred to as autocomplete. It is essentially the sum of what other users are doing. So it is not really Google knowing what you want. It is you asking for things that other users are interested in, and the fact that some of these terms come up actually reinforces the importance of education among the American public because it is a reflection of how many users are, in fact, trying to seek illegal, bootleg, pirated, otherwise infringing content out there.

Mr. Goodlatte. Well, let me ask you this. Would Google think it appropriate to, when these things are called to your attention, review the things that you anticipate and put up there and block some of them from occurring?

Mr. Walker. Absolutely. In fact, we have committed to do just that. And the challenge in doing it, obviously, is making sure that the terms we are blocking are uniquely or highly correlated with infringing material and not with other sort of material. So, for example, if you put in "cheap" or "free," many of those are perfectly appropriate and legitimate searches. You wouldn't want to not suggest that. Even terms like "faux" or "replica," in many cases it is faux leather, or even to go farther, terms like "knock-off," there are knock-off dresses that are sold by Macy's and Nordstrom's. So we have to figure out what are the list of terms that really are pushing people to something that is almost unambiguously, to Mr. Abrams' point, infringing material.

And we have started that process, and in fact, we are in dialogue with the content community to ask them what are your key terms. What terms would you like us to include in that list, and how can we do that analysis and move forward?

Mr. Goodlatte. Thank you.

And let me follow up on that. As I think you know, many Members of the Subcommittee are interested in your December 2 policy blog post regarding steps Google would take to address the growing number of issues involving the use of its services in connection with copyright infringement. Interesting among them was a pledge to, quote, prevent terms that are closely associated with piracy from appearing in autocomplete, the Google feature whereby Google's search engine will suggest search terms to its users as the users type, based on its prediction of what they might be looking for.

As you know, I am the co-chair of the bicameral congressional International Anti-Piracy Caucus, along with Congressman Adam Schiff. Last year we released our annual international piracy watch list which included six foreign websites that are notorious for providing access to infringing copies of works by U.S. creators. These included sites like the Pirate Bay, whose principals have been criminally convicted or their activities in Europe, and isoHunt, which is a file sharing site that is the subject of an injunction issued by a U.S. court for copyright inducement and whose owner is described another Federal court as, quote, an admitted copyright thief.

I am told that a review of the 15 sites identified 6 weeks ago by the USTR as notorious markets for piracy show nearly identical results. In other words, Google continues to suggest each one of those sites as search terms through the autocomplete function.

I would like to know what you are doing to address this problem and if you are doing your best to prevent terms that are closely associated with piracy from appearing in autocomplete. Again obviously somebody looking for something, they can type out that whole word and will not get to it, but I think it would help Google's reputation as not aiding and abetting the infringement by not having these pop up on your autocomplete.

Mr. Walker. We understand the optics of it, and we are working on it. I think it is an extension of our prior conversation. The challenge is that a lot of those sites are broad-based sites. The Chinese search engine Baidu, for example, I believe appears on that list, and Baidu does allow a large amount of pirated and infringing material to be accessible through its search engine. And yet, we are in a difficult situation essentially discriminating against a search competitor and leaving them out of autocomplete.

But I think the spirit of my answer here would be the same as before, which is we really want to identify things that are unambiguously infringing and we are open to removing those from the autocomplete list.

Mr. Goodlatte. Thank you, Mr. Walker. I appreciate your answering those difficult questions.

And to not single you entirely out, I have one for Ms. Jones. You mentioned that Go Daddy strongly prefers DNS blocking by registrars, registries to DNS filtering by ISP's as a strategy to shut down rogue websites because DNS filtering will not provide 100 percent protection. Is DNS blocking, as you describe it, effective against websites hosted and registered through overseas companies, and doesn't DNS filtering provide a better way to disable access to those types of foreign-based websites? Should both types of technologies be employed to combat the problem?

Ms. Jones. To answer your last question first, yes, I think that is absolutely necessary, and it is a pretty complicated technical explanation. I will try not to get too much into the weeds. But if you block DNS at the definitive root level, nobody can access the website from anywhere. The problem comes where you don't have cooperation from entities who are willing to do the blocking, and then if you want to block at least some access, you may have to engage in some filtering. And we know that both blocking and filtering take place today in a variety of contexts.

The Internet community is a little bit remiss to employ these kind of tactics because the more you filter, the more you splinter, the less stable and secure the root becomes, and you end up with a giant grid, a three-dimensional grid actually, of things that are blocked by people, from people in various geographies, and it gets very shaky. So really, that suggestion is more of a technical approach as opposed to a policy approach or a policy belief.

I was going to answer one of Mr. Walker's questions, but I know I am not allowed to ask questions here. So I will just leave it at that.

Mr. Goodlatte. That is good advice to yourself. [Laughter.]

Now I will recognize the gentleman from North Carolina, Mr. Watt.

Mr. Watt. I can't resist. I got to let her answer whatever question she wanted to answer. [Laughter.]

Mr. Watt. If she is willing to answer it, I am willing to listen to the answer.

Ms. Jones. It just occurred to me that once in a while we have foreign websites that we can't block because they are foreign, and we don't have a good, cooperative U.S. company that is willing to do it. So the example that the ICE gentleman put up here of the fake Louis Vuitton or the fake Nike, those are almost certainly— I don't know—I haven't looked them up, but they are almost certainly foreign registrars and foreign hosting providers, and they won't take them down. No offense, Mr. Walker, but that doesn't mean that we can't disable the search to those because I can almost guarantee you that Louis Vuitton and Nike have contacted somebody to say could you please stop sending people to those websites. It is an approach.

Now he is going to have to answer.

Mr. Watt. What do you say to that, Mr. Walker?

Mr. Walker. Thank you, sir.

It is exactly right. I am sure we are contacted by many of those sites, and we remove them. And that is the way the system should work. Louis Vuitton and Nike are in the best position to know what is appropriate and what is not. In many cases, when you put those search terms in, you may get ads for competitors, for example, and that is a good thing. Competitive advertising, comparative advertising helps consumers, helps them find out about more products that are out there, pay less money for them.

Mr. Watt. What do you say to that, Ms. Jones?

Ms. Jones. I happen to hear from the Louis Vuitton and Nike lawyers all day every day, and they are very willing to tell you which sites they want you to take down. So I don't have the data from any of the other providers except for the ones that I represent. So I don't know if they have the lists, but I would be shocked if they hadn't provided those.

Mr. Watt. Mr. Morton, would it be more effective to block them or filter them?

Mr. Morton. Well, as Ms. Jones noted, it gets very complicated, the sort of technical arrangements. What I will say is, first of all, on those sites, they weren't seized or terminated by industry. We seized them, both of those sites. We seized them and we forfeited both of those sites because they were notorious counterfeiting sites and they were referred to us by industry. And those are the instances in which you can have good cooperation between the Government.

I think what you have heard going before suggests, however, that industry can do a lot more and on a much greater scale than Government ever can. We are part of the solution. We are not the solution by a long shot.

Mr. Watt. Mr. Abrams, any free speech implications in any of those situations?

Mr. Abrams. You know, everything we are talking about today is suffused with a danger of free speech violation. We don't want Google taking down sites just because people are angry at them or upset. We don't want the public to have less access unless we are talking about genuinely infringing or otherwise criminally or civilly violative sites.

It seems to me that the hard issue here is that we are often talking about taking down an infringing movie, say, taking down an infringing design when the real problem is very often that these sites are only infringing sites. Everything on them is infringing. And there the question is, as a congressional matter, what can you do about that? That is what the Senate focused on in its attempt to draft legislation, and I suggest to you that when you focus on drafting anything, that you ought to propose legislation which focuses not just on individual files, not an individual movie or an individual design only, but on the sites themselves which contain them.

Mr. Watt. But wouldn't a convenient way, quick way around that be just to

Mr. Abrams. I am sorry. I didn't hear.

Mr. Watt. Wouldn't a quick way around that be just to put up some legitimate stuff on the same site? I mean, seldom are you going to have a criminal that is not—if you tell him that all you are doing is taking down sites that are exclusively dedicated to criminal activity, he is going to mix in a little legitimate stuff, don't you think?

Mr. Abrams. That is a fair point. Therefore, what I am talking about will never be a complete solution.

But law enforcement authorities deal with that when they deal with stores that sell 90 percent of child pornography. They can close down the store in that circumstance. If you get to a much lower amount. A, you have done something. You have accomplished something I think of a serious public policy nature, and then, yes, you have to go after the individual sale of an individual book. All I am saying is that it is a step forward to try to deal with the sites which is the reality, as I understand it, today where there are many sites which are either nothing but or almost nothing but infringing entities.

Mr. Watt. I am sure I have plenty more questions, Mr. Chairman, but out of respect for other Members, I will come back around the next time I guess.

Mr. Goodlatte. I thank the gentleman.

The gentleman from Arizona, Mr. Quayle, is recognized for 5 minutes.

Mr. Quayle. Thank you, Mr. Chairman, and thank you for holding this hearing.

Annually billions of dollars are being stolen through pirated or counterfeited goods. In the last hearing that we had, a number of us, including myself, had mentioned some of our concern of how illegal streaming was being treated. I am actually very pleased that the IP Enforcement Coordinator, Victoria Espinel, issued a white paper recently which states that illegal streaming should be a felony and not a misdemeanor as it currently is. And I know the Chairman of this Subcommittee and the full Committee have been working on this, and I look forward to seeing a piece of legislation soon.

I would also like to specifically thank Mr. Morton and ICE for all their good work in enforcement against illegitimate sites, and I thank you for being here today.

My first question is for you, Mr. Walker. Now, does Google currently have algorithms in place that allow ads that are paid for to show up during search results based on the search terms that are placed into the query?

Mr. Walker. Yes. That is fundamentally how what is called the AdWords side of our business works.

Mr. Quayle. So those algorithms are basically personalized for each search result based on the search terms that are utilized. Correct?

Mr. Walker. They are personalized based on a lot of different factors. So, for example, a different part of a country, different time of day, different time of season, et cetera, but there is a correlation that takes a lot of things into account.

Mr. Quayle. Are these updated regularly, daily, weekly, and monthly?

Mr. Walker. Almost instantaneously because it looks at the quality of different websites, the amounts that different advertisers are paying, user preference. The more users click on an ad, the more popular it becomes and therefore more relevant. There are a lot of factors that go into that. But it is almost in real time.

Mr. Quayle. I went to law school. I wasn't an engineer. So that sounds pretty

Mr. Walker. That makes two of us.

Mr. Quayle. That sounds pretty sophisticated.

So based on that, I mean, Google has extremely sophisticated algorithms that it uses in its search results and queries, and because of that, Google has really become a noun, not just a verb. But based on that, a recent report stated that domains classified as digital piracy attracted 32 million daily visits. Do you think that a company that has sophisticated algorithms like Google could create an algorithm in which search requests, using words that are among the most frequently associated with a crime, are able to filter out those results? Have they tried to do this or have you chosen not to?

Mr. Walker. The challenge is that it is sort of a different kettle of fish. It is a different task to solve. In the context of trying to come up with what is most relevant or related to a keyword, taking all those different factors into account, you can use user feedback. As I referred to, if you rank something fourth and all your users click on that, well, you probably made a mistake and it probably should be ranking higher and vice versa.

In the context of trying to target what is authorized and what is unauthorized on the Web, that is a much harder challenge. And the feedback loop we use there is essentially DMCA notices. We referred to before our process for when we get a notice of something from the rightsholder, then we know it is illegal and we remove the link from our system. We don't just demote it. We take it out entirely.

Mr. Quayle. I remember an article in the New York Times—I think it was earlier this year—regarding J.C. Penney and how it had been pushed to the top of the search results for everything from SkinnyJeans to grommeted top curtains. Anything that you put into the search query in Google came up J.C. Penney.

Now, when you guys were actually notified of this, you changed your algorithm so that that wouldn't happen. How can you not then use that type of sophistication that you do—I mean, I know you just explained that portion of it, but I think that it would seem to be feasible that those common search terms that are used to find pirated works on the Internet could be put into the algorithm so that those searches and the results are actually filtered out of that.

Mr. Walker. There are two problems there. I mean, one is that a lot of times searches, queries that are used to find pirated stuff are also used to find all sorts of other things as well—the word "cheap" or "discount" that I talked about before. So you are trying to separate the wheat from the chaff. That is problem one. You don't want to be over-inclusive and knock out a lot of legitimate sites.

Problem two is figuring out what the wheat is, and there we need to partner with the content industry because there are lots of sites out there that make fair use of items, that have remixes and different sorts of things that are protected under the DMCA again that we don't want to knock out. So we rely on the content industry to say that is bad. That site is bad, pull that out of your index.

We don't want—and I don't think the Members of the Committee want—us or any company to be the judge, jury, and executioner against an entire site.

Mr. Quayle. I agree with that, but you have got to understand the frustration. I think Google does understand the frustration of those that have copyrighted work that is being infringed because recently, just last week, you reached a settlement—Google did— with six companies in which Google was suing because the companies were misusing Google's trademarks and name. In addition, I have read other pending lawsuits Google was involved in over domain names that are oddly similar to Google's domain name and logo. In all of these instances, other companies were profiting off of Google.

So I think you can see where I am going with this. I think you can understand the frustration of copyright holders because they are having their content being illegally sold via the top results from searches on your search engine, and they are actually making a profit from that.

So can Google play a more proactive role in this in combating some of the deliberate illegal sites without infringing on any other —

Mr. Walker. Yes, I think we can. And look, we not only understand the frustration, we share it. As you said, we are a big IP owner ourselves. We went after some bad guys who were misusing our name in scammy sort of ways that were misleading consumers. You know, buy the Google work at home kit which, of course, had no association with Google, and pay 100 bucks to get a bunch of worthless paper. And we went after those guys and won that case. And we are committed to doing that against all these bad guys when we can identify them and clearly know who to go after. It is one thing for us, though, to be able to remove the individual links to stuff that we can look at and say, yes, that is infringing, and another to try and go after the entire domain. That is a harder procedural thing for us as a private company to do.

Mr. Quayle. Thank you very much.

Mr. Goodlatte. I thank the gentleman.

The Chair now recognizes the Ranking Member of the Judiciary Committee, the gentleman from Michigan, Mr. Conyers, and as I do that, I will ask the Vice-Chairman of the Committee, Mr. Quayle, to take the Chair.

Mr. Conyers. Thank you.

Attorney Christine Jones, why can't you organization build intellectual property protections into its user agreements and terminate customers that provide or facilitate online piracy?

Ms. Jones. I am sorry. I missed the last word. Online privacy?

Mr. Conyers. Piracy.

Ms. Jones. Oh, piracy. I think we do substantially build those protections into our agreements, and the agreements are written generally very broadly.

Like Google and other providers, we do rely on the content industry to let us know when they find things that are inappropriate.

But what we do that is somewhat more aggressive than most is if there is some infringing content and the person who runs the website doesn't cure it, we disable the entire website because you either are engaged in unlawful activity or you are not. There is no such thing as halfway. So if your domain name contains bad stuff and you don't take it down, we kill the entire domain. Period. If you fix it, we will put it back up. But we don't incentivize people to make part of their website good and part of their website bad because as our First Amendment professor—I call him a professor—says, some of it is good and some of it is bad, and you have to be able to make a decision.

Mr. Conyers. You say you are doing it already.

Ms. Jones. I think we do it already, yes, to the extent that we can.

Mr. Conyers. Mr. Kent Walker, when someone types in child pornography into a Google search, Google doesn't connect the user to images of child abuse. Now, that means to me that the technology exists to block illegal material from appearing in your searches. Why don't you employ the same technology to block searches for illegal content and illegal goods?

Mr. Walker. When it comes to child pornography, we do two things that are unique compared to the problem of online counterfeiting and infringing material. Child pornography is recognizable to some degree with filters. You can build a filter that will detect flesh tones, for example, most flesh tones, and that gives you a clue. And then you can use human reviewers to look at the sites one at a time, and to some degree, as the Supreme Court has put it, you know it when you see it. And we have people who are working on that.

In the context of unauthorized goods where it is not clear who has got the legal rights to something, it is much harder. You may remember the case that Viacom brought against YouTube not long ago. Viacom itself sued us over thousands of clips from their files that they had actually authorized—they or their subsidiaries had authorized be uploaded to YouTube. So they themselves didn't actually know what was legitimate or what wasn't. So it is a harder problem.

Mr. Conyers. So why can't you block the searches? Tell me the answer again.

Mr. Walker. Sure. We can in cooperation with the content owner. If they let us know that a given item is unauthorized, we block that search. We take that link out of our results if it is for copyrighted material.

Mr. Conyers. Could I ask the Director of ICE? I am glad you didn't mention all the lack of due diligence and collateral damage that occurred February in your organization during recent seizures where legitimate sites were taken down in droves. Do you want to admit that before we get to the question?

Mr. Morton. Either way.

Mr. Conyers. What do you mean "either way"?

Mr. Morton. If you want to continue with your question —

Mr. Conyers. I mean, didn't that happen?

Mr. Morton. What happened in that case? Ranking Member Conyers, was this. That wasn't an IP investigation. It had to do with child pornography. We were investigating 10 sites that were offering images of children as young as 4 and 5 engaged in—you know, in sex —

Mr. Conyers. Yes, but how did you get the good guys involved? That is what I am getting to.

Mr. Morton. What happened in that particular case was that in one of the 10 sites that we were seizing, the seizure was overbroad and the site we were going after was a subdomain of a secondary domain level. And we seized for a little less than 2 days more than that site. Two people contacted us. We noticed our error and we put all the sites back up.

Mr. Conyers. Okay.

The last question, with your forbearance, Mr. Chairman, to Professor Abrams. What did you think of the Senate attempt on the same subject we are working on?

Mr. Abrams. I thought the Senate attempt was constitutional.

I think the notion of trying to define a rogue site in a way which requires a very stiff showing, a very difficult but a possible showing, of a site itself or a domain itself being so devoted, dedicated in the draft statute's language to infringement works—and I think that it works in a way which goes beyond the simple question of what can happen to that site. It raises issues, at least, about intermediaries. If you have a court and the court says this whole site at this moment as it is today, this whole site is an infringing site, and you get a court order to that effect and you serve it on ISP's, it seems to me perfectly constitutional to require the ISP not to carry material from the site. And that would be true of other intermediaries as well at least with respect to direct links to the site.

I mean, I don't think you can limit information about the sites. I don't think Google can be limited any more than the Washington Post can be limited in writing about, containing a summary, describing, mentioning the website involved. But I think intermediaries might well be able to limited after being served with a finding by a court from linking to a site that has been held by a court to be an infringing one.

Mr. Quayle [presiding]. Thank you.

The Chair now recognizes the gentleman from North Carolina, Mr. Coble, for 5 minutes.

Mr. Coble. Thank you, Mr. Chairman.

Good to have you all with us, I will say to the panel.

Mr. Abrams, I think you touched on this. I was going to ask you how precise does the definition of rogue websites need to be in order to be constitutionally sound. Did you want to add anything to it? I think you have touched on that.

Mr. Abrams. Not really. I mean, obviously, language has to be very carefully drafted, but I think the notion at least of the Senate bill which focuses on dedicated to infringing with no other commercial purpose than infringing, which as I said is a very tough standard to meet, but if that can be met, I don't think there is a constitutional right of that site anymore to continue as it had been operating previously.

Mr. Coble. I thank you, sir.

Mr. Walker, some have alleged that Google benefits from illicit websites through advertising revenue. What do you say in response to that allegation?

Mr. Walker. These sites cost us money, sir. They cost us money to try and get rid of them. They cost us money when we find them and we refund money to advertisers. They cost us money when they use fake credit cards or stolen credit cards to pay for what they are doing. We have no interest in having advertising on these sites. We have no interest in having advertising leading to these sites.

There are two separate problems here. One is a problem of the digital piracy, songs and videos, which typically are given away for free on the Web. Those sites have no trouble drawing traffic. Everybody wants something for free. Those sites have a problem with monetization and so they use ad services to try and raise money, and we want to block that. And in fact, every time you see a Google ad on one of those sites, if they have gotten through our systems, there is a way to click on that ad and report that site for having infringing content on it.

There is a separate problem with regard to people selling counterfeit and real goods, analog goods, and traditional stuff. Those sites have no problem making money because they are making the good for this much and they are selling it for that much. Their problem is they are trying to drive traffic. And so on that side for our systems, that is an AdWords problem, and so we go through the ads on the Google sites and try to make sure that we don't have ads going to sites that are infringing like the Louis Vuitton sites that we talked about before. And when we find it, when we hear about it, we pull them out.

Mr. Coble. I thank you, sir.

Let me ask you another question, Mr. Walker. If Google learns that certain websites are illicit or illegal, can it restrict those websites from its searches?

Mr. Walker. So we have been talking sort of on the advertising side. The search is more challenging, and again, to Mr. Abrams' point, we need to be very focused here. It is correct that if we have the Government come and tell us that a given site is illegal, we can address that problem in our search results. But we want to do that in a way that, obviously, has appropriate due process involved and doesn't put us in the position of having to make those evaluations. Right now, we need to work together with the content industry to do that.

Mr. Coble. I thank you, sir.

Ms. Jones, what is your recommendation for the best approach to eliminate these websites in the United States and abroad? Or do you have a recommendation?

Ms. Jones. Sure. I always have a recommendation.

We have had a really good —

Mr. Coble. Truth is a good defense. If you can do it, it ain't bragging.

Ms. Jones. We have had a really good string of luck with voluntary cooperation from all of the players on the Internet to take action against operators of websites that are engaged in bad action, whatever their service is. So I recommend that we as an industry do that first and foremost. So, in other words, if I send to Google the 36,000 domain names that we took down under the Ryan Haight Act in 2010, I think Google ought to disable the search to those sites, and I think Visa and MasterCard and PayPal and Discover should disable the payment processing. And I think FedEx and UPS and the United States Postal Service should stop shipping drugs for those companies, and so on and so forth.

However, we know that not everybody cooperates and not everybody is a good guy. So in addition to that, I think we have to have legislation that says if you don't, there is a consequence. If we give you notice and you take down your services, you're good. If we give you notice and you fail to respond, you're not good. That is my recommendation.

Mr. Walker. Mr. Coble, could I jump in on that for a moment?

Mr. Coble. Sure.

Mr. Walker. I want to make the point that the real way to go after these guys is to go after these guys and get them off the Web. Because if they are out there just saying they can't be in a search engine or they can't be in Facebook or they can't be on a blog or a link to them can't be there isn't going to solve the problem because people are going to talk about them, and when they talk about the Pirate Bay or someone else, those links are going to come back up in any search engine worth its salt. So our worry is that we can cut—we would recommend cutting off the money to these guys. Cut off the advertising. Cut off the financial services. When you start to go after the pure search side of it, the risk is that you are both overbroad and ultimately ineffective in doing it.

Mr. Coble. I see my red light has illuminated. I yield back.

Good to have you all with us this morning. Thank you.

Mr. Quayle. Thank you.

The Chair now recognizes the gentlewoman from California, Ms. Lofgren, for 5 minutes.

Ms. Lofgren. Thank you, Mr. Chairman. I think this is an excellent hearing and it shows how complicated some of these issues are, and yet it is important that we deal with the challenges in a way that is serious but also works as a technical matter and also with an eye to our Constitution, not only the First Amendment, but the Fourth Amendment. We want to make sure that we are effective but smart.

And along those lines, Mr. Morton, I was interested in the Operation in Our Sites effort. How many of the owners of those sites that were the subject of your action were arrested? And for the seizures that have not been followed by an arrest, has ICE attempted to make arrests, and if not, why not?

Mr. Morton. I will have to get you the exact numbers, Ms. Lofgren, but a couple of things are going on. Several of these cases are part of an ongoing criminal investigation. So I can't really predict one way or another how they are going to end up. A few people have been arrested and I can get you those stats.

But the real challenge, as I alluded to in the beginning, is that in many of these cases, we have a criminal investigation but most of the actors are, for practical purposes, outside of our reach. They are not in this country. They are in —

Ms. Lofgren. Perhaps what I can do off calendar is just get the stats because you are going to court, you are bringing a criminal action, you are getting a matter signed by a magistrate, and I want to know then what. How many criminal prosecutions? How many arrests? And I am eager—I understand if somebody is outside our jurisdiction, that is a more complicated factor which goes to the other question I have which has to do with the jurisdiction itself.

Now, my understanding is that the customs part of ICE—they have jurisdiction over goods that cross international borders. What is the limit on ICE's authority over the Internet? Is it the international aspect of it, or is it ICE's position that you have jurisdiction over the Internet itself?

Mr. Morton. That latter proposition is not our position. Our position is that we have jurisdiction over the relevant Federal offenses provided there is the necessary constitutional nexus to the United States for the Congress to assert jurisdiction. So in practical terms, that means there needs to be some element or instrument of the crime occurring here in the United States.

Ms. Lofgren. So it is wrongdoing crossing into the United States. Is that your position?

Mr. Morton. That is right, involving the United States or United States rightsholders, some U.S. interest.

Ms. Lofgren. But it has to be an international component to it.

Mr. Morton. That is right. So if you were engaged in counterfeiting of Indian goods in China and there was no nexus whatsoever to the United States at all, that is not a case we would investigate.

Ms. Lofgren. Let me ask you this, and it is something that I think people—obviously, we have a need for enforcement, but we also want to make sure that things are done in a proper way. Recently—obviously, we are not the same, but Russia used copyright enforcement—it was pirated copies of Microsoft software. They used those pirated copies as an excuse to go in and take computers and shut down dissident groups. And there was, in fact, infringement going on, but they used it really for a political reason. What do we have in place that would prevent the Government from that sort of activity here?

Mr. Morton. Well, I am not familiar with that particular case, but I think the short answer to your question is that we have a wonderful judicial system in this country. We have a great sense of the rule of law. We have a great sense of ethical behavior on the part of Government. I have to go

Ms. Lofgren. No, but procedurally. Right now there is an ex parte communication. You go to a magistrate. You say what you think. There is nobody on the other side saying what they think. You get, in most cases, the order. You take it down. What constraint is there on you?

Mr. Morton. I have to demonstrate that there is probable cause for the seizure to the Federal judge, and the day we do it, you can walk into court and challenge that seizure immediately in addition to the separate rights you have to challenge the ultimate forfeiture if the Government pursues a permanent seizure of the site. So there is a tremendous amount of process that is provided upon seizure. The seizure itself follows the traditional rules in rule 41 where we go to a magistrate judge ex parte, and we say we believe a crime is being committed.

Ms. Lofgren. I have about five pages more of questions for you. So, Mr. Morton, I will deliver those to you in writing.

As I listened especially to the testimony from Go Daddy and Google, I am reminded that this stuff is more complicated than is obviously understood and how useful it might be to have some of the big tech presences engage in more deep conversations with content holders who are understandably concerned about what is happening to them. That might yield an effective result that is far superior to what the non-engineers in the Congress might craft. So I would just leave that suggestion with the panel. They don't need the permission of the Congress to do that. But I think that might be a good outcome of this hearing.

And I yield back the balance of my time.

Mr. Quayle. Thank you.

The Chair now recognizes the gentleman from California, Mr. Issa, for 5 minutes.

Mr. Issa. I thank the Chairman.

I think I will take the liberty of taking us a little off IP for a moment since we have a representative of ICE here. What is the financial threshold for you to care about counterfeiting?

Mr. Morton. Typically there isn't one. We are quite aggressive when it conies to intellectual property enforcement. Obviously, the various prosecutors, the United States Attorney's offices we deal with do have at some point some limitations. There is enough work out there

Mr. ISSA. Why don't you give us an idea? You know, there was a movie back, I think, in the 1930's with Cagney, "Never Steal Anything Small." It was actually a union organization, but it was a great one because basically he stole enough to be the hero of the union.

How do we change the system, which Congress has the right to do, so that every single crime that you know is a crime can, in fact, be pursued in a way that will allow a change of behavior? Now, I am not talking about going after the P2P swapper who is exchanging his own library with somebody down the street. But I am talking about somebody who commercializes the selling of counterfeits. And I did not say intellectual property. I said counterfeits. I don't see a difference. I don't think anyone on this panel should see a difference of whether it is tangible and you can feel and touch it or it simply plays through a speaker.

What change in the law would allow you to pursue everyone for all practical purposes where today you probably pursue what? One-half, one-quarter, one-tenth of 1 percent? Certainly you pursue less than 1 percent in the tangible world, don't you? If you find—and I will get to the question.

And I will take an example from my own life. If you find 500 Viper alarms inside a shipment of—my former life, if you will— clothing and it is designated as clothing and you find it, basically you seize it and that is the end of the story. Isn't it? So you found tens of thousands of dollars of value. You found registered trademarks, copies of the images that make the product real, patented product, tangible, and the most you will do is destroy it. That is the practical reality today.

And you are shaking your head yes. That is the record that I hope we will make here today. And I appreciate all the people in the IP world. We are talking about organizations. We are saying you have to do better. You have to get it down to zero.

What can we do, in your opinion—and I will take it from each of you, please—to get to a zero tolerance? And I am not trying to get you to go after fake Viper car alarms or any of the other things from my own past. But I will give you a recent one, and I will give it to you as anecdotal.

About a year ago, my congressional office ordered a USB thumb drive. They were tired of me carrying three different thumb drives. So we ordered one of the new 256-gig thumb drives. We ordered it from one of the major companies not represented here today. Their vendor was a group, which I will give, called Fantastic Deal. Now, today they are called Good Old Deal and Fantastic Deals, but if you Google them, you will get the actual company selling on that other company. So the meta-data that they put in to make sure that they still come up under their old name of Fantastic Deal—and by the way, they are still Fantastic Deal when they tell you that we at Fantastic Deal are committed to your satisfaction. Please don't hesitate to contact us. They flat shipped on its face—it was 256 gig, but it was not made by Kingston. It was not authentic in any way, shape, or form. And they shipped it out. They are still selling. They paid no price for it. The most they had to do was live up to that company's guarantee of letting me cancel the credit card, which I did around them anyway.

What change from the dais here will allow you to not let those go because they didn't meet a financial threshold that was in the tens or hundreds of thousands of dollars?

Mr. Morton. Let me start and then I will try to be brief so the rest of the panel can give you their thoughts as well.

Some of it is a resource issue. Some of it is—take ICE, for example—a question of balancing competing enforcement priorities. Obviously, we have to go after the cartel members and child pornographers and other things of weighty importance to the Nation.

I think the big challenges are focusing on the foreign actors who are in the game as a form of organized crime and have no intention whatsoever of coming to the United States, of basing their operations here. They are able, sadly in many instances, through the Internet to commit a crime on the United States on a grand scale, on a repeated scale from afar.

So we need, I think, a balance of authorities. Criminal authorities will never get us all there. Civil authorities that address that, aggressive seizure, penalties for where we can bring U.S. enforcement action. International cooperation is critical. You could give ICE triple the number of agents it has. We have no authority to arrest people in China. We have no authority to —

Mr. Issa. I appreciate that, although all the examples I gave had a U.S. nexus.

Could the rest of you weigh in please?

Mr. Abrams. I agree with Mr. Morton. I think all we can do— but it is important—is to do everything we can to drain actions of this sort of the profits that have been building up over the years and increasing, indeed, more and more as time passes because I agree that the criminal law is not going to work very easily or comfortably when you deal with foreign actors that never come here. So we are going to have work, I think, in the main through changes in our civil legislation to take all the steps that we can to make it impossible or at least very difficult for these entities to continue to engage in the criminal—and it is criminal—activity that they are currently engaged in.

Mr. Issa. Mr. Walker?

Mr. Walker. I would have three thoughts building on the comments here.

First, go after the bad guys directly whether that is more resources for ICE or otherwise.

Second, it is an international problem. Right now the MEAT process, the Multilateral Legal Assistance Treaty process, is broken. It can take months, sometimes up to 6 months, for international law enforcement to cooperate with each other in going after these guys. That doesn't work for them and it doesn't work for us in trying to stop it.

And then lastly, I agree again: follow the money. If we can cut off the funding sources, if we can identify the bad guys and then cut off advertising on their sites, that will be powerful.

Mr. Issa. Ms. Jones?

Ms. Jones. Thank you, sir. I would second the comments of my fellow panel members, but also from the dais what you can do to be helpful to us, to answer your question, is give us cover so that if we take action against these people, we have a safe harbor. We don't have people suing us. We are not going to jail. We want to help you but you have to help us help you.

Mr. Issa. Thank you for the best of all answers.

I yield back.

Mr. Quayle. Thank you.

I just want to put everybody on notice we have been called for a vote, but the Chair recognizes the gentlelady from California, Ms. Chu, for 5 minutes.

Ms. Chu. Well, thank you, Mr. Chair, for convening this important hearing.

As you know, this issue of online piracy is of great concern to my Los Angeles district, given the importance of the motion picture and recording industry to the city and the many residents who are employed by them. So I hope that we can all work together to come up with a solution that gives law enforcement a real tool to stop this practice.

While the Combating Online Infringement and Counterfeits Act that was introduced in the Senate last year is a great start, I am concerned that it doesn't address the problem of cyberlockers that are flooded with infringing content. It is important that we don't hurt legitimate business interests, but these businesses that reward these customers for uploading infringing content and refuse to penalize the offenders are not legitimate business interests. So I hope that we can address these infringing websites and cyberlockers.

I also want to thank Mr. Morton for joining us today and for all the great work that he has done on the Operation in Our Sites.

And let me just start then by asking Mr. Walker. I am very concerned, of course, as you heard, about the infringement facilitated by the cyberlockers, but I don't want to affect legitimate developments in cloud computing. How can Congress help law enforcement go after the bad actors in the cyberlocker space without interfering with legitimate economic interests?

Mr. Walker. It is the right balance to draw. Congresswoman. The challenge with cyberlockers, which are really just a different way of describing storing content online, is a real one because, as you can tell, the entire direction of the industry is in favor of moving toward the cloud, allowing people across the country, across the world to access music, video, content, documents, email in much more flexible ways than they were able to even a dozen years ago. That is a great thing for consumers and then we think ultimately a great thing for the content industries because it provides more platforms and more ways that people can consume content lawfully and legitimately. iTunes is in a sense a version of the cyberlocker that allows you to download information from the cloud. We have seen other significant companies launch ways of offering online storage.

When you get into the question of the legitimacy of the business or not, it really goes to the question of an intent to induce infringement, and the existing copyright laws have been used in some cases to go after companies that clearly, again, are sort of dedicated to just having illegal content hosted and promoting that kind of activity, distinguished from legitimate companies who may have broad-based, multipurpose storage that is abused by some of their users. That does raise more difficult First Amendment questions.

Ms. Chu. How about you, Ms. Jones? I understand Go Daddy also provides remote storage services. How can we ensure that law enforcement has all the tools that it needs to go after cyberlockers that intentionally promote the sharing of infringing content without impeding legitimate businesses?

Ms. Jones. We are a very large provider of cloud-based services. And it is difficult for us to go, say, scan all of the files that are stored on our online file folder product. But what we can do is limit storage, limit bandwidth usage, and know patterns of behavior so that if there are very, very, very large quantities of data and they all seem to be copies of movies, our system might pick that kind of thing up.

But short of that, it is really important to us to have information from the content providers. So if it is the song makers, the movie makers, the video producers, whatever those people are, to help us be helpful and also so that it helps law enforcement to know which ones to go after because it is not enough for me to just say customer A has 47 dedicated servers and they are all filled with video stuff. It is not good enough because I don't know if it is legitimate content or not. That guy could have bought 47 dedicated servers worth of videos.

So it is really important for us to be able to identify—and I think Mr. Walker has pointed this out as well—what is the legitimate content and what is not. Again, we don't want to be facilitating bad guys, but we need help to identify which ones they are.

Ms. Chu. Thank you.

And, Mr. Morton, what are the next steps in Operation in Our Sites?

Mr. Morton. Well, we are going to continue to work with industry. We have been very careful not to focus on any one industry over the other. As you know, sadly the whole landscape of American industry is under assault right now. So we will focus on pharmaceutical sites. We will focus on entertainment sites. The counterfeiting sites we can do all day long, sadly; there are so many of them. And we are just going to keep at it. Wherever we can, we are going to pursue a full criminal investigation for those sites. Where all of the elements of the crime, other than the domain name, are outside of the United States, we will focus on the domain names and take them down as aggressively as we can, recognizing that is not the long-term solution. It is one part of trying to combat this problem.

But we got to do something. My perspective is do nothing and you fail, and so we have tried very hard to get out there, do something, and work with the other parts of the system to get us to a better, more comprehensive solution.

Ms. Chu. Thank you.

I yield back.

Mr. Quayle. Thank you very much.

As previously noted, we have a vote. So this hearing shall be temporarily adjourned until immediately following the vote. Recessed. Thank you, Mr. Watt.

[Recess.]

Mr. Goodlatte [presiding]. The Committee will reconvene.

Before I turn to the gentleman from California, I would like to ask unanimous consent to enter in the record two letters: one from the National Center for Missing and Exploited Children dated March 30, 2011, addressed to Chairman Smith and pertinent to the issue raised by the gentlewoman from California; and another a letter to the Members of the United States Congress from a coalition of groups dated March 30, 2011 on a related subject. [The information referred to follows:]

NATIONAL CENTER FOR MISSING & EXPLOITED CHILDREN®

Charles B. Wang International Children's Building
699 Prince Street
Alexandria, VA 22314-3175
U.S.A.

Telephone 703.224.2150

Facsimile 703.224.2122

www.missingkids.com

www.cybertipline.com

Other Offices
California
Florida
New York
Texas

March 30, 2011

**VIA E-MAIL**
The Honorable Lamar Smith
Chairman
Committee on the Judiciary
United States House of Representatives
2138 Rayburn House Office Building
Washington, D.C. 20515

Dear Chairman Smith:

I am writing to express our appreciation for the work that U.S. Immigration and Customs Enforcement (ICE) is doing in response to the explosion of child pornography. We are pleased that ICE is taking proactive steps that maximize the scarce resources necessary to investigate and prosecute every case. A comprehensive approach to the problem of child pornography on the Internet must focus not only on the arrest of perpetrators but also on the rescue of child victims and the reduced availability of their sexually abusive images on web pages.

As you know, the National Center for Missing & Exploited Children (NCMEC) operates the CyberTipline, which receives reports of apparent child pornography from both the public and electronic communication service providers (ESP). To date, we have received and processed more than 1 million reports regarding child sexual exploitation. Per federal law (18 U.S.C. §2258A), ESPs have reported more than 8 million images of apparent child pornography. ICE agents working at NCMEC headquarters have direct and immediate access to these reports. NCMEC is proud to be a partner in Operation Predator, ICE's ongoing initiative to investigate and arrest individuals who victimize children.

I'd like to highlight two examples of this partnership:

NCMEC received a report from an ESP regarding an individual who sent apparent child pornography via email. ICE agents determined the email was sent by a New Mexico church youth minister and former teacher. In addition, he had prior convictions in another state for corrupting minors and criminal solicitation to commit deviate sexual intercourse. His computer had thousands of sexually explicit images and videos of child pornography. NCMEC's Child Victim Identification Program determined that more than 2,200 of these images and videos contained child victims previously identified and rescued by law enforcement. The offender pled guilty to distributing/attempting to distribute a video depicting an minor boy engaging in sexually explicit conduct with an adult male and was sentenced to 18 years in prison.

April 4, 2011
Page two

In another case, a 29-year-old convicted sex offender from Dallas, Texas, was recently sentenced to more than 14 years in prison for possession of child pornography. The investigation began when an ESP made a CyberTipline report to NCMEC regarding a subscriber and apparent child pornography. In the course of ICE's investigation, the man admitted to possessing child pornography, including images of prepubescent children and images that depicted sadistic and/or masochistic acts.

These are just two of many such cases demonstrating the strong collaboration between NCMEC and ICE. Please don't hesitate to contact me if you need additional information.

Sincerely,

Ernie Allen
President and Chief Executive Officer

March 30, 2011

**TO THE MEMBERS OF THE UNITED STATES CONGRESS:**

We are writing to express our strong support of the efforts of the Immigration and Customs Enforcement (ICE) agency to combat digital theft and counterfeiting for a range of U.S. industries. In the case of the entertainment industry, the theft of motion picture and television productions threatens the economic vitality of our business, and the millions of American working men, women and local small businesses that depend on it. The websites targeted by ICE—via a transparent process that requires a judicial finding of probable cause—are not "innocent" Internet users; they are illegal for-profit businesses knowingly trafficking in stolen and counterfeit goods. They pose a threat to us, to movie theaters large and small, to the American public who unknowingly gives over personal financial income to unscrupulous traders, and to the health of the U.S. economy. ICE, by initiating Operation In Our Sites in June 2010, has stepped forward to protect U.S. industries and citizens from this form of cybercrime.

As you know, the U.S. intellectual property (IP) industries—of which ours is one—are critical to the health of our economy. Our industry alone produces billions in tax revenue each year, consistently generates a positive balance of trade with every country in the world, and has shown it can contribute to the economic recovery of areas hard-hit by the recession. We are woven into the fabric of the U.S. economy.

More than 2.4 million working Americans, residing in all 50 U.S. states, rely on the motion picture and television industry for their livelihoods. While it is true that our industry employs some well-known artists, that is not the real story of our business. Whether they are set builders, costume designers, electricians, assistant directors, or cast members, the overwhelming majority of those who work behind the scenes in our industry are middle class workers who are proud to be part of a business that has created a quintessential American product for almost 100 years: filmed entertainment. The major motion picture companies represent only a fraction of the businesses that make up our industry, as there are a host of U.S. companies who play a critical role in the creation of filmed entertainment providing technologies and services utilized in every step of the post-production process. More than 95,000 small businesses—93 percent of whom employ fewer than 10 people—are involved in the production and distribution of movies and television. Those individuals, small business owners and their families are extremely vulnerable to changes in the production economy.

Digital theft threatens the jobs of all who work in our business. Such theft destroys the ability of those who finance and produce filmed entertainment to recoup their investment, and in turn, the ability of film artists to continue to create. The majority of films produced must secure financing and distribution partners prior to production. Digital theft damages the confidence of those partners in their ability to do so, the end result being a diminished number of films being made and American jobs disappearing.

We are not talking about a distant future. Over the last three months, no fewer than three reports have demonstrated that infringing content represents a significant percentage of global Internet traffic. Most recently, a report released by Envisional, an independent Internet consulting company, estimated that almost a quarter of global Internet traffic and over 17 percent of U.S. Internet traffic is copyright infringing. This is a level of theft that cannot be sustained without significant damage to the motion picture industry, the workforce it supports and the American economy.

We commend Congress for providing resources dedicated to investigating and prosecuting counterfeiting and IP theft. The Intellectual Property Enforcement Coordinator's (IPEC) Joint Strategic Plan on Intellectual Property Enforcement released in June 2010 committed to using these resources and existing resources to increase law enforcement activity. ICE, the Department of Justice, and the IPR Center have stepped forward to carry out that mandate. Operation In Our Sites has not only put illegal sites out of business, but has raised public awareness about this specific form of crime on the Internet. Most importantly, these enforcement efforts have resulted in most of these entities ceasing their illegal activity. Movies and TV programs, some of the biggest draws on the Internet, are in many ways the "canary in the coal mine." Stealing and illegally selling this content may appear to be victimless crimes or a harmless form of theft, but they are neither. If it is not made clear that this kind of activity is illegal, it has the potential to become the harbinger of even more forms of illegal activity on the Internet.

Last month, the IPEC released its first annual report to Congress, reiterating not only the detrimental impact of copyright infringement on the economy but also the need to work with Congress to update intellectual property law to improve law enforcement effectiveness. We fully endorse that proposal, as we endorse the actions of ICE and the IPR Center.

We look forward to working with Congress and the Administration to support strong IP enforcement and to secure the additional resources that will protect our industry—and American jobs—from those who engage in the illegal activity of digital theft with disregard.

Sincerely,

American Federation of Television and Radio Artists (AFTRA)
Deluxe Entertainment Services Group Inc.
Directors Guild of America
Independent Film & Television Alliance (IFTA)
International Alliance of Theatrical Stage Employees (IATSE)

Motion Picture Association of America, Inc. (MPAA)
National Association of Theatre Owners (NATO)
News Corporation
Screen Actors Guild (SAG)
Sony Pictures Entertainment Inc.
Universal City Studios LLC
Viacom
Walt Disney Studios Motion Pictures
Warner Bros. Entertainment Inc.

Mr. Goodlatte. At this time, it is my pleasure to recognize the gentleman from California, Mr. Berman, for 5 minutes.

Mr. Berman. Well, thank you very much, Mr. Chairman, and thank all of you for your testimony.

Mr. Morton, I want to join with others in praising some very effective initiatives you are undertaking to deal with the problem we are discussing today.

Mr. Walker, I appreciate your testimony and your comments about the Digital Millennium Copyright Act. I am sure the Chairman of the Subcommittee does. He spent a great deal of time negotiating that legislation, and a lot of us were involved in it. But if that legislation were really working, I don't think we would be having this hearing. I don't think there would be a Senate bill. I don't think Customs would be undertaking the initiatives it is undertaking.

Ms. Lofgren is right. This is a complicated subject. But there is one element that is quite simple, and that is truly billions of dollars and thousands of jobs are being lost because of digital theft. I think we are focused on trying to do something about it.

In terms of a legislative approach, I wanted to take off on what you said. You said that Google doesn't want to be the judge, jury, and executioner. But right now under the Digital Millennium Copyright, you are the judge, jury, and executioner. You don't just take down anything that you are asked to take down. You go and try and go through some process to determine if it is a valid request, if in fact it is directed at infringing material.

The legislative approach is an approach to try and create a process where a judge is the judge and all you have to do is be the executioner. I am wondering if in that sense this might be something you would be more enthusiastic about because it puts the onus of looking at the whole site and whether it is—I mean, nothing is going to be 100 percent infringing because some things will be in the public domain that could be on that site. But fundamentally it is a site that is marketing illegally placed content, content without permission of the copyright owner.

So I guess I would like your thoughts. Let me ask a few questions and you can answer them. One is I would like your thoughts on whether having a judge rule that a site itself is dedicated to infringement and blocking that site may be a far more effective way of ensuring due process while actually making a difference, and also your reaction to the notion that the DMCA, as good as it is, in the context of today's technology, yes, you get that takedown letter.

You try to do it expeditiously, although there is testimony submitted for the record which says that it frequently takes as much as 20 days for you—or maybe that is an average of time before actually the link comes down. And I believe Google has said they are going to try and do this within 24 hours. But I do notice that the searches and the algorithms take a few seconds. And when you are talking about a newly released film or music, 24 hours on a site is disaster in terms of the millions of people who can then get it for free.

But your notion of why a judge doing this isn't more effective than putting all the onus on you.

And correct me if I am wrong, but when you get such a letter, you take down the link to that site. I don't even know if you have the legal ability or the functional ability to take down that site as a site. So all you are doing is taking out a link to one of what could be thousands of different works that are on that site. It is a little bit like trying to empty the ocean with a bucket. And I would like to get your reaction to some of those things.

Mr. Walker. Sure. There were a lot of comments there, so let me try and address them all, and if I miss one, please let me know.

I would say our fundamental position is that we agree that there is a way to complement the DMCA. The DMCA has been very effective for what it has done, but there are additional measures that can be taken to go after the money, to go after some of the advertising, to go after the payment processors that may reach some things that are outside the copyright domain, counterfeiting and the like. And we have indicated we are happy to work with the Subcommittee on that.

There is a balance, obviously, because there are millions of dollars—billions of dollars on each side of the table. Google accounts for $54 billion in economic activity in the United States.

Mr. Berman. Yes, that is important and innovation is important. But to the extent that some portion of that billions of dollars is coming from giving people access to copyrighted works that they didn't have their permission to use, it is fruits of poisonous trees.

Mr. Walker. Sure. No, we understand and we don't want money from illegal services and never have. But most of it, the vast majority is going to small businesses, small publishers, advertisers whose businesses actually exist because the Internet is out there. So we are trying to, again, separate the wheat from the chaff and do it in the most effective way we can.

The DMCA has been a good model for what it has done. That notice and takedown has been very robust and the work of this Committee and Congress has been adopted around the world in Europe and elsewhere. So we want to be careful about doing something that would undercut that. But that is not to say we are opposed to additional sort of targeted measures that go after things.

To your comments and Ms. Lofgren's comments earlier, we are in fairly frequent conversations with the general counsels and representatives of the trade associations, of the major motion picture studios, the RIAA, et cetera to try and refine and improve and streamline our processes. In many cases it is challenging. It does take a long time—and we are hoping to make it a much shorter time—to go back and forth through the different DMCA notices we get. There are a lot of people out there who just don't understand copyright law or are using them for abusive purposes to try and take down competitors' sites without a legitimate legal claim. And we need to sort through those, but I think we can do it, especially with regard to some of the online tools that we are soon to be launching in a much faster way than we are doing now.

You had asked also with regard to question of—there was one question about pre-release movies. We have actually talked to the studios about that and are there ways of being able to address that in an even more expedited fashion where there is real economic injury at issue there.

And then lastly, I would say we do have—focusing on your question with regard to whether or not a court finding would be useful in this, before anyone takes significant steps of taking away a domain name or cutting off advertising to a site, I think it is appropriate for a court to weigh in with appropriate due process to review that. And the model of doing that in a way that is targeted on the truly bad sites—and I think for some reasons we have talked with the staff on the Senate side with regard to the bill that was introduced in the last session. In some ways that definition was somewhat overbroad and created some of the free expression and due process issues we have talked about. But we are optimistic that we can work together to get to a more focused definition and we would be prepared to support that.

Mr. Berman. Mr. Chairman, my time is quite expired. Could I squeeze one more in here, though?

Mr. Goodlatte. Without objection.

Mr. Berman. In your testimony, you say the DMCA has practical and real effect on thwarting infringement, and legislation that targets the worst of the worst should not increase liability for online services that are playing by the rules.

What if we maintained the level of liability, not increase the liability, but required more affirmative steps to be undertaken under that standard of liability?

Mr. Walker. Well, I think much of the proposal, again, on the Senate side would have required affirmative steps based on a finding that a given site was dedicated to illegal content by having us remove it from our search results. And we are

Mr. Berman. But that doesn't increase your liability.

Mr. Walker. No. I think generally not. Ms. Jones has raised concerns about needing to have a safe harbor on that side, but generally speaking, we have been able to terminate people for violating our policies without getting suits back from the bad guys in response.

Our focus has been mostly on the collateral consequences of undermining the DMCA. For example, if a site is judged to be bad and that URL is out there and then somebody using our services posts that URL in a Google doc or in an email—I send you an email that includes that URL—well, Google is now hosting that content in a sense. Are we liable for including that URL? I think the common sense answer is no we shouldn't be and that the DMCA insulates that from liability, but if just that sort of in rem order were deemed to be de facto red flag knowledge, there would at least be an open question. So we need to clarify those kinds of unintended consequences.

Mr. Berman. Thank you.

Mr. Goodlatte. The gentleman from Florida, Mr. Deutch, is recognized for 5 minutes.

Mr. Deutch. Thank you, Mr. Chairman.

Director Morton, you and I have spoken many times about the recent ICE seizures of rogue websites, and I have been very open about my admiration for the way that your office took the absolute worst of the worst of these websites hosting illegal content. And I would just like to say publicly again that more agencies, I think, ought to take a look at their existing authorities and find new ways to use those clear and established powers to combat and recognize problems, and I hope that others will learn from your excellent example.

Mr. Walker, I wanted to follow up on two online points and then shift slightly.

You had spoken earlier about autocomplete and the fact that autocomplete really reflects what people are searching for. That is how it actually works. Is there anything that you can do to change that? For example, drugs, pornography. Is there any way that you ever modify autocomplete so that it doesn't show the list of search terms that might actually be a popular search term?

Mr. Walker. There are, in the pornography realm, for example, terms that are facially offensive to virtually every user of the site that are blocked. Yes.

Mr. Deutch. So it is possible. It is not simply the will of the masses that will dictate what autocomplete shows. It is possible to actually

Mr. Walker. No. Absolutely, and we have already said that we are doing that in this context as well.

Mr. Deutch. And then one other follow-up. The issue of searches and the efforts that you have taken on specific websites and specific searches where it is clear that they lead to pirated material, stolen material. In addition to those terms, do you also include specific websites that are provided to you? I mean, a lot of times people who search the Web who go on Google are fairly sophisticated. They know what they are looking for. They don't need to search free movies or free music. They know the site that they heard about in their high school class. That is what they go to search for. So have you taken steps and can you take steps to stop so when someone starts typing in whatever that violating website is, that that website name won't come up as well?

Mr. Walker. Yes, and that is consistent with the effort we have already announced. And we are working with the content industries to try and focus on that.

Mr. Deutch. Great.

And so I would like to just shift then and move on to really where the world is going and that is apps. There was a conversation earlier, an exchange that you had, where there was some discussion of this Grooveshark app that was removed from your marketplace. I just wanted to pursue that a little bit further. That was ultimately taken down. When were you first made aware that that site was available—that app was available in your marketplace?

Mr. Walker. I am not sure. Congressman. We can get back to you.

I will tell you that the apps marketplace has probably been in existence for a little bit more than a year. During that period of time, we have removed something on the order of 2,000 different applications for a variety of reasons, including intellectual property infringement.

Mr. Deutch. Okay, because I played around on one of my staff member's Google phones and went to the App Store, and still when you type in "free," the autocomplete on the phone will finish and you can find free music. And if you go to free music within the marketplace, you can still find what appears to me to be hundreds of sites that deal in stolen music, stolen movies as well, perhaps stolen books. I couldn't quite tell. That wasn't as easily identifiable.

So if you could speak to the efforts being made to crack down. There is one example, this one app that you took down. But what steps are taken? What do you do to actually take them down?

And if I can suggest, when you are in the store, there is an opportunity for you to flag as inappropriate the app that comes up and I would respectfully suggest that in addition to the reasons that you list already, sexual content, graphic violence, hateful or abusive content, and other objection, that it might be helpful for those of us who are concerned about these issues and who monitor this to include a specific check-off box for stolen content, pirated content, whatever you think is most helpful. I think that might help you investigate.

But if you could speak a little bit about the steps that you do take.

Mr. Walker. It is a helpful suggestion. Congressman, and we are, across our products, trying to have a more standardized approach to Web forms that allow people to report all of the kinds of content that we are talking about here today and create cues for review and processing that in an expeditious way.

We do have a team of people who review the apps in the App Store. It is sometimes challenging because any number of people have an incentive to get their app in there. In some cases those apps are camouflaged or difficult to determine. There are legitimate apps that will allow you to obtain free content, and there is a lot of legitimate free content out on the Web. And so we are trying to distinguish the apps that are well intentioned from the apps that are essentially designed to induce infringement. And that is the approach that we have taken there and continue to take as we review these, as well as apps that are trying to get malware out and various other sort of negative content.

Mr. Deutch. And again, what I am concerned about is your marketplace. And if you could actually help me understand this a little better. Your marketplace functions essentially as an online mall, and stores open in this mall. In a traditional bricks and mortar mall, those stores would pay rent. Can you explain how Google is compensated by these apps that pop up in the marketplace?

Mr. Walker. Sure. It varies which is perhaps one of the reasons why it is not as clear as it could be. Many apps are free, so there is not compensation per se. Some of those are supported by advertisements; some of them are not. And then some of them where you actually pay for the app, and in that case, Google takes a small amount of money as a fee for its service in providing the platform.

Mr. Deutch. On the free apps, the ones that are free to the consumer, is there any other way that Google is compensated for those? Are there advertisements that —

Mr. Walker. Yes. They may choose to use advertisements or they may not. And they may use Google ads or other forms of ads.

Mr. Deutch. I hope that you can understand my concern here. In a traditional shopping center, there would be no place for any store that opens that sells illegal goods. In this case, Mr. Morton and his good folks are effectively playing the role that the sheriffs in Palm Beach County would play if a shopping center opened in my district that wanted to sell illegal merchandise. And those stores would immediately be shut down as soon as they were notified.

Just trying to bring this full circle, I would ask that you can provide the Committee with some details on the Grooveshark example since it has been touted as a great example of your efforts to try to crack down on these apps that merchandise in illegal goods. I would like to understand when you were first notified and how long it took to investigate. If there is any way for you to determine how many songs might have been downloaded illegally during the period of that investigation, that would all he most helpful, I think, as we go about this.

And finally, Mr. Chair, if I could also ask—I know you are going to be requesting some additional information as well. I hope that you can broaden your request to focus on the application world as well, given that this is really the direction that we are going.

Mr. Goodlatte. Yes. If the gentleman would yield. If the gentleman would work with the Committee staff, we will be happy to incorporate your question into the questions that we will submit to the members of the panel.

Mr. Deutch. I appreciate it, Mr. Chairman, and I will yield back.

Mr. Goodlatte. I thank the gentleman.

The gentlewoman from Florida, Ms. Wasserman Schultz, is recognized for 5 minutes.

Ms. Wasserman Schultz. Thank you, Mr. Chairman.

Mr. Chairman, Ranking Member Watt, who I know is not here at the moment, I really want to start off by thanking you for holding this hearing today and for officially opening this investigation into rogue websites here in the House.

As our economy continues to recover, we really must take every action that we can to create jobs and meaningfully address intellectual property theft. It is a great place to start.

That is why I have been having a conversation with Google about this for almost 3 years now. Mr. Walker, it is good to see you.

In the last hearing, Mr. Chairman, I focused on the problem of advertising on rogue sites, advertising which not only lines the pockets of those who facilitate theft, but also advertising that makes many of these rogue sites seem legitimate to unwitting users.

Today, Mr. Walker, I would like to talk with you about two related issues, as you have spent the morning doing talking about your autocomplete feature on search and your notice and takedown times under the DMCA. First I want to start with autocomplete.

In your testimony, you say that Google is committed to prevent terms that are closely related with piracy from appearing in autocomplete. And you go on to say that you are working with the industry stakeholders to suggest specific terms that shouldn't appear in autocomplete.

And you were kind enough to come see me in my office almost a month ago, March 10th, and I raised this issue with you then. So I know you won't be sandbagged by my raising it here now. I showed you—let me just grab it—this screen shot, and it was a screen shot that lists what comes up in a search when you type in the word "knock-off."

Then Google's algorithm automatically filled in the suggested search terms that I described, some of which UGGs and Coach were the names of specific brands. I showed you this screen shot which showed all the suggested autofills when I typed in the word "knock-off" into the search engine window. It showed knock-off handbags, knock-off UGGs, knock-off Coach handbags, knock-off shoes, knock-off watches, and knock-off sunglasses, among others.

Now, all I typed in was "knock-off." I didn't type in anything else, and that is the list that came up. These weren't words that I typed. It is what your autofill automatically filled in.

Mr. Chairman, I would like to ask unanimous consent to admit this screen shot into the record.

Mr. Goodlatte. Without objection.*

Ms. Wasserman Schultz. And then we searched the word "fake" and got similar results. Fake Rolexes and fake Louis Vuitton purses.

Now, I realize—and from our conversation—fake can be attached to a lot of different kinds of things. As we discussed in my office, "knock-off" doesn't really conjure up anything other than trying to steal something that is someone else's intellectual property. And I know you referenced that they sell knock-off dresses and other kinds of products in Nordstrom's and Macy's. It would be very simple to simply have your autofill put those search terms in after knock-off if that is really what someone is searching for. But instead, your autofill brings up things that are not appropriate and are, in fact, facilitating illegal content and illegal products.

Now, I had my staff perform—this was a month ago that we had this conversation. I had my staff perform the same test yesterday, and they got the same results as they did

* The information referred to was not received by the Subcommittee at the time this hearing was printed.

before I shared these concerns with you a month ago. So nothing has changed since we talked. And I am concerned that your autocomplete feature continues to suggest that people visit websites with pirated content, that Google enables and facilitates theft by suggesting words that people haven't even typed in yet.

And I want to suggest to you, Mr. Walker, the word "knock-off," as I just said, is probably a word you don't need to get consensus on from the Nation's designers of purses, handbags, watches, shoes, and furry boots. It is probably okay to eliminate those words after the word "knockoff." What other meaning is there for the word "knock-off" than a fake product that is meant to be passed off as the real thing? Couldn't you instead redirect that traffic to legitimate sites?

Now, Chairman Goodlatte brought up Taylor Swift earlier. Way back in 2008, Mr. Walker, I sat down with some of your colleagues. Several of them are here today. And way back then, I showed them screen shots of unauthorized Hannah Montana songs on Google-hosted blogger sites with Google's ads on them on top of that. We talked about Google's obligations under the DMCA and we asked for you to help rightsholders by designing a product that would help them identify infringing content and pull it down more quickly. You said you would try to work with us, but that was 3 years ago. I continue to hear from the rights community that it was taking too long for Google to pull down pirated content.

So a year later, in November 2009, I facilitated a meeting between your lobbyist and RIAA President Cary Sherman. In that meeting, Google said you would try again to develop a product cooperatively. That was 2 years ago. Again, no real impact.

In May 2010, Google sent Rick Klau to meet with my staff, and I was so excited by what I believed was finally a new attitude at Google that I actually drafted a letter commending you for your leadership and your willingness to address these issues. Mr. Chairman, if I can ask that—well, is there a Chairman? [Laughter.]

If I can ask unanimous consent to admit this into the record. Sorry.

Mr. Goodlatte. Yes, Virginia, there is a Chairman. [Laughter.] Ms. Wasserman Schultz. Thank you.

Mr. Goodlatte. Without objection, so ordered.

[The information referred to follows:]

Chairman Bob Goodlatte
Subcommittee on Intellectual Property,
Competition and the Internet House Judiciary Committee
Committee on the Judiciary B-352 Rayburn
House Office Building Washington, D.C. 20515

Dear Chairman Goodlatte:

Thank you for convening the Wednesday, April 6 hearing on "Promoting Investment and Protecting Commerce Online; Legitimate Sites v. Parasites." I share your frustration with the ease with which you conducted a Google search to find "free Taylor Swift MP3s" and welcomed your saying that you would "do the same search in a week, a month, three months, six months" to see if there is any change. I presented similar search results to Google representatives in 2008 and again in 2009 and, therefore, believe that an ongoing assessment by the subcommittee is warranted and necessary. I believe members of the subcommittee from both sides of the aisle would agree that we need to follow the implementation of the promises made during Mr. Walker's testimony.

Mr. Chairman, I suggest that as part of the subcommittee's ongoing study that we also ask rights holders to provide evidence of the speed with which Google responds to DMCA take down notices. Mr. Walker's testimony states that, "the critical foundation for [Google's] anti-piracy efforts remains the DMCA" and that, "through the DMCA, Congress established a notice and takedown process that provides copyright owners expeditious recourse when the discover infringement online..." Section 17 use 512(c)(1)(C) requires that online service providers respond "expeditiously" to remove or disable access to, the infringing material.

As I mentioned during the hearing, I am told by many copyright owners that Google often takes over a week to remove infringing material after it receives notice and was glad to read in the testimony that Google is, "designing new tools that will enable us to act on reliable copyright takedown requests within 24 hours."

I suggest that the subcommittee ask both rights holders and Google to track the process and timeliness of DMCA take-downs and allegations that something violates Google's terms of service involving its search engine, Google Blogspot and Android Apps.

Thank you for your attention to this request. I know that you are crafting legislation to address online theft and look forward to working together to achieve our mutual objectives.

Sincerely,

Debbie Wasserman Schultz
Member of Congress

Ms. Wasserman Schultz. Thank you.

And I realize that my time has run out. If I can ask unanimous consent for just a couple of extra minutes, Mr. Chairman. I am wrapping up.

That was a year ago. But I have learned since then that there still has been very little improvement on notice and takedown times. According to the IFPI, for the month of February 2011, the latest month for which they have records, 46 percent of the blogspot infringement notices sent to Google remained active for longer than 7 days.

So, Mr. Chairman, would it be possible to include notice and takedown times as part of your investigation? Chairman Goodlatte?

Mr. Goodlatte. Yes. The answer is yes.

Ms. Wasserman Schultz. That would be great.

Mr. Walker, you really have an obligation to take those down within 24 hours. You know that you do. We have discussed it. But for a blogger in February, almost half were still up after a week. There really isn't a question here, Mr. Walker. You are Google. You helped overthrow the head of an entire country in a weekend. I mean, really, you are Google. Okay? So really, to suggest that this is difficult, too difficult for Google to accomplish, it seems to me that it is more expression of a lack of will, and I think that is unacceptable. I know that you say your heart is in it. Prove to use that you want to go beyond the boundaries that the law requires you to do because that is the right thing to do. Short of that, you are essentially promoting trafficking of stolen property, and that is just unacceptable.

Thank you, Mr. Chairman.

Ms. Lofgren. Will the gentlelady yield?

Ms. Wasserman Schultz. Oh, I would be happy to yield.

Ms. Lofgren. As you were talking, I just went on my little android and typed in "knock-off Coach purses," for example, on Google search. The first one, if you go to it, there is a site from ICE saying it has been taken down. The second one, if you go to it, the site is not found. And the third one is how to spot a fake Coach bag. So I think we can get overwrought here. The World Wide Web is a great big place, and we need to make efforts to get these counterfeit goods taken down.

Ms. Wasserman Schultz. Reclaiming my time. I don't really have any more.

Mr. Goodlatte. The gentlewoman's time has expired, and I think it would be only fair to allow Mr. Walker to respond to both comments.

Ms. Wasserman Schultz. Thank you very much.

Mr. Goodlatte. Mr. Walker is recognized to respond, and then we will move on to the next Members of the Committee.

Mr. Walker. Thank you very much, Mr. Chairman. I will look forward to addressing both of those points. Thank you.

And congratulations. Congresswoman, on your appointment yesterday.

Let me do it in reverse order, if I can, because the most important thing to me and to us is that you do believe and recognize that we are actually making progress here.

Over the last 6 months or so, we have announced commitments to this 24-hour turnaround time. It is about to be unveiled in the next week or 2. We actually have it up and running now in a test mode, and that goes to both copyright and the counterfeiting materials that we have talked about. So that is a dramatic change and streamlining with the sort of key tools that we have been able to implement. There is engineering work there and there is also partnering work there with the key companies we are working with.

Beyond that, in the last month or so, we have unveiled a Web tool, a Web form that goes across many of our products because one of the problems we were having was that we were getting so many low quality notices from people who didn't understand copyright. In some cases things were abusive, meaning one competitor was taking down another competitor's materials, fans of one football team were trying to take down the websites or links on another football team's listings using the DMCA. These are the kinds of things we need to sort out. The Web tool replaces a lot of the old paper and faxes and emails we were getting with a more standardized process.

And as a result of that, the good news is it is much easier for rights owners to be able to file material. The bad news is we have had blip in terms of being able to respond as quickly as we would like to, but we are looking forward to getting those response times down as we go forward. And that is above and beyond the 24-hour commitments we have talked about with the express tools.

So I think we are seeing progress. I recognize it has been a continuing conversation with you and your office. But judge us on— as we are going forward, I think we are making really material progress.

And to Congresswoman Lofgren's earlier comment, we spent a lot of time working with the content industry on this. I have talked to most of the general counsels of most of the MPAA and RIAA and their trade association. We understand where they are coming from. While there may always be some difference with regard to scope of fair use and these sorts of issues, there is no reason for grit in the system to be slowing down the operation of the DMCA, and we are trying to really make sure it is an efficient tool for everybody.

Ms. Wasserman Schultz. Mr. Chairman, I realize I am yielding back time I don't have, but I do appreciate your willingness and expression that there is will. And I will just point out that when I did type in "knock-off," it was simply "knock-off" and those other words came up in your autofill.

Mr. Goodlatte. This discussion is going to go on for quite a while.

Ms. Wasserman Schultz. Thank you very much. I yield back the time I don't have.

Mr. Goodlatte. I have been very generous.

And now we will recognize the gentlewoman from California, Ms. Sanchez.

Ms. Sanchez. Thank you, Mr. Chairman. I want to begin by thanking Mr. Morton for the initiative you have shown in being proactive in going after infringers. I do have some questions for you that I will come back to, but I want to start with Mr. Walker.

Mr. Walker, I want to address your AdSense program, if I may. In your written testimony, you stated that you respond swiftly when notified by rightsholders that an ad is being placed on an infringing site. And I am just curious to know on average how long does it take Google to comply with a DMCA notice.

Mr. Walker. It varies dramatically. Congresswoman, based on the different products and the different nature of the request. We get requests in foreign languages, paper, they are incomplete, et cetera.

Ms. Sanchez. Ball park figure?

Mr. Walker. Our gold standard right now is YouTube where we are typically able to process DMCA requests in a matter of minutes, and we have a very sophisticated system. That is above and beyond the content ID system that we have already talked about that automates the process for rightsholders.

With regard to other products, our goal is to move that within 24 hours for people able to use our sort of advanced and sophisticated tools. There will always be some cases that take longer, in some cases days, as we go back and forth with the rightsholders to clarify or correct defective DMCA notices, DMCA notices that aren't really about copyright, for example, and the like.

Ms. Sanchez. Okay. So there really isn't a typical time that you can say a ball park figure that it takes?

Mr. Walker. Unfortunately, it is very different for different products.

Ms. Sanchez. Okay. Let us start this way then. What is the shortest length of time it takes Google to respond?

Mr. Walker. I would say it is the YouTube example, a matter of minutes.

Ms. Sanchez. And the longest amount of time?

Mr. Walker. Well, some notices

Ms. Sanchez. I am just trying to get a scope here of time.

Mr. Walker. I don't mean to be evasive. Many notices are actually never processed because they are incorrect.

Ms. Sanchez. But for a correct notice. Let's qualify that and say for a correct notice. What is the longest amount of time it has taken?

Mr. Walker. You know, I think it is certainly in days and might even be in weeks depending on the nature of the notice, if it is in a foreign language, if it is submitted in a way that is difficult for us to process or we have questions.

Ms. Sanchez. Let's leave that topic

Let me ask you what happens to the ad revenue that was generated by that site while it was hosting infringing material. Does the ad revenue go to the rightsholder?

Mr. Walker. There are different scenarios with regard to our AdSense product which is the product that puts ads up against publisher websites and our AdWords product which are ads on Google essentially or hosted ads that go out. But when we discover somebody who is infringing, we stop payments to them if they are on the publisher side of it, and we refund money to the advertisers if money has been paid out.

Ms. Sanchez. But none of that money goes to the rightsholder who is being infringed upon.

Mr. Walker. It is in many cases difficult for us to determine who the rightsholder is in some of these situations. In the case of music, as you know, there are labels and publishers and artists.

Ms. Sanchez. Sure. So somebody is making money off of these sites, but it is almost like the rightsholder is—it is sort of a double whammy. They are being infringed upon by somebody else who is using their content in a way that isn't authorized, and then somebody who is selling ad revenue then on those sites is also making money and that is not going to the rightsholder.

Mr. Walker. I want to be clear. We are not making money really because we are refunding the money back to the advertiser when we discover that the site that the ad was appearing on was infringing. So it is not as though Google is holding that money.

Ms. Sanchez. Well, you and I will have to disagree on whether or not there is profit to be made in advertising on infringing sites.

I want to go back to Mr. Morton and your public education efforts. Now, you mentioned a successful symposium that you had last year and you talked about one that is also planned for this year. And the question that I have for you—and I am not trying to be impertinent here, but it seems like symposiums, which are a great idea—it is sort of like preaching to the converted because the folks that are attending those symposiums are probably the most informed or at least the most aware of the problem of IP theft. And I am talking specifically about industry leaders. Government officials, and congressional staffs. And reinforcing information to those folks may be beneficial, but if we are talking about the vast scope of IP theft, I would think that probably education efforts are probably better aimed toward a younger audience and the people who are actually doing the infringing.

So I want to know if you are taking any steps to inform, say, teenage kids who are looking for the new album of their favorite artist or a college student who is looking to watch a movie online or that type of crowd. Are there any efforts that you are dedicating toward making them more aware of the issue?

Mr. Morton. It is an excellent question. The Government has not typically been expert in the public education arena in this area, but it is exactly where we need to be.

So one of the things that we have been thinking about is the seizure banners that we use right now are static, and they just say we have seized this site. One of the things we have been contemplating is when we actually forfeit a site that was dedicated to infringing or counterfeiting, can we use the fact that so many people are going to see our banners. I mean, they have become a sort of unanticipated Internet phenomenon. Can we use those as an educational opportunity and instead of them just being static, have a public service announcement?

The other thing that we need to do and work on is working with the rightsholders so that we have—let's take the entertainment industry—updated public service announcements in the movie or maybe it is on iTunes or using the platforms that already exist that people are going to that are legitimate to help preach the gospel as it were. So we are very much focused on that. It is a need. It is a work in progress.

Ms. Sanchez. Great. Thank you.

And I thank the Chairman and I yield back.

Mr. Goodlatte. I thank the gentlewoman.

The gentlewoman from California, Ms. Waters, is recognized for 5 minutes.

Ms. Waters. Thank you very much, Mr. Chairman.

And to our Ranking Member, all of the Members of this Committee, this is a fascinating discussion and one that is very much needed, and I am really appreciative for the opportunity to engage our folks who have come here today to help us to learn about this problem of rogue sites and infringers, et cetera.

And while I thank everyone, I am particularly drawn to Ms. Christine Jones of Go Daddy Group who is so confident about what she is attempting to do and your description of the volunteer effort that you are attempting to get everyone involved in.

I notice in your testimony, I think you said you had identified 36,000 infringers or websites and that you told Google about them, and you expected them to take them down. Is that what you meant, or did you mean something else that you didn't have time to discuss about what you expected of Google? Would you elaborate a bit on that?

Ms. Jones. Sure. In 2010, we disabled 36,000 websites that were engaged in selling drugs illegally online. We worked together with the Intellectual Property Enforcement Coordinator from the White House and Google who has co-led this effort with me the entire way to form a group that would address those sorts of things. So if I suggested that I gave them a list that they did not act on, I misspoke and let's correct the record on that.

Ms. Waters. Okay.

Ms. Jones. What I am saying is that is exactly the sort of thing that voluntary cooperative group is designed to address, and I think it can be done effectively and successfully in other contexts as well.

Ms. Waters. Is there some way that we could be helpful incentivizing everyone so that there is more cooperation and that people are looking out for each other? Is there something that we can do legislatively?

Ms. Jones. Well, one of the things that we have heard from some of our brethren in the industry is that, look, we are not as big as Google and we are not as big as Go Daddy. You guys have scale. You have resources to effort against these problems. We don't.

Some registrars have 10 employees in the entire company. We have thousands. So one of the things that they have specifically asked for—and I think I can speak on their behalf here—is help them know when a site is engaged in illicit activity. Don't leave it to them to decide. And frankly, we would like to have that too. It is just that we might have some experts on our staff who have some knowledge and some judgment. So I think help them know. Don't threaten them with a lawsuit if they take action against a website. Give them a safe harbor if they do what they are supposed to do and then provide a consequence for the people that refuse to do it.

I mean, I think we have to keep in mind here we are vilifying Google because they are big, and they have the ability to influence a whole lot of what happens on the Internet. And some people vilify us because we are big and we have the most domain names under management of anybody in the whole world. But we don't engage in infringing other people's intellectual property. Right? So I think you have to be a little careful about throwing the spears against the people who are trying to make it better. And that is my one single defense of Mr. Walker today. [Laughter.]

Mr. Walker. And for the record, Mr. Chairman, I don't feel particularly vilified here.

Ms. Waters. Well, let me turn to Mr. Walker. I am glad you don't feel that you have been vilified. Perhaps you don't know it when you see it. [Laughter.]

But I would like to know what you think you can do better. You obviously have identified ways that you have tried and the complications of that. What else can you do?

Mr. Walker. I think we can continue to work with the content industry to make the process faster. We have a common goal on that and we are in the late stages of actually being able to deliver in a big way on that. And that has been an initiative that we announced in December and has been universally applauded, I think, by the folks on that side of the aisle.

Also as we have said, we are open to working on the advertising side, which is really the right complement to the DMCA process, to try and cut off advertisements to sites that courts have adjudicated to be illegal essentially and dedicated to infringing content. That makes sense to us as a complement.

We are also doing a lot of things to try and make life easier for rightsholders. We have hundreds of people working on this problem now. We spend, as I have told you, tens of millions of dollars to try and address it in a better way. We are trying to take the friction out of the system. And there are a lot of ways of doing that. Having a simplified Web form is one. Faster turnaround time is another. Working on the advertising system is a third.

Ms. Waters. Thank you.

I yield back the balance of my time.

Mr. Goodlatte. I thank the gentlewoman.

The gentlewoman from Texas, Ms. Jackson Lee, is recognized for 5 minutes.

Ms. Jackson Lee. Let me thank you very much, and I think you can just look at the activity on the dais of Members coming in and out that this is an important hearing. And Mr. Chairman and Ranking Member, I thank you for holding this hearing. Many of us are in a number of different hearings, and so we are very appreciative of this particular meeting.

I would like to focus on some of the issues that you have addressed but allow me the benefit of just trying to delve in it further.

I don't take ownership of this, but what I will take ownership of is the very interesting and important byline here, "Fight Online Theft." And I think each and every witness here, from the Government on, would say that you are unanimously in support of fighting online theft. I think I need yeses so it will be audible.

Ms. Jones. Yes, Congresswoman.

Mr. Walker. Yes.

Mr. Abrams. Yes.

Mr. Morton. Yes.

Ms. Jackson Lee. In the course of that, the documentation notes 2.5 million jobs lost to counterfeiting, $135 billion total global sales of counterfeit goods—I have seen it as I have traveled—$75 billion, cost of global piracy of copyright, $1.77 trillion by 2015. I think that is an enormous dent in the genius of America and the creation of jobs. I really think we are talking about jobs.

Let me just go right to Google because I frankly think it is important that you are here. I feel that there is going to be legislation, but it will not be punitive and it should not be punitive. It should be collaborative, and I encourage the collaborative process.

I will use the term "web crawling" to identify—and I want to know the difficulty that Google would have in identifying and working with better site placement and, as well, the taking down. You are committed, know that there is a job issue here. But I want you to know there is a genius issue here. We are proud of Google. We are proud of all of the witnesses that are here as it relates to their input into this economy, into the new job creator of the 21st century into the 22nd century. We are discovering something every single minute. The better discoveries we make—or as my son explains to me, the development side of the business and, if you will, the programmer or the person who is coming up with the ideas— the better off we are.

But can you tell me what would be the challenge for a greater engagement in the work of taking these sites down?

Mr. Walker. Sure. Congresswoman, thank you.

The key issue is the need for collaboration and identification of who the bad guys are, sorting out the baby from the bath water. We already do a lot of that on the DMCA side. We hear from the content industry.

Ms. Jackson Lee. So do you have a team? Do you have a department, a section that deals with that?

Mr. Walker. Yes, we do.

Ms. Jackson Lee. That has the expertise.

Mr. Walker. Yes.

Ms. Jackson Lee. So those individuals could give us input into the crafting of the legislation, to be honest with you.

Mr. Walker. No, absolutely, and we would be delighted to work with both this Subcommittee and the folks over at the Senate to try and make sure that we are coming up with a refined definition of who the bad guys really are.

Ms. Jackson Lee. So I get to other witnesses, just quickly what do they do in the pulldown? You are pulling down now. What can you do better to pull it down even more?

Mr. Walker. Sure. We can do it faster. We can do it with less friction. We can make it easier for rightsholders, and we are working on all three of those things.

Ms. Jackson Lee. Mr. Morton, you need help. Your staff is dwarfed by the employees that are in these companies that are sitting with you, but behind you I know are people in different industries. Musicians are being impacted. People with unique, inventive talents—their products are being taken. In the old days, you would go to a certain country and find people's pocketbooks were labeled and weren't the correct pocketbooks that you thought you were purchasing.

What tools do you need? I think you need an expanded team in ICE, to be frank with you, that is dedicated solely to this issue. But give us a point that we can hang our hats on.

Mr. Morton. A couple of things. Just a real focus on additional tools for foreign actors where there really isn't much based here in the United States, particularly either the defendants or the server.

Help from Congress understanding that the challenge here is so much broader than simply the traditional entertainment industry. This has gotten to a point where it is an assault on U.S. industry.

Ms. Jackson Lee. So the foreign element is something we need to include in the legislation and give you tools to reach. Is that what I am understanding?

Mr. Morton. It is really a collaborative one. It is not just Government. It is again allowing Government to work with the people to my left and to encourage the people to my left to work on this in a collaborative way. They can do so much more on a grander scale than we do. We are a specialized tool in the toolbox. It is important to have us, but we are not the end all and be all.

Ms. Jackson Lee. Let me just quickly, Mr. Chairman, if I could. Mr. Abrams, the First Amendment. This whole question of cyberlocking, this whole question of these parasite sites, your leadership on the First Amendment. And I am thinking about people stealing people's ideas. We have got to do a statutory fix I believe. Is there a comment that you want to expand on?

Mr. Abrams. All I would say is that I agree with you that you need to do something which involves additional methods, that enforcement of the copyright law that already exists. We have a copyright law. We are talking about entities that are already routinely and increasingly violating our copyright law by taking, stealing intellectual property that doesn't belong to them. And I think one of the main things that you can do which would be constitutional is to come up with a definition, difficult as it is, but a definition of a site or a domain that by its nature is so overwhelmingly dedicated to copyright infringement that a court can enter an order so designating it and that that order can be used and is available to entities such as, but not limited to, Google but the whole range of intermediaries in this area who, once they have it, can at least not be in the position of having to decide for themselves on an ad hoc basis all the time whether this is too much taking or that is too much taking. If we can get a judge, if we can get a magistrate to play that role—and I think a properly drafted statute can—I think that would be a very, very big step.

Mr. Goodlatte. And with that, the time of the gentlewoman has expired.

Ms. Jackson Lee. I thank the Chairman.

Mr. Goodlatte. Mr. Abrams' comments are a good note to end the hearing on with one exception. We are going to submit many questions to the panel for you to answer in writing and any other Members who wish to do so will have an opportunity to do so.

Mr. Watt wants to pose one of those questions which you can answer in writing, but he wants to pose it verbally. So we are going to yield to him for that purpose and then we will conclude the hearing.

Mr. Watt. I thank the Chairman for providing me this opportunity. I do this not to get a response today. It is addressed to Mr. Walker and Ms. Jones, but it is also addressed to people in the audience who are invested in this issue in various ways.

It has occurred to me that one of the areas we are going to have to look more aggressively at is this safe harbor notion. I am not sure I understand how it is being applied, but it seems to me that one possibility might be to impose some of the greater obligation and risk on the people who are requesting these takedowns, rather than just you having potential liability. The people who are best positioned to identify the culprits are the owners of these intellectual property, songs, materials that are being counterfeited. And when they request you to take something down, what I need to know is there some viable way to structure something that would put them at risk, in addition to putting you at risk, as opposed to just providing an absolute safe harbor here because safe harbors, it seems to me, are subject to being more abused than if somebody has some skin in the game, so to speak.

Ms. Lofgren. Would the gentleman yield?

Mr. Watt. Well, I am not sure the Chairman is going to let me yield.

Ms. Lofgren. Just on the point. One of the things we worried about when we wrote the DMCA—at least I worried about and expressed at the time—was that when you have notice and takedown request, who is going to stand up for the First Amendment. If it is somebody who has a different agenda, you know, the smartest thing for the person who it is directed to is just to comply. I think that gets to the issue you are talking about.

Mr. Watt. All I am trying to do is get all of these issues out. So I would welcome written comments from anybody on this whole notion of how the safe harbor works, whether it could work more effectively if we put some additional incentives in for people to put something on the line when they assert that they ought to be given a safe harbor.

And with that, Mr. Chairman—my, you have changed. [Laughter.]

Instantly you changed.

With that, I yield back.

Mr. Marino [presiding]. And I am not going to touch that statement.

Thank you, Mr. Watt.

Mr. Marino. I think I am the one left that has some questions, and I apologize for running in and out of here, but it is one of those days where several Committees are going at the same time. Actually I will be brief

First, there was a statement made earlier, and I think it was by Attorney Jones, and Attorney Walker responded to it to a certain extent on giving notice. And I liked that idea of people within the industry giving each other notice of rogue websites and getting them shut down.

Does anyone on the panel—and I will start with you, Mr. Walker—have any problem with that?

Mr. Walker. The challenge, Mr. Chairman, is the verification of what is legitimate and what is illegitimate. Some of the bills that are being talked about here would have appropriate due process and a court review, and that is, I think, where we are most comfortable before we are talking about something like taking down somebody's website or cutting off access to their services or advertising.

There have been other examples in the pharma case and the like where there are a limited number of authorized websites out there.

You know, there may be only 20 people who are allowed to buy ads for pharmaceuticals. That is somewhat different than in the content industry where there are a million different people. Everybody who posts something on YouTube, including their home movies— that is a copyrighted act, copyrighted work. So we have to be a little careful about that.

That said, we are delighted to work with the rest of the industry to share information. We have worked, in fact, with ICE. We have somebody down at the IPR Center today helping them get up to speed on some of the technology issues at play here, and we are delighted to do that.

Mr. Marino. Does anyone else care to respond to that?

Ms. Jones. I will briefly. I mean, I suggested it. We like getting information from people and we like sharing information with other people.

I think it might be slightly disingenuous to suggest that somebody can't verify that a pharmacy is selling drugs without a prescription. That is a pretty easy case. I will agree that it is much more difficult to determine a genuine Louis Vuitton bag or a song recording that has been authorized by the production company, the distributor, or the writer, and so on and so forth. So the issue is very complicated, but the sharing of information is really, really important.

Mr. Marino. Attorney Walker, you noted that defining a rogue site is not simple. Would you be able to come up with at this moment a definition of what you would propose?

Mr. Walker. Absolutely, at least at a level of principle. Because we thought the comment may come up, forgive me as I refer to my notes here.

Mr. Marino. Sure.

Mr. Walker. I think we are in the process of actually sharing specific statutory language we propose, but at a high level, we would say there are four key principles to be looked at. One is that the site is knowingly violating copyright law. Second is that it contains complete copies of works or counterfeit goods. Third is it has a commercial purpose. And four is that it refuses to respond when notified by rights owners. Within that construct, I think we are comfortable with a notion of a site that is dedicated to infringement.

Mr. Marino. Would you agree with me—and see if my research is right. You were an Assistant United States Attorney.

Mr. Walker. That is correct.

Mr. Marino. And I was a United States Attorney. Many times we have prosecuted people for omission, turning a blind eye. A scenario I could use is when I made a drug arrest and went into a crack house, and there were several individuals who were not particularly selling the drugs but they were facilitating the dealers and knew that it was going on. Would you agree with me that those individuals could be prosecuted for aiding and abetting?

Mr. Walker. So long as there is a finding of specific knowledge and intent to have the transaction proceed, yes, sir.

Mr. Marino. Sure. I would think a specific knowledge is here I have the cocaine in my pocket and I am going to give it to the guy at the door so he can sell it. So I think we get over that hurdle.

But not equating the industry with that, but don't you think there could be a situation where it may appear that industry is turning an eye and simply saying because of cost or other reasons, this is just too much for us to address?

Mr. Walker. I want to be very clear that we are not saying that. I recognize it is a growing problem, and as I say, it is a frustration for us, as it is for the content industry. When the bad guys' sites proliferate or change their identity or Congressman Issa earlier referred to a site that changed its name to avoid detection, we have that problem too. And it is important to not confuse the message with the messenger. It is a difficult problem and we work on it hard every day.

Mr. Marino. And please continue.

One more question I have for the Director. How would enforcement be affected if prior notice of seizure blocking orders was given to parasites before they were shut down, and how easy is it for websites to change domain names or redirect traffic to other websites?

Mr. Morton. The answer to your question depends on whether or not we are in a civil or criminal context. I think the Government's view in the criminal context would be that we shouldn't alter basic criminal procedure which doesn't provide notice in most instances to Government search warrants or arrests prior, obviously, to the execution of the search or the arrest.

In the civil context, it is a different story, and I think there is plenty of room for prior notice. That is a common hallmark of civil enforcement, and I don't see why it would be any different than it is in other areas of the law.

Mr. Marino. Anyone else wish to make a comment pursuant to my questions to the Director?

[No response.]

Mr. Marino. No? Well, I think that concludes our hearing today. I would like to thank our witnesses for their testimony, and I really appreciate your being here. I certainly want to thank my colleagues for the in-depth questions.

And without objection, all Members will have 5 legislative days to submit to the Chair additional written questions which we will forward to the witnesses and ask them to respond to as promptly as possible so their answers may be part of the record.

Without objection, all Members will have 5 legislative days to submit additional materials for inclusion in the record.

With that, I again thank the witnesses.

This hearing is adjourned.

[Whereupon, at 2 p.m., the Subcommittee was adjourned.]

*Chapter 7*

# SUBMISSIONS FOR THE RECORD

## PREPARED STATEMENT OF THE HONORABLE DARRELL ISSA, A REPRESENTATIVE IN CONGRESS FROM THE STATE OF CALIFORNIA, AND MEMBER, SUBCOMMITTEE ON INTELLECTUAL PROPERTY, COMPETITION, AND THE INTERNET

Chairman Goodlatte,

Thank you for holding this second hearing today on legitimate versus parasite websites.

Counterfeiting and Online piracy continue to run rampant on the internet; stifling legitimate online commerce and costing manufactures and content producers billions of dollars a year.

Many of these websites are run by entities with links to organized crime and other criminal elements. The structure of the internet has made it difficult in the past for law enforcement to make a substantive dent in these elements; however, I appreciate the recent efforts of U.S. Immigration and Customs Enforcement to employ innovative methods to take down parasite sites.

There are many different ways that legitimate web-based companies have unintentionally supported the efforts of counterfeiters and online pirates; whether through providing them with ad based revenue, or facilitating financial transactions to their overseas locations.

I look forward to hearing recommendations from our panel of witnesses today as to how we can deal with illegitimate online sites versus legitimate ones. It is my hope that some thoughtful ideas will come from this discussion that can be incorporated into a balanced piece of legislation.

Whatever actions we end up taking on this important issue we must make sure that they do not tread upon individual's legitimate usage of the internet.

Thank you Mr. Chairman and I yield back.

## Congressman Tim Griffin (AR-02), Statement for the Record, Subcommittee on Intellectual Property, Competition, and the Internet, "Promoting Investment and Protecting Commerce Online: Legitimate Sites v. Parasites, Part II", April 7, 2011

I commend Chairman Bob Goodlatte for convening this important hearing as Congress reviews past efforts to enforce copyright law and considers legislation to protect the intellectual property rights of our nation's innovators. The need for this hearing and for legislation to address copyright infringement on the Internet is clear: copyright infringement costs American jobs, and creators have and will continue to lose billions of dollars every year unless Congress acts. The Internet is a dynamic system, and Congress should recognize this fact by passing adaptive legislation that protects copyright holders in the digital age.

U.S. Immigration and Customs Enforcement (ICE) has taken a positive step toward stronger copyright enforcement by implementing "Operation in Our Sites." This first-of-its-kind program protects American jobs by providing aggressive enforcement of copyright law on the Internet. I applaud the leadership of ICE Director John Morton and look forward to the continued success of this program.

Copyright protection is first and foremost a jobs issue. From the sale of counterfeit software to CDs to DVDs, and pharmaceuticals, copyright infringement undermines job growth and weakens our Nation's constitutionally guaranteed respect for intellectual property rights. As the Internet continues to reinvent itself. Congress is duty-bound to pass legislation that keeps current our ability to take down rogue sites and to protect copyright law in America. 1 stand ready to work with my colleagues on the Committee to pass legislation that addresses this urgent need.

The Register of Copyrights of the United States of America
April 1, 2011

The Honorable Zoe Lofgren
U.S. House of Representatives
1401 Longworth House Office Building
Washington, D.C. 20515

Re: Hearing of the Subcommittee on Intellectual Property, Competition, and the Internet on Promoting Investment and Protecting Commerce Online: Legitimate Sites v. Parasites, Part T'

Dear Representative Lofgren:

During the Subcommittee hearing, you requested information regarding the Copyright Office's discussions with stakeholders about the rogue website issue. As I described during my testimony, our legal and policy staff are immersed in an ongoing series of meetings with a large number of diverse stakeholders. To date, we have had discussions with content owners,

Internet service providers, payment processors, companies that provide search engines, public interest groups, and various additional players in the Internet ecosystem. We are continuing these meetings to further expand our knowledge of the legal and technical considerations relevant to rogue websites and to support the work of the Subcommittee.

I have enclosed here a list of the fifty-four stakeholders we have seen thus far in thirty-seven meetings. Thank you for your request and please do not hesitate to contact us if you need additional information.

Respectfully submitted,

Maria A. Pallante
Acting Register of Copyrights
Enclosure
cc: Hon. Robert Goodlatte
Chairman, House Judiciary Subcommittee
on Intellectual Property, Competition, and the Internet
Hon. Mel Watt
Ranking Member, House Judiciary Subcommittee
on Intellectual Property, Competition, and the Internet

## U.S. COPYRIGHT OFFICE
## ROGUE WEBSITES STAKEHOLDER MEETINGS

April 1, 2011

1. American Express
2. American Federation of Television and Radio Artists (AFTRA)

3. American Society of Composers, Authors, and Publishers (ASCAP)
4. Association of American Publishers (AAP)
5. The Authors Guild, Inc.
6. Broadcast Music, Inc. (BMI)
7. Business Software Alliance (BSA)
8. Center for Democracy & Technology (CDT)
9. Computer & Communications Industry Association (CCIA)
10. Comcast
11. Directors Guild of America (DGA)
12. Disney
13. Doxpara
14. eBay
15. Entertainment Software Association (ESA)
16. Electronic Frontier Foundation (EFF)
17. Facebook
18. Federal Communications Commission (FCC)
19. G2
20. Go Daddy
21. Google
22. Information Technology and Innovation Foundation (ITIF)
23. Interactive Advertising Bureau (IAB)
24. International Alliance of Theatrical Stage Employees (IATSE)
25. Internet Corporation for Assigned Names and Numbers (ICANN)
26. Major League Baseball (MLB)
27. MasterCard Worldwide
28. The McGraw-Hill Companies
29. Microsoft
30. Motion Picture Association of America, Inc. (MPAA)
31. MovieLabs
32. National Basketball Association (NBA)
33. National Football League (NFL)
34. National Music Publishers' Association (NMPA)
35. NBC Universal
36. News Corporation
37. NetCoalition
38. Paramount Pictures
39. PayPal
40. PolicyBandwidth
41. Public Knowledge
42. Recording Industry Association of America (RTAA)

43. Reed Elsevier and Elsevier
44. RosettaStone
45. Screen Actors Guild (SAG)
46. Sony Music
47. Software & Information Industry Association (SIIA)
48. TimeWarner
49. U.S. Chamber of Commerce
50. U.S. Immigration and Customs Enforcement (ICE)
5I. VeriSign
52. Verizon
53. Viacom
54. Visa

MACMILLAN
Brian Napack

## Statement Submitted by Brian Napack, President. Macmillan House .Subcommittee on Intellectual Property, Competition, and the Internet Hearing on "Promoting Investment and Protecting Commerce Online: Legitimate Sites v. Parasites, Part II" Wednesday, April 6, 2011

Mr. Chairman and Members of the Committee

We applaud the work that the House Judiciary Committee has done to promote and protect the work of American authors and publishers, and I appreciate this opportunity to submit written testimony to the Committee as it seeks to address the critical problem of digital piracy and counterfeiting.

Macmillan is one of our nation's leading publishers with well-known imprints such as St. Martin's Press, Farrar Strauss & Giroux, Henry Holt, Picador. Tor, Macmillan Audio. Bedford Freeman A Worth. i>clicker, and Hayden McNeil As publishers, we create books, textbooks, and a myriad of digital products and interactive services that contribute directly to our nation's culture, to our educational system, and to the asset base of intellectual property that is the engine of the American economy.

Our industry is built upon the creative drive of many thousands of authors, educators and technologists. Together, we are embracing the incredible opportunity that technology presents to create powerful new content that inspires and educates, and to get this content in the hands of more readers and learners as their reading goes digital. Unfortunately, the rise of the new digital book formats, distribution channels, and devices that make such innovation possible has also brought with it a steep rise in digital piracy,

Today, we believe that the economic ecosystem that supports the creative output of publishing is deeply threatened by a competing, illicit economic ecosystem, one fueled by the wholesale theft of American intellectual property.

We, like those in the ether creative industries, look forward to working with Congress to craft solutions that take a comprehensive approach to reigning in piracy by curtailing the activities of rogue websites and by disrupting their ability to profit from theft.

## The Problem Facing the U.S. Book Publishing Industry

At this very moment, a large portion of Macmillan's catalog of copyrighted books and textbooks are easily found and freely available for download from unauthorized websites all over the Internet. These websites, which include some of the most heavily trafficked websites in the world, operate out in the open. They carry advertisements from well-known companies, they accept major credit cards, and at first blush appear perfectly legitimate. And consumers are downloading copyrighted books from them by the millions.

Although the problem of distal piracy is relatively new to the book business, its contours and scale have quickly become clear and appear quite familiar to those that have watched the recent history of the music and movie businesses.

- At Macmillan, we have seen a rapid rise in the availability of our titles on pirate sites worldwide. We currently issue well over 3,000 takedown notices every month under the provisions of the Digital Millennium Copyright Act and this number is rising.
- In October of 2010, the anti-piracy firm Attributor found that there were between 1.5 and 3 million daily searches online for pirated e-books and that this figure is increasing 50 percent annually.[92]
- An earlier study released by Attributor tracked 914 book titles over a three month period and found that 9 million individual copies these books had been downloaded from pirate sites in just a three month period.[93]
- A study by Verso Digital in January 2010 found that 28% of eReader owners had used file-sharing sites to download free eBooks.[94]

[92] http://attributor.com/blog/a-first/book/at/demand-for-pirated-e-books-across-the-web/.
[93] http://attributor.com/blog/book-piracy-costs-study/.
[94] http://www.versoadvertising.com/invers/?p=213.

- A story entitled "Digital Piracy hits the e-book industry" by CNN in January 2010 tracked best-selling author Dan Brown's latest novel "*The Lost Symbol*" as it was illegally downloaded over 100,000 times on pirate sites within the first few days of its release.[95]

Not surprisingly, free is a very compelling value proposition. And, of course, each pirated version online can translate into many lost sales as they are downloaded repeatedly and passed around from reader to reader, even accounting for the probability that not every free download will equate to a lost sale.

Making our content available in digital formats is a vital part of our business model, allowing us to deliver content to readers when, where, and how they want it. But just as we look to innovate using devices such as Barnes & Noble's Nook, Amazon's Kindle, and Apple's iPad, pirates look at these new devices as new opportunities to expand their lucrative businesses. We have, in fact, seen sharp rise in activity on pirate websites in the year since the introduction of the iPad. We have also seen the advent of widely distributed tools that facilitate the removal of anti-piracy protection from our eBooks so that they can be freely distributed. Unfortunately, the opportunity to distribute pirated materials will only accelerate as the new platforms proliferate.

Looking across the sectors of copyright-intensive industries, a dark picture of the future emerges for anyone whose livelihood depends on the creation and distribution of books:

- Rogue sites engaged in copyright piracy receive over 53 billion visits a year.[96]
- Nearly one quarter of all Internet traffic worldwide is reportedly associated with infringing activity.[97]
- The value of digitally pirated products is as much at $75 billion and appears to be rising very rapidly.[98]

## How Books Are Being Stolen

Books are being pirated online today through a wide variety of websites, each of which presents unique challenges, Today, the primary concerns of publishing are the following:

---

[95] http://www.cnn.com.2010/TECH/01/01/ebook.piracy/index/html.
[96] MarkMonitor, "Traffic Report: Online Piracy and Counterfeiting," 2011.
[97] Envisional. "Technical Report: An Estimate of Infringing Use of the Internet," 2011.
[98] Frontier Economics, "Estimating the Global Economic and Social Impacts of Counterfeiting and Piracy," 2011.

- Cyberlocker sites are currently the venue of choice for book pirates. These personal file storage sites are known to host countless individual pirated book files and are easily searchable by consumers looking for free files using major search engines. They offer little protection for copyrighted works. To attract users and pirated content, these sites often offer payments and other incentives in exchange for uploads of content files. Not surprisingly, popular copyrighted books wind up being popular downloads on these services.
- Peer-to-peer (P2P) sites and services play matchmaker for uploaders and downloaders who can share files directly between using technologies that eliminate the need for a central server. Due to the distributed nature of this model, there is no central server. This renders the notice and takedown procedure of the DMCA of limited application and ineffective,
- Pirate stores are online retailers that offer large collections of infringing eBooks for free or at deep discount. Often the works are available on pirate stores before publication, which severely damages the potential sale of a book. These sites are among the most nefarious infringers since they often appear to be legitimate online retailers, promoting products, taking sales, and carrying advertising.
- Feeder sites, also known as link sites, are websites that do not host infringing files, but rather provide links that enable downloads from cyberlocker sites. They exist in order to attract large volumes of traffic that they can monetize through means such as advertising and "referral" commissions from cyberlockers which pay them a percentage of their premium subscription revenues.

While there can certainly be legitimate uses for some of these sites, a great many of them engage in, condone, and even encourage massive trafficking of stolen IP. These sites are real businesses that are supported by common commercial models such as the sale of advertising, premium subscriptions, and unauthorized versions of products such as our books. They have robust economic models yet they provide no compensation to the creators of the IP that sustains their businesses. Increasingly, they have located themselves outside the reach of U.S. law and enforcement agencies.

From our perspective as publishers, it is as if there was a chain of beautiful bookstores, well-lit and fully stocked, located on prime sections of Main Street everywhere, sitting right next to Barnes and Noble or Borders superstores. The only difference is that the books in the first store are actually stolen and offered for free or close to free. If you were walking by which one would you walk into?

In the physical world, we would have no qualms about shutting down the store engaged in the sale of stolen goods. Yet, today there is currently little that we can do stop the illegal activity of these obviously bad actors.

## What Macmillan Is Doing to Confront Digital Piracy

At Macmillan, we consider protecting the work of our authors one of our top priorities. Thus, we are taking aggressive steps to confront digital piracy:

- We devote a significant amount of time and money to searching the Internet for unauthorized and infringing versions of our books and then issuing takedown notices under the DMCA, We now issue thousands of takedown notices every month, only to see such materials reappear almost immediately on the same sites. Unfortunately, the volume of works found online continues to grow despite these efforts.
- Where possible, we and other publishers have taken legal action against leading file-sharing sites overseas. While this has had some limiting effect on the infringing activities of the specific targets, much of the pirate traffic appears to simply shift to other infringing sites.
- We work diligently to protect our content throughout the publishing process to prevent our pre-publication books from winding up online. To this end, we have invested considerable sums in sophisticated systems and processes to track and protect our content as it works its way through the publishing process. Of course, once a book is published, it is easily copied or scanned and distributed.
- We work closely with our business partners to implement practices and technologies that can limit piracy. Just this week, a leading tablet manufacturer agreed to pull the app of one of the leading pirate cyberlocker sites from their app store. In another case, our work led to the same device manufacturer refusing to accept the app of a significant facilitator of eBook piracy for distribution in their app store. As a result, the infringing company decided to ''go legit." A year later, they remain "legit." In yet another case, a major US-based online book community decided to implement content filtering in response to pressure from publishers. This filtering technology, while admittedly imperfect, is allowing the site to identify infringing content and prevent its upload before it appears on the site, available for public consumption. This action is paving the way for commencing commercial relationships with publishers such as Macmillan.
- Above all, we work to make the vast majority of our content widely available at fair prices and in the formats that consumers want. Although the existence of piracy could motivate us to keep our content offline, we believe that broadly restricting the availability of digital books would limit market innovation and would only serve to increase a consumer's motivation to steal our content, and for pirate sites to fill the void.

Despite all of these actions, digital piracy of books continues to grow very rapidly, largely fueled by the existence of large commercial websites and services that profit from the creative output of our industry. As has occurred in other IP-based industries, rampant online piracy threatens to undermine our ability to nurture creativity, to develop new technologies that will enhance knowledge development and education, and to create a publishing platform for the next generation of great American authors.

For these reasons, we must now pursue strong legislation. Our simple goal is to begin to shut down the very worst offenders and choke off the economic incentive that they now have to steal and trade in the work of authors and publishers.

## A Comprehensive Legislative Approach

Macmillan strongly supports the introduction of legislation that enables us to address the "worst of the worst' infringers. Further, we believe that any such legislation must address the problem in all of its forms, including all categories of infringing sites as mentioned above.

From our perspective as publishers, this would mean that any legislation must specifically include cyberlocker sites due to the massive and flagrant book piracy they are facilitating today. We recognize that the inclusion of cyberlockers presents a challenge because they can, in theory, be used for legitimate purposes. To address this concern, we propose a rubric that enumerates criteria that may be indicative of whether a site is legitimate or is primarily disseminating pirated or counterfeit goods and services. Proposed criteria could include:

- Does unauthorized copyrighted content comprise a substantial portion of the material publicly offered by or through the site such that the operators of the site must know of and acquiesce to this activity?
- Does the site have substantial, repeated, and persistent features that directly enable trafficking in unauthorized copyrighted content?
- Does the site take reasonable steps, including well-known technologies such as filtering, to prevent the distribution or sharing of infringing content?
- Does the site take reasonable steps to remove or disable access to infringing content in an expeditious and reasonable manner upon notification by or on behalf of the copyright owner, and are reasonable efforts made to keep such infringing content off of the site?
- Does the site market itself as a source of free, copyrighted content and prominently feature verbiage that is associated with pirated or counterfeit product distribution?

- Does the site's domain name incorporate a trademark or service mark that indicates the availability of pirated or counterfeit products or services?
- Does the site offer financial or other incentives to upload and broadly share stored content?

This list is certainly not exhaustive, but it does encompass key characteristics that define the bright line between legitimate sites and those that are aggressively pursuing business models primarily based on piracy and counterfeiting.

## Engaging Key Industry Partners

A second critical element of any effective legislation must be the engagement of key members of the legitimate Internet economy whose services are unwittingly used to enable the piracy-based business models. These players include ISPs, search engines, payment processors, and advertising service providers, each of whom is responsible for a key piece of the rogue website economic ecosystem.

Said differently, consumers cannot find rogue sites without search engines and cannot go to these websites without ISP's who manage internet traffic. Further, the rogue sites cannot sell illegitimate product without the services of credit cards processors and cannot sell adds without ad networks. Thus, we need the help of these key players, and any legislation should not contain substantial carve-outs that would otherwise allow some entities to be part of the solution only when it is convenient for them.

Specifically, it has become clear that search engines provide a vital link to rogue sites for consumers. It is also clear that the search engines can quite effectively remove and/or block specific websites from their search results. We have seen search engines make ongoing iterative changes to their search algorithm to decrease rankings of websites that capitalize on loopholes, or that offer generally low quality content.[99] Presumably, these companies could do the same for other sites that blatantly traffic in pirated content.

To date, we have made progress working with some of these industry partners. However, it is clear that legislation is needed to lay the appropriate legal framework that will allow ISPs, search engines, payment processors and ad service companies to fully tackle this problem alongside rights holders. For instance, some intermediaries may require immunization from liability, along with clear direction from judicial authorities, in order to take concerted action against rogue sites.

[99] http://googleblog.blogspot.com/2011/01/google-search-and-search-engine-span.html.

## Conclusion

For the book publishing industry, the obvious end result of continued, unfettered growth of rogue websites will be simple: the large scale loss of sales, profits, and jobs. From our point of view as publishers, a more dangerous effect lies behind the simple economics.

As book sales evaporate the incentive for writers to write and publishers to publish will decay. It is truly demoralizing for authors to see their work, which may have taken many years to create, online for free the instant it is published. Moreover, for many authors and publishers the migration of a small share of sales from "paid" to "pirated" will be the difference between continuing to create books and having to find another line of work.

As publishers, we believe that this outcome will result in long term damage to our knowledge-based economy, our culture, and our standing in the world. Thus, while the direct effect of piracy can be quantified but the cost to our nation's future will be immeasurable.

Again, Mr. Chairman, we appreciate this opportunity to share our views with the Committee and would look forward to the opportunity to work with you and your colleagues as you continue to address the important issue of protecting American intellectual property.

# Statement of the Motion Picture Association of America, Inc., Before the House Judiciary Committee's Intellectual Property, Competition, and the Internet Subcommittee Hearing: "Promoting Investment and Protecting Commerce Online: Legitimate Sites v. Parasites, Part II," Rayburn House Office Building, Room 2141 Washington, D.C., April 6, 2011,10 AM

## A. Background and Introduction

We want to thank the Committee for holding a second hearing on promoting legitimacy online and addressing the economic impact to our industry by parasitic websites that traffic in stolen content. We appreciate the opportunity to submit this

Statement on behalf of the Motion Picture Association of America, Inc.[100] and its member companies regarding the serious and growing threat of Internet sites that profit from the theft and unauthorized dissemination of creative content. As the primary voice and advocate for the American motion picture, home video and television industries in the U.S. and around the world, we have witnessed the proliferation of web-based enterprises dedicated solely to stealing the product of our industry's workforce and are gravely concerned about the detrimental impact that digital theft has on the millions of American men and women who work in our industry.

The U.S. motion picture and television industry plays a unique role in today's American economic infrastructure, providing high-paying jobs to workers in all 50 states; fueling small business growth; injecting capital into local, state, and national revenue pool and consistently generating a positive balance of trade. Of the 2.4 million American workers who depend on the entertainment industry for their jobs, about 12 percent are directly employed in motion picture and television production and distribution—from behind-the-scenes production technicians to make-up artists and set-builders—across all 50 states. These are high-paying jobs, paying an average salary of nearly $76,000, 72 percent higher than the average salary nationwide. More than 95,000 small businesses—93 percent of which employ fewer than 10 people—are involved in the production and distribution of movies and television. On-location filmed productions infuse, on average, $223,000 per day into a local economy. Nationwide, our industry generates more than $ 15 billion in public revenue. As one of the few industries that return a positive balance of trade, our industry is critical to the U.S. export economy.

## B. Websites Peddling Stolen Digital Content Create Consumer Confusion, Harm the Online Marketplace and Damage the Motion Picture and Television Industry

High-speed broadband networks present tremendous opportunities for exchanging information and ideas; unfortunately, the laws and regulations put in place to protect consumers and innovation in the physical marketplace have not kept pace with the growth of illegal conduct online. The illicit use of online networks can facilitate the anonymous theft and rapid, ubiquitous illegal distribution of copyrighted works. The key foundation of American industry—the expectation that hard work and innovation is rewarded—is imperiled when thieves, whether online or on the street, are allowed to steal America's creative products and enrich themselves along the way.

---

[100] The Motion Picture .Association of America and its international counterpart, the Motion Picture Association (MPA) serve as the voice and advocate of the .American motion picture, home video and television industries, domestically through the MPAA and internationally through the MPA. MPAA members are Paramount Pictures Corporation, Sony Pictures Entertainment Inc. Twentieth Century-Fox Film Corporation. Universal City Studios FFC. Walt Disney Studios Motion Pictures, and Warner Bros. Entertainment Inc.

Rampant theft of American intellectual property puts at risk the livelihoods of the workers who invest time, energy and fortune to create the filmed entertainment enjoyed by millions. To these men and women and their families, digital theft means declining incomes, lost jobs and reduced health and retirement benefits.

Currently, the most pernicious forms of digital theft occur through the use of so-called "rogue" websites. The sites, whose content is hosted and whose operators are located throughout the world, take many forms, but all materially contribute to, facilitate and/or induce the distribution of copyrighted works, such as movies and television programming.

These websites present a two-pronged threat: They simultaneously weaken the film and TV industry by undercutting, eliminating or reducing the market for, and thus the financial support for, film and television production, which millions rely on for jobs, bringing down the U.S. economy as a whole, as well as undermining the online marketplace. In addition, these websites expose consumers to criminals who routinely pilfer personal and financial information from unsuspecting targets, putting consumers at risk to identity theft. Furthermore, legitimate companies that want to usher in new business models and provide high-quality content and more consumer choice online, have a limited potential for growth when they are forced to compete with entities that are distributed the exact same content through illicit means.

Rogue websites typically engage in one or more of the following forms of online theft of copyrighted content:

- Streaming an unauthorized copy of a copyrighted video;
- Downloading an unauthorized copy of a copyrighted video;
- Streaming or downloading of an unauthorized copy of a copyrighted video by linking to a torrent or other metadata file that initiates piracy;
- Linking to a specific offer to sell an unauthorized copy of a copyrighted video;
- Hosting an unauthorized copy of a copyrighted video.

These rogue websites are increasingly sophisticated in appearance and take on many attributes of legitimate content delivery sites, creating additional enforcement challenges and feeding consumer confusion. Among the steps taken by rogue websites to deceive consumers into believing they are legitimate are:

- The use of credit card companies, such as Visa and MasterCard, to facilitate payments to rogue websites;
- The use of "e-wallet" or alternative payment methods such as PayPal, Moneybrokers, AlertPay and Gate2Shop to allow for the receipt of payment from the public for subscriptions, donations, purchases and memberships;

- The use of advertising, often for mainstream, Blue Chip companies, on the websites;
- Reward programs for frequent purchasers.

The impact of this nefarious activity is documented in a recently published report by Envisional, an independent Internet consulting company. Envisional's "Technical Report: An Estimate of Infringing Use of the Internet" estimates that almost a quarter (23.8 percent) of global Internet traffic and over 17 percent of U.S. Internet traffic is copyright infringing. This staggering level of theft cannot be sustained without significant damage to the motion picture industry and the workforce it supports.

Our studios are not alone in grappling with this threat. According to Deluxe Entertainment Services Group, the leading provider of post-production creative services for the film industry, hackers from around the world attempt to penetrate Deluxe's network 20 million times a month on average, seeking financial gain by stealing movies and television content while it is in their possession, four million attempts—a quarter of the hacker hits—come from Chinese IP addresses. These criminal networks are undermining U.S. competition abroad and banning American workers.

Unfortunately, American companies—knowingly or not—often provide the financial fuel that enriches the criminals profiting from these rogue sites. Online advertisement brokers such as Google's AdSense advertise their clients on these sites, paying the website operators for the right to do so. Online pay processors and credit card companies similarly operate on these websites, turning a blind eye to the willful infringement of copyrights that they are facilitating. Internet service providers (ISPs) allow these websites to operate on their networks. Search engines present a menu of illicit materials with a few strokes of the keyboard, while demonstrating over the past few months that they are, in fact, able and willing to change their search algorithms as they see fit. These American businesses are contributing to the problem.

## C. Legislative Action and Administration Enforcement Is Effective and Necessary to Address the Assault of Online Theft

We are encouraged by the strong commitment this Committee and this Administration have shown to protecting intellectual property and the American workers who create it. The positive effects of government's willingness to intervene have been palpable: Since U.S. Intellectual Property Enforcement Coordinator (IPEC) Victoria Espinel was confirmed by the Senate, we have seen increasing cooperation from our partners in the private sector intermediaries— whether pay processors, ad brokers, or ISPs. To combat online infringement of copyrighted material, many industries must work together to exert reasonable efforts to prevent, detect and deter infringement. This is a shared responsibility for all intermediaries and third parties, including search engines.

## D. Motion Picture Industry Efforts to Address Online Copyright Theft

In recent months, industry efforts to address online copyright theft have been called into question. It is important to point out that private litigation has its limits, with suits left unresolved for years. This is particularly damaging since swift action is paramount to our industry. Most films make the bulk of their box office returns in the first few weeks of release. By the time a lawsuit is even filed, the damage is already done.

Nevertheless, the MPAA and member studios have filed over 25 copyright infringement lawsuits in the last five years against owner/operators of rogue websites or "parasites," or other companies infringing our copyrights.

The MPAA and member studios spend an enormous amount of time and financial resources on identifying and seeking removal of unauthorized, copyrighted content online or links to such content. On average, a motion picture studio identifies several hundred thousand pieces of, or links to infringing content online per month. In addition, a number of companies must hire private vendors to assist in locating and responding to additional hundreds of thousands incidences of unauthorized content. Unfortunately, not all content owners have the resources to protect themselves.

To respond to such illegal activity, a content owner must file countless copyright infringement notices pursuant to the Digital Millennium Copyright Act (DMCA). For those sites that are responsive to notices, it can still take days or weeks before the content is removed. With sites that are dedicated to providing unauthorized copyrighted content online, it is a virtually fruitless exercise. In one example, a piece of infringing content was re-posted by the same individual over 40 times on the same website before finally giving up. Furthermore, many of these sites will not even respond to take down notices submitted pursuant to the DMCA.

The MPAA and member studios also invest substantial financial resources to generate digital fingerprints and watermarking of their copyrighted content. Fingerprints are provided to cooperative online user-generated content sites, such as YouTube, MySpace, and Daily Motion, in order to provide for identification and removal of unauthorized copyrighted content that a user might seek to upload. Watermarking is used to protect film content in theatrical release; where a device manufacturer is willing to install watermark detection technology, a bootleg DVD copy of a film camcorded in a theater will be disabled from playback on such a device. These measures only have a limited impact given the small number of sites or entities willing to cooperate with us.

## E. Effective Enforcement by the U.S. Government

Last week MPAA and member studios joined our colleagues in the filmed entertainment business to express our strong support for the Immigration and Customs Enforcement (ICE) agency in a letter to all Members of Congress. We commend their efforts to combat digital theft and counterfeiting for not only our industry but also a range of U.S. industries dependent upon intellectual property protection.

The combined efforts of ICE and the Intellectual Property Rights (IPR) Center have not only put numerous rogue sites out of business but have also raised awareness with the public, deterred bad actors, and resulted in many websites voluntarily ceasing criminal activity or becoming legal platforms for online content.

Recently, the Office of the TPEC released its first annual report to Congress pursuant to the PRO-IP Act, as well as a white paper outlining intellectual property enforcement legislative recommendations. Both the report and white paper emphasized the detrimental impact of copyright infringement on the economy and the need to work with the Congress to update intellectual property laws to improve law enforcement effectiveness.

We believe that rogue sites legislation, combined with the Administration's work with intermediaries and enforcement by the IPR Center, will go a long way towards shutting down the unauthorized distribution of copyrighted works and close a gap in the intellectual property law.

Again, we thank the Committee on behalf of our member companies for the opportunity to provide this Statement to underscore the severity of the pernicious threat posed by digital theft to our workers, whose jobs, pensions and benefits are most vulnerable to its impact. We look forward to working with you. Chairman Goodlatte, Ranking Member Watt, and other Members of the Subcommittee on crafting legislation to deal with this criminal activity.

MiMTiD
Report
The World's Leading Content Protection Company
April 1, 2011

The Honorable Lamar Smith
Chairman, Committee on the Judiciary
2138 Rayburn House Office Building
Washington. D.C. 20515

The Honorable John Conyers
Committee on the Judiciary
B-351 Rayburn House Office Building
Washington D.C. 20515

**Subject: Hearing "Promoting Investment and Protecting Commerce Online: Legitimate Sites v. Parasites, Part 11"**

Dear Chairman Smith and Ranking Member Conyers:

The production and distribution of creative works, such as television content, motion pictures and music, has been an unassailable strength of our Nation, and the protection of this American intellectual property is now more than ever absolutely critical to our future economic growth.

## Background on MiMTiD and DMCA-Complaint Take Down Notices

Our company. MiMTiD Corp., acts as a copyright enforcement agent for some of the world's leading motion picture, television/sports programming and music companies. On a monthly basis, MiMTiD sends to various websites several thousand infringement notices demanding that infringing content on tho.se websites be removed.

Each take down notice sent by MiMTiD on behalf of copyright owners complies with the rigorous requirements set forth in the Digital Millennium Copyright Act (DMCA). This means that, among other things, each of these notices contains identification of the copyright owner of the work infringed; an attestation to the copyright owner's good faith belief that the identified links are infringing and not authorized by the copyright holder or by law; a sworn statement under penalty of perjury that the issuer is authorized to act on behalf of the relevant copyright holder; and an attestation that the information provided in the notice is accurate. Accordingly, before a notice is submitted, the copyright owner and/or its agent must undertake an appropriate investigation confirming the accuracy of the infringement allegation and the other information provided in the notice.

MiMTiD sends DMCA-compliant notices ("take down notices") to sites that host (store) infringing files, torrent sites that facilitate peer-to-peer infringement, streaming sites that link to and stream infringing content, and to search engines that provide links to infringing content. For instance, over the past two months (February 1, 2011 through March 30, 2011), MiMTiD has issued 4,701 take down notices to hosting, torrent, and streaming sites offering infringing content, and 19,237 notices to all search engines we monitor that are linking to infringing content. 13,219 of those search engine notices were to Google in particular. Over the past 6 months (September 2010 through March 2011). MiMTiD has issued over 262,722 take down notices in total. For perspective, this work was conducted on behalf of a small number of copyright owners for a limited number of titles; it constitutes an accurate representative sample but it should be noted that it is a mere fraction of the infringement perpetuated by these sites and on the Internet in general.

Monitoring of popular search engines for links to infringing content, and sending take down notices to the search engines, is a specialty of our company. MiMTiD is one of the largest, if not the largest, submitter of such take down notices to search engines. Consumers regularly utilize search engines to identify sources for content online, and the search engines' prompt compliance with our take down notices through the removal of identified infringing search results, would help to prevent countless consumers from knowingly or unknowingly accessing infringing content.

## Data on Search Engine Compliance with DMCA-Complaint Take Down Notices

Unfortunately, in most cases, the take down notices we send to search engines on behalf of copyright owners are not complied with expeditiously. For example, over the past two months (February 1, 2011 through March 30, 2011), Google has delayed for an average of 20 days before taking action on our notices, and many notices are not actioned by Google for more than 4.5 days. During this delay, the Google links to infringing content (with Google ads running next to the infringing search results) remain live, which causes irreparable harm to the copyright owners that created and own the valuable content that continues to be stolen in the interim. By comparison, over the same period, Yahoo and Bing took 4 days and 5 days, respectively, to act on our take down notices, which we believe is several days longer than necessary or appropriate for the simple task of removing an infringing link, but still in a different category of delay than Google. Moreover, Google willfully refuses to comply at all with a significant subset of take down notices; indeed, over the past two months, Google refused to remove 39% of the links identified in the take down notices we submitted. By comparison, over the same period, Yahoo and Bing have complied with 98% of our notices by removing the infringing links.

Why the material difference in search engine responses and response time? From what we understand, Google takes it upon itself to conduct a manual investigation of each infringing link identified and ultimately decides, using unpublished criteria, whether or not Google agrees with the copyright owner that the link is indeed an infringement of the relevant copyright owner's rights. As noted above, all notices sent by MiMTiD on behalf of copyright owners are DMCA-compliant, so they satisfy the extensive, carefully-crafted criteria that Congress established for a notice to be valid. The DMCA also provides other built-in safeguards and checks and balances, such as a counter-notice process for a party to object to the removal of its content and penalties against copyright owners that abuse the notice process. Nonetheless, Google inserts itself as an extra-statutory, self-appointed arbiter of the validity of DMCA-compliant notices that Congress has already determined as valid under the statute. If Google does not unilaterally agree that the links submitted in a take down notice are infringing, under whatever standard it chooses to use, Google informs the copyright owner or its agent as follows: "In accordance with the Digital Millennium Copyright Act, we have completed processing your infringement complaint. ... At this time, Google has decided not to take action on these URLs: [*list of ignored links*]." We believe Google's self-appointed arbiter role is improper because it interferes with the carefully-crafted and balanced statutory process, causes undue delay, and deprives copyright owners of their right to have infringing content removed expeditiously on the basis of their valid take down notices, as expressly contemplated by the DMCA statute. It is our position that any website that intentionally delays processing DMCA-compliant infringement notices for any reason cannot be said to be acting "expeditiously" and therefore does not satisfy the requirements for safe harbor eligibility set forth in the Digital Millennium Copyright Act.

## The Role of Egregiously Infringing Sites

An additional challenge with the DMCA take down notice process is that all search engines currently choose to remove only the specific infringing link that the copyright owner or its agent detects and includes in a take down notice. This may make sense with respect to an occasional link to a legitimate site that has incidental infringements. However, our data shows that a significant number of the specific infringing links detected and noticed are for a small number of egregious, repeat infringing sites that are dedicated exclusively to infringement. Over the past 6 months, the top 10 infringing sites monitored by MiMTiD have accounted for 65% of the total take down notices we have submitted. Presently, the search engines do not consider these egregiously infringing sites to be "repeat infringers" under the DMCA and therefore choose to do nothing to stop the influx of infringing links from these sites in their search engines. For example, even after receiving dozens or even hundreds of infringement notices about a particular egregiously infringing website, the search engines do not deindex these infringing sites as whole. To the contrary, the search engines continue to frequently and affirmatively "crawl" these egregiously infringing sites for more links to display in their search engine results.

Copyright owners are forced to try to constantly and reactively respond to new infringements from these egregiously infringing sites that appear before the old ones are even removed. It is an impossible task, and this is one reason we strongly support legislation that would establish procedures for obtaining a Court determination that a specific egregiously infringing website is dedicated to infringing activity and include search engines as parties bound by such a Court determination. Once a Court determines a site to be dedicated to infringing activity, the search engines should be required to deindex the site, including by removing existing links and by not crawling the egregiously infringing site for more links.

## The Role of Advertising

In the course of our monitoring and enforcement work, MiMTiD also captures evidence of the advertising networks that are monetizing our customers' infringed content by placing ads alongside those infringements. Many of the websites that we notice to search engines repeatedly for copyright infringement are dedicated to infringing activity and are among the top several hundred most popular sites in the world. Publicly available data suggests that many millions, if not billions, of dollars are being monetized annually through advertisements appearing on sites dedicated to copyright infringement. For instance, available tools for estimating website advertising revenue (websiteoutlook.com and cubestat.com), indicate that the top 10 infringing sites monitored by MiMTiD alone earn over $70M in advertising revenue annually.

Our data also shows that Google is the principal advertising network, or is participating with the advertising networks, appearing on many websites dedicated to copyright infringement. Specifically, Google is a direct or indirect advertising network for 29% of the top 100 repeatedly infringing websites most frequently identified in take down notices sent by MiMTiD.

For instance, one repeat infringing site that we have recently noticed to Google over 2,000 times for 137 separate infringing links on behalf of a diverse set of content owners is TORRENTZ.EU (http://www.torrentz.eu). TORRENTZ.EU is ranked as the 173rd most popular site in the world by Alexa, the world's leading company that ranks a website's global polarity (by comparison Reuters.com is ranked #172). The advertising networks that MiMTiD detected as monetizing the infringing content on TORRENTZ.EU include: Adperium, Google Syndication and Google Doubleclick. Of 137 TORRENTZ.EU links included in our notices, Google has taken an average of 26 days to process only 37 of these infringement notices. The other 100 links remain active in Google search results.

Another such site that we have recently noticed to Google over 300 times for 163 separate infringing links is TARINGA.NET (http://www.taringa.net). TARINGA.NET is ranked as the 127th most popular site in the world by Alexa (by comparison Google's GOOGLE.CN (Google China) is ranked #128). The advertising networks that MiMTiD detected as monetizing the infringing content on TARINGA.NET include: Google Syndication and Google Doubleclick. Of 163 TARINGA.NET links included in our notices, Google has taken an average of 24 days to process 131 of these infringement notices. The other 32 links remain active in Google search results.

Google, through a direct relationship with TORRENTZ.EU and TAR1NGA.NET or through its relationship with the other advertising networks that are present on those sites, is necessarily receiving a tangible financial benefit from these sites' infringing activity. Google continues to maintain direct and indirect advertising relationships with these sites and includes these sites in its search database, despite recent notice of over 100 separate instances of infringement on each site. As long as the infringing websites and the specific infringing links remain included in the Google search database. Google also continues to profit off of keyword advertising associated with consumer searches that include links to those sites in the search results. The continued inclusion of egregiously infringing sites in search results also materially helps the infringing sites by generating traffic to those sites. This traffic generates additional advertising revenue for the sites and their advertising networks. Increased traffic tends to elevate sites in search engine results, giving them even greater visibility. All of this results in a perpetual cycle of infringement, generating traffic and revenue, which can then be applied by the infringing sites back into the business of infringement.

In our opinion, search engines that also ran advertising networks tire disincentivized from taking action to stop the flow of consumer traffic to, or advertising revenue from, even the most egregious sites dedicated to infringement. It remains in their financial interest to continue to enable the cycle of commercial infringing activities, including by delaying action on specific infringing links noticed by content holders and refusing to deindex egregiously infringing sites. For this reason, we strongly support legislation establishing procedures for obtaining a Court determination that a specific egregious repeat infringing website is dedicated to infringing activity and, specifically, the inclusion of search engines and advertising networks within that legislation's framework as parties obligated to cut off their support of such sites.

Sincerely,
David Wallace Cox
President and Chief Enforcement Officer; MiMTiD Corp.

iab.

April 4, 2011

## IAB Launches First and Only Quality Assurance Certification for Ad Networks & Exchanges

**Program Gives Advertisers Confidence Certified Ad Networks & Exchanges Provide Safe Environments for Brands**
**First 17 Companies Receive Compliance Seal**

**NEW YORK, NY (April 4, 2011)** – To enhance buyer control over ad placement and context, the Interactive Advertising Bureau (IAB) announced today the in-market debut of the Ad Network & Exchange Quality Assurance Certification program, a first-of-its-kind compliance mechanism and the only industry-endorsed certification program that exists today. Only companies that undergo rigorous training, conduct an intensive internal audit and assign a compliance officer to ensure they maintain the IAB's Quality Assurance Guidelines (QAG) will receive a compliance seal from the IAB. The seal, which can be placed on the company's website and marketing materials, certifies that the company is adhering fully to the only industry established criteria as outlined by the QAG, finalized in June 2010.

The IAB also announced the first 17 ad networks & exchanges that have completed the training and received the seal:

- 24/7 Real Media
- Adap.tv
- Adconion
- AOL/Advertising.com
- AudienceScience
- BrightRoll
- Burst Media
- Casale Media
- CONTEXTWEB
- CPX Interactive
- Google
- Specific Media
- SpotXchange
- TubeMogul
- ValueClick Media
- YuMe
- Traffic Marketplace

"IAB congratulates this first wave of companies and looks forward to announcing additional compliant companies in 2011," says Randall Rothenberg, President & CEO, IAB. "The Ad Network & Exchange Certification Program is the next step of the Quality Assurance Guidelines and gives marketers an extra level of comfort that companies carrying the IAB seal are brand safe and deliver what they promise. Buyers who want to ensure they are getting the highest level of quality assurance can now look for the IAB compliance seal and know they are dealing with an ad network or exchange that has made a commitment to transparency, accountability and trust in advertising."

"We are grateful to the IAB for creating the Ad Network & Exchange Certification Program. Knowing that the IAB is making sure ad networks & exchanges with a compliance seal are following the Quality Assurance Guidelines is very reassuring," says John Montgomery, COO, North America, GroupM Interaction. "If an ad network or exchange has an IAB compliance seal, we can trust they are working with our agency and the brands we represent to deliver ads to relevant audiences in appropriate content. This commitment will now be a very important factor when we are considering campaigns."

Seven other IAB member companies are currently enrolled in the Ad Network & Exchange Certification Program, and along with those that have received their seals, they represent more than two thirds of the top 25 ad networks ranked by comScore based on site traffic or audience.



IAB is allowing buyers to file complaints via the IAB website about compliant companies that might be falling short of their commitment to maintain the highest industry-established standards of quality. The IAB will then investigate with an independent third party under the direction of a Steering Committee of IAB member ad networks and exchanges, which can result in revocation of the seal. The guidelines and contact information for the compliant companies can be found at: http://www.iab.net/ne_guidelines

**About the IAB**
The Interactive Advertising Bureau (IAB) is comprised of more than 500 leading media and technology companies who are responsible for selling 86% of online advertising in the United States. On behalf of its members, the IAB is dedicated to the growth of the interactive advertising marketplace, of interactive's share of total marketing spend, and of its members' share of total marketing spend. The IAB educates marketers, agencies, media companies and the wider business community about the value of interactive advertising. Working with its member companies, the IAB evaluates and recommends standards and practices and fields critical research on interactive advertising. Founded in 1996, the IAB is headquartered in New York City with a Public Policy office in Washington, D.C. For more information, please visit www.iab.net.

**IAB Media Contact**
Marnie Black
917.828.7308
marnie@iab.net

# INDEX

## A



## B



## C

## D



## E

## F



## G



## H

## M



## N



## O

## P



## Q



## R

## S

## T



## U



## V



## W

## Marketing Research: Fundamentals, Process, and Implications

**Author:** Rajagopal, Ph.D. (EGADE Business School, Monterrey Institute of Technology and Higher Education, ITESM, Mexico City Campus, Mexico)

**Series:** Business Issues, Competition and Entrepreneurship

**Book Description:** This book examines and emphasizes the differences in marketing research designs across cultures, paying attention to differences between international consumers and cultural norms that affect marketing initiatives, and several factors for consideration in international marketing research.


**Hardcover ISBN:** 978-1-53613-029-4
**Retail Price:** $195


## Strategic Human Resource Management: Perspectives, Implementation and Challenges

**Editors:** Max Lucas and Jill Grant

**Series:** Business Issues, Competition and Entrepreneurship

**Book Description:** *Strategic Human Resource Management: Perspectives, Implementation and Challenges* aims to fil the existing gap in this regard by exploring the effect of coaching on employee performance in the Lebanese banking sector through the investigation of one of its variables, namely Organizational Citizenship Behavior (OCB), that links coaching to performance improvement.


**Softcover ISBN:** 978-1-53613-158-1
**Retail Price:** $82

## Pensions: Global Issues, Perspectives and Challenges

**Editor:** Alexandra Webb

**Series:** Business Issues, Competition and Entrepreneurship

**Book Description:** Understanding the strategies underlying pension investing is important because pension assets are one of the largest pools of investment assets in the world. Chapter One reports on how the widespread application of robots and artificial intelligence may dramatically reduce the number of human workers in employment, such that more people will be either unemployed or out of job market altogether.

**Softcover ISBN:** 978-1-53612-462-0
**Retail Price:** $82

## Contemporary Conviviality of Trade Unionism: Perspectives from the Power Sector

**Authors:** Sreenivasan Poornaiya (General Manager (Human Resources) Indian Renewable Energy Development Energy Limited, New Delhi, India); Krishna Nath Pandey (Dean, Department of Business Management, Lingya's University)

**Series:** Business Issues, Competition and Entrepreneurship

**Book Description:** This book has been written by an academician who provided the concept, articulated the changed dynamics in the global arena in trade unionism and has been delineated by a professional who had keenly observed a new situation which has compelled management to seek the cooperation of trade union functionaries.

**Hardcover ISBN:** 978-1-53612-772-0
**Retail Price:** $195